# Human

WORSHIP RESOURCES FOR AN AGE OF CHANGE

Compiled and edited by Hannah Ward and Jennifer Wild

MOWBRAY

Mowbray
*A Cassell imprint*
Wellington House
125 Strand
London
WC2R 0BB

215 Park Avenue South
New York
NY 10003, USA

First published 1995

**British Library Cataloguing-in-Publication Data**
A catalogue record for this book is available from the
British Library

ISBN 0–264–67334–4

Printed and bound in Great Britain by
Biddles Ltd, Guildford and King's Lynn

# Contents

# Introduction

The purpose of this book is to provide a collection of services and rituals that demonstrate 'liturgy from the ground up'. In other words, we have not set out to rival existing prayer books, or those collections of liturgical writing offered by some one author with considerable creative gifts backed up by a more or less explicit theory of liturgy. When we were asked to compile this anthology, we sent out letters to upwards of eighty people who, we thought, might have something to offer us in the way of rituals for occasions or circumstances not catered for in the churches' prayer books. Many of them wrote back sending samples of their own or others' work, or else they gave us names of other people to approach. The generosity of all who responded was heart-warming and encouraging. In the meantime we also went round various denominational and ecumenical bookshops to see what was on offer — and we two Anglicans were greatly impressed by what others, particularly Free Church people, are producing; though, as far as we could find, no one was working on a collection quite like this. In the event, this is a thoroughly ecumenical collection, and we are proud of the fact. We should also point out that we have not made it our business to worry about church legalities, so that this collection aspires to no official standing.

There are in this book liturgies written or compiled by known and respected liturgists — the names of Jim Cotter and Nicola Slee come instantly to mind — but, more typically, the pieces printed here, liturgies of the people, have a history of their own, arising from the variety of experience of those who have taken part in producing and performing them. An obvious example is 'Waiting for God-O' (pp.18–20), based on a reflective Advent evening (Womenspace, London, 9.12.94), where the starting-point was the ancient antiphons (refrains) sung with the Magnificat on the days leading up to Christmas, words which for centuries expressed in largely biblical imagery human longing for the coming of God-with-us, Emmanuel. The person leading the evening then introduced Jim Cotter's additional O refrains; after that those present worked in small groups to create their own 'O's; and the evening ended with a rather moving reading of the Magnificat interspersed with the O cries we ourselves had written. This is indeed 'raw' material, but it had life, and movement and feeling, for women who, like everybody at the time, were weary with end-of-year, pre-Christmas activity. In other parts of the book may be found a greater 'rawness' of emotions, also typical of this collection – for instance in some of the funeral rites, and in the reminders of homelessness and of personal experience of violence and abuse. We hope it is clear that some of these liturgies were used in a church context, that is, in public worship, while others were specially designed for small groups in private or semi-private settings – women's needs and capacities for creating ritual have found expression in both contexts. Public or private, some of these rites are printed here with the names of those who took part, others have dashes or initials or other formalizing devices. Our hope is that this mix of the formal with informality will encourage readers to look on all or any of the contents of the book as likely to be of use to themselves or their friends. Ministers and pastors may find, in fact, that they can learn something about the pastoral needs of those they serve.

Some of the liturgies given here rely on an ASB or other denominational rite for their basic shape and wording, but with parts of the service reworked to provide for the particular needs of those taking part (for instance some of the marriage or covenant promises). Clearly, many clergy are doing this kind of thing on some scale much of the time: this book reflects some of the what and how and where this is happening. In such ways there is a breaking down of the barriers between liturgy providers and liturgy users, when these people work together; and it is noticeable that it is not only participating in liturgies and rituals that helps people to change in creative ways – the process of creating liturgy, and the theological effort involved, itself changes lives (recorded most movingly in connection with the designing of a Jewish–Christian marriage ceremony on p.119).

In this book we are not arguing a particular cause or party line. But our theme is change; and we do see it as a special task or challenge for people at this time to act creatively in face of change. No doubt all times are times of change, but how we deal with our own particular shifting sands is important. We see around the world one reaction: the retreat towards fundamentalism, together with the violence and the destructive operations of the human spirit which this sort of attitude tends to produce. We have reflected at some length on the challenge of living creatively with change in our recent book *Guard the Chaos*. It is clear from the way people still turn to churches for appropriate rituals around birth, marriage and death that ritual is important in helping individuals and societies to make changes. We find the most helpful way of looking at the role of ritual in change is that offered by Arnold van Gennep in his now celebrated *Rites de Passages* (1907). Van Gennep and those who followed him, notably Edith and Victor Turner, and in recent years the anthropologist and liturgist Roger Grainger, show convincingly the vital function of ritual in enabling people to make and cope with signficant change in their lives.

Not all the rituals included in this book are rites of passage, although most of them could be seen in that way, because there is a kind of movement within all ritual, which includes that moment of 'no-time' which is characteristic of the rite of passage. Van Gennep allows us to identify the three phases of movement in a change: the time when we let go of what has been; the time when we are neither one thing nor another; and the time of arrival, when we rejoin the community in our new state, e.g. as married people. As we have argued in our book, all change and decision-making involves this same process.

This book, then, is very largely about people's experience of change: coming to terms with change, struggling with change, and coping with change. But we cannot all change on all levels at once; and this book reflects different attitudes to language about God, and different uses of language about God. Although we ourselves are committed to the use of inclusive language within public worship, we have not thought it appropriate to censor material sent to us; nor have we censored any image of God. We positively want to see lots of different images, rather than a few safe and neutral ones. In short, we would prefer to risk offending everyone than no one.

So how do we see this book being used? We hope that it will inspire and give ideas rather than provide ready-made 'alternative' liturgies, although we hope that by including some whole liturgies, people will find ideas for ways of structuring rituals. But in general we are offering starting-points rather than transferable finished products, even though some of the formularies here included, for instance the partnership promises, could be used in other settings.

We have given this collection the title *Human Rites* because we wish to encourage the humanizing of our religious rituals. We believe that this age needs a greater degree of personalization in ritual than did previous ages. Ritual itself is or should be deeply humanizing: all of life needs to be brought into it, including the messy bits, the pain and the anger, as well as the hitherto unacceptable and uncatered-for happenings like abortion, or divorce. It is true also that even the great basic ritual moments, the namings, couplings, buryings, all need personalizing, and this is possible to a degree greater than many have yet envisaged. Nevertheless, a good part of the material sent to us concerns other moments of life-change, relating for instance to retirement, emigration, adolescence, and various forms of separation and of healing, all produced to meet the needs of particular individuals or groups. We notice that not everyone feels the need for a formal ritual to mark an occasion or change; but everyone does need to give themselves permission to mark change in ways suitable to themselves, and especially to give change time. Reflection often reveals to us ways in which we have marked change: spring-cleaning the house, getting a new outfit, going on holiday with a friend, having a special meal, and so on.

It needs to be said that words are not everything, though that is almost all that the printed page can include. Words by themselves are incomplete, and can be very misleading. Other things are important too: gesture, context, symbol and above all silence. One way of widening one's understanding might be to make a scrap book of words — prayers, poetry, prose — and pictures that from time to time present themselves as throwing light on the process of the various changes that happen in human life. The whole process of preparing, enacting and reflecting on a ritual marking an important life-change can have incalculable effects on us; it can be a true movement of the spirit for those who find themselves 'drawn by God over their parochial fence and outward into the cosmos' (Edward Hays).

Finally, it will be noticed that the structure of this book parallels stages of the life of Jesus. It would have been possible to arrange the contents in a variety of ways, but we believe that we have chosen one that is peculiarly appropriate, in that it reflects our belief that our lives and Jesus' life meet in a way that is revelatory.

> Christ, crucified and risen,
> is set free —
>
> > from one time
> > > for all times
> > from one community
> > > for all communities
> > from one sex
> > > for both sexes
> > from one culture
> > > for all cultures
> > from one world
> > > for all worlds
> > from life as one individual
> > > for life within every
> > > trusting heart.

(Kate Compston)

Hannah Ward
Jennifer Wild

# I

## *In whom we live . . .*
### *Changing images and experience of God*

Our first chapter of worship material has as its thread changing images and experience of God. It is a thread throughout the whole book, but we wanted to highlight it at the beginning to emphasize that it is our experience of God which leads us to create liturgies and to write prayers. The writings that follow express the way God touches our lives and reveal the particular times we feel either touched or the need to be touched by God.

We should not be surprised or alarmed to discover here images of God that are new or 'odd' to us. Some will speak to us, others will not. The important thing is that we should feel able to express the truth of our experience; we can encourage one another out of the constraints of thinking God can only be addressed and imaged in certain respectable formularies. This does not mean we have to set out to shock one another but that, in sharing the colours of our own faith story, we might open a window for others.

Amongst all the material we were sent that spoke of new and changing images of God, there was a handful whose inspiration and quality echoed and took us back to the 'in-the-beginning' quality of the Hebrew and Christian Testaments. This was the case in particular with the first two liturgies here: A Celebration of Faith Development and the celebration of the Wessex United Reformed Church on the theme of Treasure. The first reminds us of the ways in which faith itself is full of changes and chances, all of which hold the possibility of God-encounter and therefore growth in human be-ing. The 'Treasure' liturgy is itself a wonderful example of the treasure waiting to be discovered by those who are willing to seek God in different images and different places, not least in the things that are given us by virtue of a shared locality. All the longer pieces in this chapter, as indeed throughout this collection, are a blend of 'things old and things new', a quality to be found wherever religious instincts seek expression in ritual words and actions.

1    *A celebration of faith development*

---

## Opening sentence and collect

LEADER Speaking the truth in love, we are to grow up in every way into him
who is the head, into Christ.

ALL    O God in whom we live and move
and have our being,
all our times are in your hands
and all our beginnings and endings
are known to you.
Help us to respond to the challenges
and opportunities you offer us
and to grow in trust and faith
into the stature and fullness of Christ.
Amen.

## Confession

LEADER Let us call to mind the times in our lives when we have refused to
trust God's goodness, when we have not taken the opportunities for
the growth and deepening of faith offered to us; when we have not
cared for others but been the cause of their stumbling or stunting in
faith.

*A short period of silence is kept.*

ALL    We turn to you, O God;
we renounce evil;
we claim your love;
we choose to be made whole.

*In the circle, each turns to her or his neighbour in turn and pronounces the
words of forgiveness, such as 'God loves you. Love yourself. Love others.'*

## Ministry of the Word
*Reading: Ephesians 4.1–16*

*A range of non-biblical readings describing the life of faith at different
stages could be used to supplement the biblical reading.*
*After the readings, there follows a time of informal discussion and
sharing.*

## Intercessions

*A period of silence follows each reader for the offering of individual petitions.*

1ST READER   O God in whom we live and move and have our being, all our times are in your hands:
We thank you for the times of beginnings in our lives, for the first steps in faith and every tentative sign of new life and growth.

We offer to God our new beginnings, with all their unknown opportunities, our fears and anxieties, as well as our hopes and expectations. We pray for any we know who are setting out into newness at this time; for new human and spiritual life in the birth of a baby, the beginning of a marriage or a job or a vocation.

2ND READER   O God in whom we live and move and have our being, all our times are in your hands:
We thank you for the times of transitions in our lives, for opportunities to change and develop and move on in our faith.

We offer to God our insecurities and anxieties about change, the hopes and fears we have for our lives, and our confusion when all our plans are disturbed by unforeseen circumstances and events. We pray for any we know who are in a time of disruption, transition and change in their lives: for any who are ill, or the victims of violence, or whose circumstances have changed suddenly for reasons outside their control.

3RD READER   O God in whom we live and move and have our being, all our times are in your hands:
We thank you for the times of stability in our lives, when we are invited to put our roots down deep into your love and to learn the discipline of faithful obedience to our calling.

We offer to God our own periods when nothing much seems to change or happen, with all the boredom and frustration of such times as well as the comfort and security of a settled existence. We pray for any we know whose lives are apparently monotonous, empty, unenlivened by any sense of growth or anticipation. We think, too, of any who are in desperate need of settledness and security but seem unable to find it.

4TH READER   O God in whom we live and move and have our being, all our times are in your hands:
We thank you for the times of ending in our lives, when we are invited to let go of the past so that something new and better can be born in its place.

We offer to God all our endings, partings and closures, with all their sense of incompleteness and imperfection, loss and grieving, as well as the joy of celebrating what has been accomplished and learnt in them. We pray for any we know who are experiencing a time of ending, the end of a relationship, a job of work, a home, or the death of someone close.

ALL    Merciful God,
accept these prayers in the name of Jesus Christ our Lord.
Amen.

## The Peace

LEADER  We are the Body of Christ.
We grow together into the fullness of God's love as we share God's peace and live God's forgiveness. Let us offer one another a sign of peace.

*The peace is shared among the group.*

## Affirmation and celebration of faith

LEADER    There's a season for everything
under the sun,
a time to do
and a time to be done,
a time to laugh
and a time to cry,
a time to live
and a time to die.

SIDE ONE  A time for dying and a time for rebirth,
SIDE TWO  A time for the spirit and a time for earth.

SIDE ONE  A time for laughter, a time for tears,
SIDE TWO  A time for courage and a time for fears.

SIDE ONE  A time to cling and a time to release,
SIDE TWO  A time for war and a time for peace.

SIDE ONE  A time to talk and a time to be still,
SIDE TWO  A time to care and a time to kill.

SIDE ONE  A time alone. A time for romance.
SIDE TWO  A time to mourn. A time to dance.

SIDE ONE  A time to keep. A time to lose.
SIDE TWO  A time to be told. A time to choose.

SIDE ONE  A time to tear down. A time to rebuild.
SIDE TWO  A time to be empty. A time to be filled.

SIDE ONE  A time to welcome and to send away.
SIDE TWO  A time to complain and a time to pray.

SIDE ONE  A time to share and a time to save.
SIDE TWO  A time to break rules. A time to behave.

SIDE ONE  A time to free and a time to bind,
SIDE TWO  A time to search and a time to find.

SIDE ONE  A time to plant and a time to uproot,
SIDE TWO  A time to be barren. A time to bear fruit.

SIDE ONE  A time of plenty.
SIDE TWO  A time of need.

SIDE ONE  A time to follow.
SIDE TWO  A time to lead.

SIDE ONE  A time to give.
SIDE TWO  A time to take.

SIDE ONE  A time to bend.
SIDE TWO  A time to break.

SIDE ONE  A time to hurt.
SIDE TWO  A time to heal.

SIDE ONE  A time for secrets.
SIDE TWO  A time to reveal.

SIDE ONE  A time to let go.
SIDE TWO  A time to hold.

SIDE ONE  A time to be young.
SIDE TWO  A time to grow old.

SIDE ONE  A time to rip open.
SIDE TWO  A time to mend.

SIDE ONE  A time to begin,
SIDE TWO  and a time to end.

ALL       There's a season for everything
          under the sun,
          a time to do
          and a time to be done,
          a time to laugh
          and a time to cry,
          a time to live
          and a time to die.
                              (Miriam Therese Winter)

LEADER    The vision will be fulfilled
in its own time.
If it seems slow in coming,
wait for it,
for it will surely come.
And as we wait,
may all things work together for good,
may we be blessed
with wisdom and discernment
and determination and patience,
may we take the time
to grow in grace
day by day.

ALL    Amen.

(Miriam Therese Winter)

**Nicola Slee**

## 2    'Treasure'

A Wessex Province United Reformed Church Assembly Celebration on the theme 'Treasure', held at Portsmouth Guildhall, 7 July 1993. The Celebration took as its inspiration the raising from the Solent of the Tudor ship, the *Mary Rose*, and the recovery of its many treasures, in the period 1979–82.

### Opening sentences

### Prayer of Approach
*Brief silence.*

### Hymn *Eternal God, your love's tremendous glory* (**17**)

### Introduction to theme

### Prayer of Confession

LEADER Shining, surprising, grace-full God, for avoiding the searchlight of your desire for us and running away from your love:

ALL    forgive us;

LEADER for preferring the safe, familiar and certain to the risky, unknown and mysterious:

ALL    forgive us;

LEADER for failing to believe in the vulnerability of power and the power of vulnerability:

ALL   forgive us;

LEADER for taking no delight in variety and insisting on sameness and conformity:

ALL   forgive us;

LEADER for fearing those different from ourselves, and projecting onto them what we cannot accept within our own depths:

ALL   forgive us;

LEADER for assuming we are superior to the rest of creation, for abusing, despoiling and failing to celebrate our relationship with the earth and the web of life:

ALL   forgive us;

LEADER for not noticing your presence in darkness as in light, in body as in spirit, in feeling as in intellect, in pain as in healing, in Good Friday as in Easter Day:

ALL   forgive us;

LEADER Set us free, we pray, to be whole human beings and to live our lives graciously and without fear.
      *(Pause)*

LEADER God forgives us:

ALL   God makes peace within us:
      we claim this healing, in faith and hope.

(Kate Compston)

## Litany: *Treasure from dark vaults*

*Between readings, the following is sung:*

Moderato
(solo)

Voice

I  shall  give  you  trea-sure  from  dark  vaults,

Piano/Org.

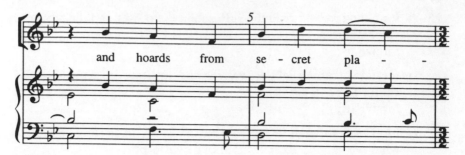

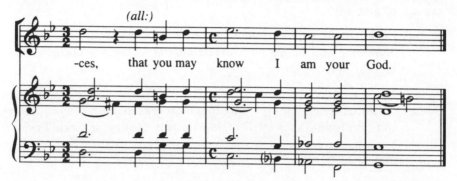

(Words: Isaiah 45.3 REB. Music: Andrew McBirnie)

## Hymn *Messenger of marvels* (**18**)

## Litany of Resurrection

*Between readings, under the following headings, all join to sing the following refrain (Taizé melody):*

**O—Christus resurrexit, Christus resurrexit**
**O—Alleluia, Alleluia!**

Let's celebrate . . . God's self-expression in creation — an opportunity for awe.

> *Refrain*

Let's celebrate . . . God in stillness and attentiveness — an opportunity for quiet meditation.

> *Refrain*

Let's celebrate . . . God's calling of women — an opportunity to redress the balance.

> *Refrain*

Let's celebrate . . . God's calling of all to ministry – an opportunity for re-thinking and re-commitment.

> *Refrain*

Let's celebrate . . . God's mission in the world – an opportunity to stretch our arms around the globe.

LEADER We pray that we may all find our humanity and our potential wholeness in God, that the entire earth may cry 'Glory!'

ALL (*rising and shouting*) Let the earth cry GLORY!

> *All remain standing.*

## Hymn *Put peace into each other's hands* (20)

## Affirmations

VOICE 1 I believe in God: creator and farmer, lover and friend, challenger and enabler; wellspring and womb of purposeful living.

ALL We believe in God.

VOICE 2 I believe in Jesus Christ: compassionate and wounded healer, wise-one and fool; liberator from oppression.

ALL We believe in Jesus Christ.

VOICE 3 I believe in the Spirit; go-between and negotiator, inspirer and encourager; barrier-breaker, community-maker.

ALL We believe in the Spirit.

VOICE 4 I believe in the community of faith: alive in the aliveness of Christ, prophetic in its solidarity with all who suffer, celebratory in its hope, its work, its witness.

ALL We believe in the community of faith.

VOICE 5 I believe in God's Kingdom: beckoning and burgeoning, dynamic and harmonious, present and future; in which we glimpse
– the satisfaction of our deepest longings,
– the healing of our painful rifts,
– the forging of justice, peace and integrity.

ALL We believe in God's Kingdom.

(Kate Compston)

**Prayer to the Spirit of God**
*(with participation by international representatives)*

**Hymn** *Christ is the King! O friends, rejoice*

**Benediction**

LEADER Sisters and brothers,
Let us claim the treasures Christ holds out to us, let us claim the
freedom he gives us by his own self-giving on the cross.

ALL      May he enable us to live and serve in faith, hope and love.

LEADER Let us, in times of sorrow, as in times of joy, celebrate the goodness
of God. Let us go in peace.

ALL      Thanks be to God. Amen.

(Kate Compston)

**Recessional hymn**

(to be sung several times as congregation depart): *We are marching in the
light of God*

(South African traditional song)

3      *Where is God in all this?*
*A liturgy for the experimental liturgy group held at St
Mark's Church, Wimbledon, 19 July 1991.*

**Opening**

*Those present stand in a circle, hands raised to shoulder height, facing
inward and each touching his or her neighbours.*

LEADER We have come here this evening, each of us bringing that which is
of God within us. Jesus said, 'Where two or three meet in my name,
I am there among them.'

*All sit.*

**Collect**

ALL      O God, our Lover and our Friend,
sometimes seeming to play hide-and-seek with us,
hiding from us in the desert times,
yet calling us by name from the midst of the burning bush,

even though we are so lost in our concerns that we do not hear your
    voice:
please join us in our prayers this night,
filling our hearts with love and your life-giving hope. Amen.

### First reading *Exodus 3.1–15*

### Litany *Where is God in all this?*

FIRST READER

    Where is God in all this?
    The trees are felled
      and a desert of ash is where the forest grew.
    The rich man's greed and the poor man's need
      have laid waste the world we knew.
    Where is God in all this?

ALL      God is in labour, panting and groaning,
    giving birth to all creation.
    And she puts into our hands the fragile Earth to nurse.

SECOND READER

    Where is God in all this?
    The rains have failed yet again,
      and the foodplants wither in the scorching sun.
    Children's bellies are swollen with hunger,
      and eyes are blind in the blowing dust.
    Where is God in all this?

ALL      God, the waterer of the fields, calls by name a man of Mali:
    'Coulabaly, dig me channels linking lakes to bring the water.'
    He dug the channels, linked the lakes, and water came
      to part of Mali, through a vision of Coulabaly.

THIRD READER

    Where is God in all this?
    The unemployment figures grow
      and stark despair disables the poor.
    The homeless huddle in the doorways,
      and our children stand begging on every street corner.
    Where is God in all this?

ALL      God is the Son of Man who has nowhere to lay his head,
    God is in the burning bush calling us by name,
    God is walking with us hand in hand,
      our Companion and our Friend.

## Intercessions

*A candle is lit for each intercession, and placed in a bowl of sand.*

## Second reading

ALL My soul praise Yahweh,
Happy is she whose helper is the God of Jacob,
Whose hope is in the God of our ancestors,
Maker of heaven and earth,
The sea, and all that in them dwells;
Who maintains faithfulness for ever,
And deals out justice for the oppressed.
Yahweh feeds the hungry
And sets the prisoner free.
Yahweh restores sight to the blind
And lifts up those who are bowed down.
Yahweh watches over the stranger in the land,
And gives support to the fatherless and widow,
But the way of the wicked he brings to ruin,
And beloved to God are those who try their best to do
   that which is right.

As long as I live I shall praise Yahweh, our Loving God;
I shall sing songs of love to our God all my life long.

(Psalm 146.1, 5–10, 2 (paraphrase))

## Song *Ubi caritas* (Taizé)

*A time of silence, followed by a time for sharing if desired.*

## Confession

ALL Why do we cry, 'Where is God in all this?'
when it is so often our selfishness, our apathy
or our fear of being made to look a fool
that makes us collude in the suffering of the world?
We are sorry God for all that we have done, or not done.
Open our ears that we may hear your voice in the burning bush
and fill us with the spirit of your presence,
that we may boldly live in the light of your love,
and serve you with joy in our hearts.

*All link hands and share silently in God's absolving love.*

**The Peace**

**The Agape**

ALL    As we share the bread and wine, we remember how Jesus gave the
bread and the wine to his friends, as he gave his body and life.

**Song** *Jubilate Deo omnis terra* (Taizé)

**The Blessing** *(from the Celtic tradition)*

ALL    May God's goodness be yours
and well, and seven times well,
may you spend your lives.
May you be an isle in the sea,
may you be a star in the darkness,
may you be a staff to the weak;
may the love Christ Jesus gave
fill every heart for you;
may the love Christ Jesus gave
fill you for every one.


**The Grace** *(said together)*

Jean Gaskin

# 4    *A ritual of confession and absolution*

---

This ritual has been used in large and small gatherings, and is useful in
ecumenical and multi-faith worship as an act of sharing.

> *A bowl, towel and bottle of oil is placed for use near the altar or place of
> leadership for the worship. In large gatherings, two or three bowls etc. can
> be placed with space between them.*
> *An assistant goes to each bowl and oil vessel.*

MINISTER

We sit in silence, open to God, to feel what is heavy upon our
hearts. We each name before God what we would like to say sorry
for, to let go that we may be renewed.

*(Silence.)*

I invite you to come forward to receive hand washing, to dry with
loving care the hands of the person behind you, and to be anointed
as a Blessing of our confession if you so wish.

*Music is played while people file to each of the bowls; their hands are washed, they dry the hands of the person behind them, and anointing is optional. Each then returns to their seat.*
  *During the washing, a voice speaks over the music, at intervals.*

VOICE    I will pour clean water upon you,
         says God,
         and you shall be clean
         from all your uncleanness;
         from all your idols I will cleanse you.                (Ezekiel 36.25)

         Wash away my guilt, O God,
         and cleanse me from my sin.                            (Psalm 51.2)

                                                            **Mary Robins**
                    (adapted from suggestions in *Women Included* (SPCK))

## 5    *Waiting for God-O*
### *A reflective evening for Womenspace, December* 1994

### Blessing of the Light

*Candles are lit as the Blessing of the Light is said.*

Light of God to give us hope
Power of God to protect us
Light of God to give us joy
Peace of God to calm us
Light of God to give us faith
Grace of God to save us
This night and for ever more.                              (David Adam)

God of tender compassion and mercy
whose Son is the Morning Star
and the Sun of Righteousness;
let him shine in the darkness
and shadows of this world,
that we may serve you in freedom and peace,
through Jesus Christ our Saviour. Amen.
                                        (from *The Promise of his Glory*)

### The Great O Antiphons

The Great O Antiphons are ancient refrains, expressing longing expectation for the coming of Emmanuel ('God with us'), sung traditionally with the

Magnificat in the Evening Office in the days leading up to Christmas.

O Wisdom, who came out of the mouth of the Most High, and reach from one end to another, mightily and sweetly ordering all things: Come and teach us the way of prudence.

O Adonai, Leader of the house of Israel, who appeared in the bush to Moses in a blazing fire, and gave him the law on Sinai: Come and redeem us with outstretched arm.

O Root of Jesse, who stand for a sign for the people, at whom kings shall shut their mouths, for whom the nations shall seek: Come and deliver us, and do not delay.

O Key of David, and Sceptre of the house of Israel; who open and no one shuts, who shut and no one opens: Come, and bring the prisoners out of the prison-house, those who sit in darkness and the shadow of death.

O Dayspring, Brightness of the everlasting Light, and Sun of righteousness: Come and bring light to those who sit in darkness and the shadow of death.

O King of nations and their desire, the Cornerstone, who make both one: Come and save humankind, whom you formed of clay.

O Emmanuel, our King and Lawgiver, the Desire of all nations and their Salvation: Come and save us, O Lord our God.

> *Those present are invited to ponder on these refrains, along with the further 'Cries of Advent' composed by Jim Cotter (see his* Prayer in the Morning: *'O Living Word', 'O Lion, Regal in Courage', 'O Swallow', 'O Salmon', 'O Voice of the Voiceless' etc.); and then gather in small groups to create their own O refrain. All these are then read out in turn between verses of the Magnificat:*

OOOOO beyond our defining and confining: Come and infuse your creation with life and connect all the parts with one another and with you.

O Snowdrop, God embodied in fragile form: Come and break through hard earth, to bring us new life and beauty.

O Water of life, you fall to renew the earth, you spray and splash, bubble and flow in river and ocean, you are still and deep, and quench the thirst of all creation: Come, refresh us, cleanse us, satisfy our thirst.

O Rainbow, created by our vision from light and water, sign of hope, continuity and renewal: Come and open our eyes, break into our awareness, and enable us to rejoice in the diversity of your creation.

O Rainbow, symbol of light and colour, appearing as a bridge across the greyness of the storm: Come to lead us from the stillness of our gloom to the radiance of our beauty.

O Candle of calm and peace, symbol of ancient light, lending your beauty and wonder to our darkened corners: Come and share your halo of light with us, to soothe, comfort and guide us as we go on our journey.

O Dancing Waters of Wisdom, ebbing and flowing with surfable waves: Come and exhilarate us who wait for the dance to begin.

O Star of Night, Dreamworld, lead us to new dawnings, guide our journey to our deepest desires, banish doubts, free us from fear, guide us to all fullness.

O Sudden Flare, you explode like a burst of match flame in the darkness: Come and illumine our inner depths, and shine within the folds of our despair.

## Concluding prayer

God our deliverer,
whose approaching birth
still shakes the foundations of our world:
may we so wait for your coming
with eagerness and hope
that we embrace without terror
the labour pangs of the new age,
through Jesus Christ, Amen.

(Janet Morley)

**Joyce Yarrow** CSF

**6**    *Cairn-building*
       *A reflective act of worship*

## Introduction

LEADER A large part of this reflective act of worship will consist of shared silence during which you are invited to pray, meditate or read the scriptures, and allow God to speak to you in the silence.

The worship will culminate in the building of a cairn, in which each person places a stone to represent some intention, prayer or burden you wish to offer to God.

From Old Testament times, the building of a cairn, or a pile of stones, was a sign commemorating an encounter with God. A cairn can take many forms and have a variety of significances:

- a heap of stones by a faint track on a mountain, reassuring the traveller in mist;
- wooden posts indicating a safe route across a trackless fen or shifting sands;
- the summit of a mountain;
- a boundary between two territories, a place of uncertainty and dreaming;
- the site of a burial or a memorial or a hidden treasure;
- signposts, waymarks, markings, indicating that we were here, exploring and finding.

The scriptures are full of images of stones, rocks and cairns, which may speak to us of many facets of God's power, as well as of the fragility and vulnerability of the created world and our own powers for wreaking evil as well as creating good. During the silence, you may like to explore some of these passages as indicated in the service sheet.

LEADER Come to him, a living stone, though rejected by mortals yet chosen and precious in God's sight, and like living stones, let yourselves be built into a spiritual house, to be a holy priesthood, to offer spiritual sacrifices acceptable to God through Jesus Christ.

ALL    Amen.

## Ministry of the Word and Reflection

LEADER We will keep silence for a considerable period. During this time, you may like to sit quietly and pray, meditating on what has been happening to you recently in your life, and being attentive to what God is saying to you.

You may also like to reflect on a passage of scripture. The following passages are all linked to the image of the cairn or the stone:

Jacob builds a cairn at Bethel (Genesis 28.10–22)
David defeats Goliath with a stone (1 Samuel 17)
The Lord is a rock and a fortress (Psalm 18)
Casting the stone at the sinner (John 8.1–10)
The stones proclaim Christ's praise (Luke 19.29–40)
Christ, God's cornerstone (Matthew 21.42–4, 1 Peter 2.4–8)
Precious stones in the foundations of the new Jerusalem (Revelation 21.9–27)

*Silence.*

## Building a Cairn

LEADER You are now invited to place a stone to form a cairn. As you place your stone, you may like to offer a word or a phrase, silently or aloud, indicating what your stone represents for you — perhaps a prayer, an insight, an offering.

*When all have placed their stones, all stand.*

## Hymn *Guide me, O thou great Redeemer*

Nicola Slee

# 7    *On entering a retreat*

---

Let silence be placed around us
like a mantle.
Let us enter into it
as through a small secret door
stooping
to emerge into
an acre of peace
where stillness reigns
and the voice of God
is ever present.

The voice of God
in the startled cry
of a refugee child
waking
in unfamiliar surroundings.

The voice of God
in the mother,
fleeing with
her treasure
in her arms,
who says
'I am here.'

The voice of God
in the father
who points to the stars
and says:

'There is our signpost,
there is our lantern.
Be of good courage.'

O Lord may the mantle of silence
become a cloak of understanding
to warm our hearts in prayer.

Kate McIlhagga

## 8     *O boundless God*

O Boundless God, beyond all naming,
awake our senses
to all we see, hear, touch, taste or smell,
that we may know you are everywhere,
forever with us and within us,
in the light and in the darkness;
that we may joyfully accept our responsibility
in the co-creation of your kingdom here on earth.

In the name of Jesus,
who looked upon the lilies in the field,
who listened with compassion to the troubles of the sick,
who touched the leper's skin,
who tasted the sweetness of the wine,
and who enjoyed the fragrance of the perfumed oil
    poured over his head in the house at Bethany.

Jean Gaskin

## 9     *The word awaited*

Sometimes,
I long to call
words of praise
to me,
so that they may settle
like doves on my palm.
I long to coax them
down from the trees
into my waiting hands.

Sometimes they come,
swift and powerful
like hawks to the wrist of the falconer,
words of challenge,
fierce words of regret.

One time you came,
the word.
Not at my call,
you came
to occupy
a cradle,
a grave,
my heart,
the universe.
You came to call me
to unleash
words of comfort
words of hope.

Sometimes
I hold out
my empty hands
and wait.

Kate McIlhagga

## 10    *Prayer in six directions*
### *An Ohlone (Native American) way of prayer*

---

*In an unhurried fashion, one greets the six directions in prayer.*

We turn to the *east* and face the rising sun. God is praised for the gift of new life, of new days, of youth, of beginnings.

Turning towards the *south*, thanks are given for those people, events and things which warm our lives and help us to grow and develop.

The sun sets in the *west*, and so we praise God for sunsets, nights, for the endings in our lives.

As we face the *north*, we remember the challenges and difficulties in life.

Bending down to touch mother *earth*, we praise the Creator for the things which sustain our lives.

Finally, as we gaze into the *sky*, we thank God for our hopes and dreams.

Centred in the Creator's universe, we remember God's mighty deeds in our
lives and can thus move into the future.

**Michael Galvan**

## 11    *God, our Companion*

---

God, our Companion on the journey,
let us not be so caught up in worldly cares
that we forget that you are with us everywhere.
Open our eyes that we may meet you
    in the people squashed against us in the crowded bus,
    in the weary shoppers elbowing their way towards the counter,
    in the sightseers sauntering along the pavements,
    in the beggars squatting in their squalid corners,
    in the noisy children kicking around an old tin can,
    and in the lonely pensioner peering out of a grimy window.

O God, our Companion,
let us never forget that you are with us everywhere.

**Jean Gaskin**

## 12    *God our mother*

---

God our mother
who brings us into life:
in the pain and risk of creating
you give birth to your children.
**God our mother,**
**we praise your love.**

God our mother
who nurtures us:
you watch over our tentative exploring
and protect us as we grow.
**God our mother,**
**we are safe in your love.**

God our mother
who stays with us:
you stand alongside us in our pain
and suffer our sullen withdrawal.

**God our mother,**
**we trust your love.**

God our mother
who lets us go:
you watch agonised as we make the choices
and decisions that lead to sadness.
**God our mother,**
**we are free in your love.**

God our mother,
you live in us:
risk-taking
nurturing
suffering
freeing.
**God our mother,**
**fill us with your love.**

Jan Berry

## 13　*Trawling the depths*

In the dead of night with fingers numb and a meagre catch,
we come to you, empty and questioning:
**Calling Christ, your time is fulfilled.**

As the waves mount up and the gale unleashes its fury,
we come to you, fearful and vulnerable:
**Calling Christ, your time is fulfilled.**

As the dawn breaks and the day is born,
we come to you, sunstruck with praise:
**Calling Christ, your time is fulfilled.**

As the sun climbs and light flashes through mist,
we feel the heat of your love:
**Calling Christ, your time is fulfilled.**

As the minutes turn to hours and the day gathers pace,
we turn to you for forgiveness:
**Calling Christ, your time is fulfilled.**

In the afternoon of enforced idleness, quotas exhausted,
we search for you in frustration and anger:
**Calling Christ, your time is fulfilled.**

As the temperature drops and the shadows lengthen,
we turn to you, speechless in our need:
**Calling Christ, your time is fulfilled.**

As the sun dips into tomorrow,
we embrace your presence, transforming the ordinary:
**Calling Christ, your time is fulfilled.**

Janet Lees

## 14

**Name Unnamed, hidden and shown, knowing and known: Gloria!**

Beautiful Movement, ceaselessly forming,
   growing, emerging with awesome delight,
Maker of Rainbows, glowing with colour, arching in wonder,
   energy flowing in darkness and light:
**Name Unnamed . . .**

Spinner of Chaos, pulling and twisting,
   freeing the fibres of pattern and form,
Weaver of stories, famed or unspoken, tangled or broken,
   shaping a tapestry vivid and warm:
**Name Unnamed . . .**

Nudging Discomforter, prodding and shaking,
   waking our lives to creative unease,
Straight-Talking Lover, checking and humbling jargon and
      grumbling,
   speaking the truth that refreshes and frees:
**Name Unnamed . . .**

Midwife of Changes, skilfully guiding,
   drawing us out through the shock of the new,
Mother of Wisdom, deeply perceiving, never deceiving,
   freeing and leading in all that we do:
**Name Unnamed . . .**

Dare-devil Gambler, risking and loving,
   giving us freedom to shatter your dreams,
Life-giving Loser, wounded and weeping, dancing and leaping,
   sharing the caring that heals and redeems:
**Name Unnamed . . .**

*Tune: Castle Montgomery*

**Brian Wren**

**15**

Great soaring Spirit,
  sweeping in uncharted flight
beyond the bounds of time and space.
  God's breath of love,
you fill the outflung galaxies,
and move through earth's long centuries
with aching, mending, dancing grace.

Great eagle Spirit,
  crying from the tallest crags
to all discarded, all distressed,
  glad gusting love,
come, scatter trivialities,
and raise envisioned ministries
to hear and honour earth's oppressed.

Great nesting Spirit,
  sheltering with mighty wings
your chattering, demanding brood,
  deep, restless love,
come, stir us, show us how to fly,
till, heading for tomorrow's sky,
we soar together, God-renewed.

*Tune: McKendrie*

**Brian Wren**

**16**   *Trinitarian blessings*

May the Sending One sing in you,
May the Seeking One walk with you,
May the Greeting One stand by you,
  in your gladness and in your grieving.

May the Gifted One relieve you,
May the Given One retrieve you,
May the Giving One receive you,
  in your falling and your restoring.

May the Binding One unite you,
May the One Belov'd invite you,
May the Loving One delight you,
    Three-in-One, joy in life unending.

*Tune: Rollingbay*

Brian Wren

## 17

Eternal God, your love's tremendous glory
cascades through life in overflowing grace,
to tell creation's meaning in the story
love evolving love from time and space.

Eternal Son of God, uniquely precious,
in you, deserted, scorned and crucified,
God's love has fathomed sin and death's deep darkness,
and flawed humanity is glorified.

Eternal Spirit, with us like a mother,
embracing us in love serene and pure:
you nurture strength to follow Christ our brother,
as full-grown children, confident and sure.

Love's trinity, self-perfect, self-sustaining;
love which commands, enables and obeys:
you give yourself, in boundless joy, creating
one vast increasing harmony of praise.

We ask you now, complete your image in us;
this love of yours, our source and guide and goal.
May love in us, seek love and serve love's purpose,
till we ascend with Christ and find love whole.

*Tune: Highwood*

Alan Gaunt

**18**

Messenger of marvels, challenger of sleep,
Light is born — and quickens life within the deep.
God, quicken us, empower and set us free:
Light is come, like treasure salvaged from the sea.

Truths, obscured and buried, speak in language plain;
Old wells are unstopped, and water springs again.
Once locked in folly, now we find the key:
Truth is come, like treasure salvaged from the sea.

Beauty's gold is rescued, dross is skimmed away;
Hoards from secret places shine anew today.
Give we our hearts to God's fierce alchemy:
Beauty comes, like treasure salvaged from the sea.

Love of Christ, rejected, buried in the tomb,
Now is resurrected, leaps the prison-room.
Called out* from death, Christ's living Body, we:
Love is come, like treasure salvaged from the sea.

Secret, silent Kingdom — jettisoned, denied —
Rises from the deep and dances on the tide:
In and around us, waiting patiently:
Kingdom come! like treasure salvaged from the sea.

* 'Ekklesia' (Church) is that which is 'called out'.

*Tune: Noel Nouvelet*

**Kate Compston**

**19**

Deep inside creation's myst'ry
Stands a table set with bread
And a cup of grapes' rejoicing
Love full-bodied, sparkling red.

Hands reach out across the cosmos;
Each is gladly taking part,
Off'ring deeply all their being
In this Eucharistic heart.

Rocks and stones rejoice together;
Insects, birds can join the song;
Flowers leap up and clouds are dancing;
All are joined and all are strong.

Human voices join the chorus;
Chant and jazz and mystic prose,
Hymns of fellowship all make the
Counterpoint of One who Knows.

Life-transforming celebration
Centr'ing eccentricity,
Shape our dancing, keep it rooted
In love's creativity.

We all bear the marks of loving
In our hearts. That is the plan.
In our own truth we shall find that
Truth in Whom we all began.

*Tune: Cross of Jesus*

June Boyce-Tillman

## 20    *Hands shaped like a cradle*

Put peace into each other's hands
and like a treasure hold it,
protect it like a candle-flame,
with tenderness enfold it.

Put peace into each other's hands
with loving expectation;
be gentle in your words and ways,
in touch with God's creation.

Put peace into each other's hands
like bread we break for sharing;
look people warmly in the eye:
our life is meant for caring.

As at communion, shape your hands,
into a waiting cradle;
the gift of Christ receive, revere,
united round the table.

Put Christ into each other's hands,
he is love's deepest measure;
in love make peace, give peace a chance,
and share it like a treasure.

*Tunes: Ach Gott und Herr, or St Columba*

**Fred Kaan**

## 21    *A hymn for King Alfred's Day*

Your supporting presence guides us through the night
So we can approach You, sparkling Source of light;
Shine through the mists, the dead'ning heavy clay.
Purifying Spirit, burn the dross away.

You are gentler weather after winter's rains,
And a wayside restplace soothing journ'ying's strains;
Though out in front, protect us with Yourself:
You're our destination and the road itself.

*Tune: Noel Nouvelet*

**June Boyce-Tillman**
(based on Alfred's translation of Boethius)

## 22

Praise to God, the world's Creator,
Source of life and growth and breath,
Cradling in her arms her children,
Holding them from birth to death.
In our bodies, in our living,
Strength and truth of all we do,
God is present, working with us,
Making us creators too.

Praise to God, our saving Wisdom,
Meeting us with love and grace,
Helping us to grow in wholeness,
Giving freedom, room and space.
In our hurting, in our risking,
In the thoughts we dare not name,

God is present, growing with us,
Healing us from pride and shame.

Praise to God, the Spirit in us,
Prompting hidden depths of prayer,
Firing us to long for justice,
Reaching out with tender care.
In our searching, in our loving,
In our struggles to be free,
God is present, living in us,
Pointing us to what shall be.

*Tune: Pond Street*

**Jan Berry**

## 23    *Daring, dancing Trinity*

Lord, your power has called to being
all that fills the earth below,
myriad stars beyond our seeing,
tiniest creatures that we know;
earth and air and fire and water
woven in the grand design,
witness to the final meaning
of your love in human kind.

Human lives are made for sharing;
joined in trust and truth we grow,
speech or silence opening pathways
to the hearts we seek to know.
Welcome love, by your renewal
worn out ways turn upside down;
weak is strong, success is failure,
and the wise becomes the clown.

From your self we take our nature,
Maker, parent, love divine.
Bound into your life we flourish,
leaves and branches of the vine.
Through the Christ we see your pattern,
life surrendered, life restored:
echoing through all creation
sounds the spirit's deep accord.

Love releases us for taking
one more risk than we might dare;
glory breaks through dark and danger,
shows the Lord transfigured there.
God who planted our affections,
help your gifts to grow more free,
fan in us the fires of loving,
daring, dancing Trinity.

*Tunes: Blaenwern, or Wangford*

**Michael Hare Duke**

## 24    *Blessing*

May the divine Wisdom hold you in the palm of her hand
and breathe into you, gently,
her own life-giving Spirit;
may she befriend you, cherish you and challenge you,
and draw you to herself in freedom;

may Jesus go with you,
and may you be with him
always and everywhere;

and may you too embody in this world
the redeeming love of God.

**Jennifer Wild**

# 2

## *The holy child to be born shall be called . . .*
### Beginnings and namings

The event of a birth seems to be universally one of the most significant human happenings. Birth is special, precious, frightening, dangerous, awesome, absolutely ordinary and a cause for wonder. Often, all these feelings accompany the birth of a single child. Not surprising then that 'birth' is one of the three times ('hatch, match and dispatch') when the church is seen to come into its own liturgically, in this case with services of baptism. However, more and more parents are seeking something different from formal baptism: naming, thanksgiving, welcoming, blessing are some of the descriptions of the services sent to us for this collection. Number 30, a thanksgiving for the birth of a child of Muslim and Christian parentage, and number 32, 'A welcome for Tristan', are both examples of making a formal, denominational service one's own.

It is a theme of this book that any experience of change nearly always carries at least some ambivalent feelings. And so it is with birth. A child will bring great joy, but great change also. Parenting will be fun and it will challenge. Whether the child will be brought up by one parent or two, the love and support of friends will be important. All these aspects are recognized in the liturgies and prayers that follow. So too is the messiness, pain and chaos of birth itself, something rarely visible in more formal church rites.

Birth is a beginning. Other life experiences are also beginnings or new beginnings and so we include in this section rites of passage for a daughter's menarche, for retirement, and for 'croning' when a woman reaches her 'third age'. We included these last two here rather than with rites of separation and farewell, wanting to say something positive about increasing age in a culture and at a time when older people are so negatively regarded. Nevertheless, it should still be remembered that these rites of passage, as with celebrations of an actual birth, involve both endings and beginnings.

**25**    *The enlightening Light*
*A service for Advent*

---

### Greeting and Introduction

LEADER During the season of Advent the Christian church seeks to identify with countless women and men who, before the birth of Christ, had intimations of his coming; and with all those in the world today who still look for the fulfilment of their expectations.

As a sign of the common heritage which Christians share with the Jewish people, a seven-branched candelabrum, or Menorah, is used as a visual focus for this service.

### Hymn *O come, O come, Emmanuel*

### The Great Advent Antiphons

LEADER The Great Advent Antiphons remind us of humanity's rich expectations of a Redeemer, and look forward to their fulfilment in the final coming of Christ.

O Wisdom, Holy Word of God, who governs all creation with your strong yet tender care; come, and show your people the way to salvation.
**Come, Lord Jesus, come.**
**Come, Lord Jesus, come** *(sung)*

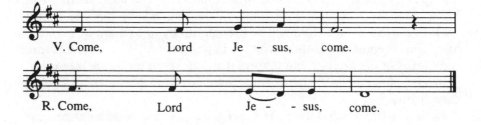

O Sacred Lord of Ancient Israel, who showed yourself to Moses in the burning bush and gave him the holy Law in Sinai; come stretch out your mighty hand to set us free.
**Come, Lord Jesus, come.**
**Come, Lord Jesus, come!**

O Flower of Jesse's stem, you have been raised up as a sign for all peoples, rulers stand silent in your presence, the nations bow down in worship before you; come quickly to our aid.

**Come, Lord Jesus, come.**
**Come, Lord Jesus, come!**

O Key of David, and sceptre of the house of Israel, you open and no one can shut, and shut and no one can open; come and free the captive from prison.
**Come, Lord Jesus, come.**
**Come, Lord Jesus, come!**

O Radiant Dawn, splendour of eternal light, sun of justice; come and shine on those who live in darkness and the shadow of death.
**Come, Lord Jesus, come.**
**Come, Lord Jesus, come!**

O King of all the Nations, the only joy of every human heart, keystone of the mighty arch of humankind; come and save us whom you fashioned from the dust.
**Come, Lord Jesus, come.**
**Come, Lord Jesus, come!**

O Emmanuel, King and Lawgiver, hope of the nations, saviour of all peoples; come and redeem us, O Lord.
**Come, Lord Jesus, come.**
**Come, Lord Jesus, come!**

## Collect

Almighty God, who spoke in time past in many and various ways to your chosen people by the prophets, and gave us in your Son our Saviour Jesus Christ a fulfilment of the hope of Israel; we pray you to speed the coming of the day when all people shall be subject to him, who lives and reigns with you and the Holy Spirit, ever one God, now and for ever, Amen.

## Psalm 85

A O Lord, you once favoured your land
and revived the fortunes of Jacob;
you forgave the guilt of your people
and covered all their sins.

B You averted all your rage;
you calmed the heat of your anger.

A Revive us now, God, our helper!
Put an end to your grievance against us.

Will you be angry with us for ever?
Will your anger never cease?

B Will you not restore again our life,
that your people may rejoice in you?
Let us see, O Lord, your mercy,
and give us your saving help.

A I will hear what the Lord God has to say,
a voice that speaks of peace;
peace for the people and their friends,
and those who turn to God in their hearts.

B God's help is near for those who fear,
and God's glory will dwell in our land.

A Mercy and faithfulness have met;
justice and peace have embraced.
Faithfulness shall spring from the earth
and justice look down from heaven.

B The Lord will make us prosper,
and our earth shall yield its fruit.
Justice shall march before our God,
and peace shall follow behind.

(Grail Psalms, adapted)

## Prophecy *Isaiah 55.6–11*

## Responsory

v I wait for the Lord, my soul waits,
and in God's Word I put my hope.

R **Jesu, tawa pano.** *(sung)*

Je - su  ta - wa  pa - no,        Je - su

ta - wa  pa - no,  Je - su  ta - wa  pa - no,

ta - wa  pa - no  mu  zi - ta  ren - yu.

(Patrick Matsikenyiri, Zimbabwe)

v My soul waits for the Lord,
  more than those who watch for the morn.
R **Jesu, tawa pano.**

v O Israel, hope in the Lord!
  For with the Lord there is steadfast love,
  and with the Lord there is plenteous redemption.
R **Jesu, tawa pano.**

v In our darkness there is no darkness with you, O Lord,
  the deepest night is as clear as the day.
R **Jesu, tawa pano.**

## Gospel *Luke 1.5–23*
*Silence.*

## Acclamation *Laudate, omnes gentes (Taizé)*

## Poem *Are you a stranger to my country, Lord?*

## Benedictus

## Litany of darkness and light

VOICE 1  We wait in the darkness, expectantly, longingly, anxiously,
         thoughtfully.
VOICE 2  The darkness is our friend. In the darkness of the womb, we have

all been nurtured and protected. In the darkness of the womb, the Christ-child was made ready for the journey into light.

ALL    **You are with us, O God, in darkness and light.**

VOICE 1    It is only in the darkness that we can see the splendour of the universe — blankets of stars, the solitary glowings of distant planets.

VOICE 2    It was the darkness that allowed the Magi to find the star that guided them to where the Christ-child lay.

ALL    **You are with us, O God, in darkness and light.**

VOICE 1    In the darkness of night, desert peoples find relief from the cruel relentless heat of the sun.

VOICE 2    In the blessed desert darkness Mary and Joseph were able to flee with the infant Jesus to safety in Egypt.

ALL    **You are with us, O God, in darkness and light.**

VOICE 1    In the darkness of sleep, we are soothed and restored, healed and renewed.

VOICE 2    In the darkness of sleep, dreams rise up. God spoke to Jacob and Joseph through dreams. God is speaking still.

ALL    **You are with us, O God, in darkness and light.**

VOICE 1    In the solitude of darkness, we sometimes remember those who need God's presence in a special way — the sick, the unemployed, the bereaved, the persecuted, the homeless; those who are demoralized and discouraged, those whose fear has turned to cynicism, those whose vulnerability has become bitterness.

VOICE 2    Sometimes we remember, in the darkness, those who are near to our hearts — colleagues, partners, parents, children, neighbours, friends. We thank God for their presence and ask God to bless and protect them in all that they do — at home, at school, as they travel, as they work, as they play.

ALL    **You are with us, O God, in darkness and light.**

VOICE 1    Sometimes in the solitude of darkness our fears and concerns, our hopes and our visions rise to the surface. We come face to face with ourselves and with the road that lies ahead of us. And in that same darkness we find companionship for the journey.

VOICE 2    In that same darkness, we sometimes allow ourselves to wonder and worry whether the human race is going to survive.

ALL    We know that you are with us, O God, yet we still await your coming. In the darkness that contains both our hopelessness and our expectancy, we watch for a sign of God's hope.

(Presbyterian Church of Aotearoa New Zealand)

## Magnificat

### Intercession

Remember your Church O Christ; send us continually your Spirit of unity, courage and holiness.
**Kyrie eleison** *(sung).*

(Music: Dinah Reindorf, Ghana)

By shedding your blood you have purified us; keep us ready to welcome the Day of your coming.

Call from among us bearers of your presence; may they go to the far ends of the earth as tokens of your friendship and signs of your light.

Give joy to all your faithful servants; may they follow you all the days of their life.

**Kyrie eleison.**

Nurture within us your Spirit of love; may we never close our hearts to any of our sisters and brothers.

Bring to an end the divisions between Christians; gather us in one visible communion.

Have mercy on all who suffer persecution for your name's sake; uphold them by your strong Spirit, that they may remain true to you in all their trials.

**Kyrie eleison.**

Comfort all who are suffering in their hearts or in their bodies; give them health and peace to sing of your power. We pray for all who are leading the nations; give them a sense of what is right, that they may work towards peace and fullness of life for all.

Give eternal rest to all who are dying; may the light that never sets shine upon them.

**Kyrie eleison.**

O God, you have brought us out of the power of darkness into the kingdom of your dear Son; may we wait for his coming in the knowledge that we

are in the world but not of the world, since he reigns in your Eternity for
ever and ever, Amen.

(Adapted from *Praise in All our Days:*
*Common Prayers at Taizé*)

## The Lord's Prayer

## Hymn *O Lord, how shall I meet you?*

## Blessing

v  Holy, Holy, Holy is the Lord our God,
R  Sovereign Ruler of all the world,
v  Who was, and is, and is to come,
R  Emmanuel, God is with us.
v  Let us bless the Lord.
R  Thanks be to God.
v  The Lord bless you and keep you;
   May the Lord's face shine upon you,
   and the Lord be gracious to you;
   May the Lord's countenance be lifted up
   upon you, and the Lord give you peace,
R  Amen.

## Recessional *Kindle a flame, to lighten the dark*

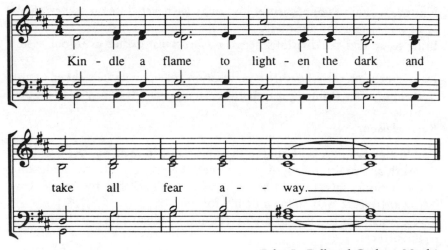

(John L. Bell and Graham Maule)

Alec Balfe-Mitchell

(based on the service outline in *With All God's People*, pp. 3–13)

# 26   *A liturgy for Advent Sunday*

Mary Robins writes:
This process can be used with any liturgy, once the essential elements have been identified.

I used this method first working with some members of the congregation of Tring Parish Church. The Tring clergy joined us and we much appreciated the experience. Our aim was to celebrate the Parish Eucharist using as much of the congregation's input as possible.

A workshop on the Saturday before the service gave an opportunity to explore 'Journeying towards Christmas'. First we explored the theme together, then we divided into groups using different creative processes. After looking together at the basic elements of the Eucharist, and those we must retain from the Rite A, we allocated tasks – the painting group produced the intercessions; the writing group put together a collect, the confession and absolution, a Proper Preface, a Dismissal; the drama group presented the readings and 'sermon'; the musicians chose hymns and other music for the theme. A few other inputs, such as the blessing, we did not have time to write and so used traditional pieces that blended. The result was the following liturgy for Advent Sunday.

## Advent Sentence

Our God is coming, he will not keep silent;
before him is devouring fire and tempest whirls about him.        (Psalm 50.3)

## Hymn *O Come, O come, Emmanuel*

## The Preparation *(as in ASB)*

## Lord have mercy *(sung)*

## Collect

O God our guide, be with us on our journey towards Christmas
as we await the celebration of the birth of Christ.
You know all our needs,
guide us along the path that will bring each one of us
to the wonder of your birth, through Jesus Christ our Lord, Amen.

## Proclaiming and responding to the Word of God

Reading: Luke 2.1–5
Drama: *of the poor, lonely, hungry, abused, finding Christ and helping each other to find a way to Christ.*
Reading: *Luke 1.46–55*
Hymn: *Come thou long-expected Jesus*
Confession

LEADER Let us take a few moments to reflect upon the things that get in the way as we journey towards Christ . . .

As we journey towards you, some of us are separated from you. If we are separated from you by our anxiety and tension
ALL **Lord, forgive us and heal us.**

LEADER If we are separated from you by our business
ALL **Lord, forgive us and heal us.**

LEADER If we are separated from you by grief or loneliness
ALL **Lord, forgive us and heal us.**

LEADER If we are separated from you by materialism and the pressure of commercialization
ALL **Lord, forgive us and heal us.**

LEADER If we are separated from you by bad relationships
ALL **Lord, forgive us and heal us.**

*A bowl of incense is carried in.*

## Absolution

Our God meets us every step of our way
with forgiveness on his lips and healing in his hands.

## Intercessions

When we pray, Lord, you listen.
Let our prayers rise before you, like incense to your throne.

*Prayers are made while children hold up paintings.*

*The Advent Candle is lit to the Iona chant,* Kindle a flame *or the Taizé chant,* The Lord is my Light.

## Peace

LEADER In the tender compassion of our God, the dawn from on high shall break upon us, to shine on those who dwell in darkness and the shadow of death, and to guide our feet into the way of peace.

CELEBRANT
The peace of the Lord be always with you.
ALL   **And also with you.**

*A sign of peace is exchanged.*

## Hymn *From heaven you came, helpless babe*

## Words of offering

Yours, Lord is the greatness, the power, the glory
the splendour and the majesty;
and yours, Lord, is the excitement, the planning,
the worry, the anxieties and the sadness.
For everything in heaven and on earth is yours.
All things come from you, and of your own do we give you.

## Third Eucharistic Prayer

## Proper preface

And now we give you thanks because you are with us on our journey, shining light on our path. We are never alone.

## Post-Communion sentence

CELEBRANT
He who gives the testimony says, 'Yes, I am coming soon!'
ALL   Amen. Come, Lord Jesus!

## Hymn *Lo, he comes, with clouds, descending*

## Blessing

CELEBRANT
Christ the Sun of Righteousness shine upon you and scatter the darkness from before your path; and the blessing of God Almighty, Father, Son and Holy Spirit, be among you and remain with you always.
ALL   Amen.

### Dismissal

CELEBRANT
   So let us set out on our journey towards Christmas.
ALL    In the name of Christ. Amen.

**Mary Robins**

## 27    *Celebrating birth*

---

*Preparation: Have seven candles on a table ready for lighting.*

**Hymn** *Hymn for a child's baptism*

**Reading** *A story of creation*

*Use several voices to read this, and if using candles, light one for each 'time' a section is read.*

Once upon a time, in the beginning,
a labour of love was undertaken.

It started with a sign, to show that
something was about to happen.
Light came forth from the deep darkness,
bright, clear and unmistakable.
And it was very good.

At the second time, the waters were broken.
At first, they gushed, then they dried to a trickle,
and a space was created.
It was exactly the right size.
By now, the creation was well under way.
And it was very good.

At the third time, a cradle was made ready.
It was comfortable and beautiful and waiting.
And food was prepared, issuing sweetly and warmly
and in precisely the right measure
from the being of the labourer.
And it was very good.

At the fourth time, rhythm was established.
Ebbing and flowing, contracting and expanding,
pain and joy, sun and moon,
beginning and ending.

The labour of love progressed.
And it was very good.

At the fifth time, there was ceaseless activity.
Fluttering like the wings of the dove,
humming like the murmur of the dragonfly,
swimming like the darting golden fish,
wriggling like the lithe serpent,
leaping like the flashing deer,
surging like the mighty lion.
And it was very good.

At the sixth time, there was a momentary,
endless hesitation.
Then a child was born.
And the child looked just like the one
who had given it life.
The child too was born with the power to create
and to make decisions, and to love.
The labourer looked at all that had been
accomplished, and rejoiced,
for it was very good.

At the seventh time, the labour was finished.
The task was complete.
And the labourer rested,
for she was very, very tired.

(Kathy Galloway)

LEADER Hear the words of two women from the Bible whose pregnancies
were particularly special: Sarah, who conceived in her old age:

READER Isaac, my son,
I feel you stir within me:
My own private genesis
Cell upon tiny cell.

I'd long believed this
Couldn't happen.
I am so old and
Have lived childless.

In this life
'Woman' means nothing
Without 'child'.

So many years
I watched with jealous anguish
The swelling bellies of other women;
Small mouths clasped to their milky breasts
And I yearned for a child.

Even now my fears are many:
Can I nurture you safely to birth?
Will I be a good mother?
Is my faith strong enough?

But you, my son,
Are gifted from God,
And you carry hope and promise
To our people.

And so I will nurture you
And raise you to be proud and strong,
For I am your mother,
And I love you.

(Philippa Brooker)

READER Mary, a young unmarried woman, asked by God to do what had not been done before, responded in these words:

*Read the Magnificat, Luke 1.46–55, preferably in a modern version; or sing it, or a hymn based on it, e.g. 'Tell out my Soul'.*

LEADER I invite you to share your own birth experiences.

Where did your support come from?
What were the positive aspects of the experience?
What were the negative ones, if any?
Was there an awareness of God in this process?

*(It may be advisable to have asked at least one person beforehand to be ready to share her birth experience at this point. Alternatively, members could be asked to share with a neighbour, rather than the whole group.)*

## Prayer *Litany of new birth*

O gracious God of life and birth,
**How you labour, how you suffer, to bring forth the new creation!**

Indeed, you cry out like a woman in childbirth.
**And the Spirit groans with you.**

But your cries become cries of joy,
**As you behold fragile new life before you.**

All creation waits on tiptoe for the revealing of your daughters and
sons;
**We ourselves long to take part in the glorious liberty of your
children.**

Who can separate us from the love of God?
**Even a mother might forget us,**

Yet you will not forsake us!
**O God, our God, how wonderful is your name in all the earth!**

(from Bread for the Journey)

*A suitable hymn may be sung.*

## Blessing

May God, who laboured in love to create all life,
continue creating within us
new hope, new joy, new visions;
and may we go from here to bring
new life to the world. Amen.

**Dorothy Brooker and others**

**28**   *From a naming ceremony and thanksgiving*
*For Leila Balfe, at the Amani Centre, Moss Side,*
*Manchester, 6 March 1993*

---

### Words of Welcome

**Hymn** *Now thank we all our God*

**Past and present** (*Linda reflects on her three children*)

Nadia —
Your name means Hope.
Your birth burst
Upon the world
Like August sunshine,
Flooding it with light,
Painting all of life
In new colours,
To be seen again
For the first time.

**Nicholas** –
After many months
Of waiting
And wondering
You came
And went
Almost in a day,
Transient as the wind
Gusting through green leaves.
The rain lashed and stung,
Then suddenly
All was still.

At dawn each day
A blackbird sang,
Whose chicks had been snatched
Cruelly from the nest
By magpies.
One by one
They died
As we looked on,
Helpless

But the song
Did not stop.

**Leila** –
Of the night.
Born in the hours
Before dawn.

You caught the old year's
Breath
In time
To start afresh
And continue.

The all-embracing
Night
Covered your birth
Like a soft blanket.

While,
In another place,
Pierced by the crystal coldness

Of stars,
It enveloped
A Middle-Eastern hillside,
Where men huddled,
Hungry for their Homeland.

The quiet peace
Of the night
Was born
With you,
The clear-speaking
Silence,
The luminous
Darkness.

The year ends
In its
New beginning.
Each birth
A resurrection.

Day breaks
On each of us
Alone
And all of us
Together.
We are all
Of the Night.


## Song for Leila

Lullaby our little baby,
who lies upon the breast,
Whose dreams are blessed with emptiness,
Whose beauty knows no beast.
Whose days, as yet uncluttered,
Are filled with peace and light,
Whose world is small and beautiful;
Whose fears must yet take flight;
For the earth as made awaits you,
With journeys harsh and long;
As you sleep to draw your growing strength
We offer you this song.

There are children now who cannot sleep,
Whose days are filled with tears,
Whose lives are bruised and broken down
By grown-ups' greed and fears.
There are those who cry with hunger,
There are those who suffer pain,
There are countless million others
Who will not wake again.
And these children are your sisters,
Your brothers, of this earth;
Each life, like yours, in need of love
To care for all its worth.

As you grow you will hear stories
Of Why and What and How,
Saying God or Man or Fate or Chance
Makes things as they are now;
And some will say all sorrow
Has some purpose, goal or good,
And some suggest we suffer
Precisely as we should!
But our gift to you, new baby,
A mortal like us too,
Is the cradle of community
Where we will stay with you.

For together we can take life on
And give all suffering hell!
We can fight all fear and prejudice,
And combat wrong as well.
We can give our suffering meaning
As we make it work for good,
As your brother did before you
With thorns and nails and wood.
For the world's as yet unfinished,
And gains from every birth
Like yours — and his — and those to come,
The hope of one whole earth.

(Alec Balfe-Mitchell and Michael Taylor)

**Present and future** *Alec reflects.*

**Lighting of candles**

*During this is sung:*

*Ubi caritas et amor,*
*ubi caritas, Deus ibi est.*

(Where there is tender care and love,
God is present.)

**Bible reading** *Mark 10.13–16*

**The Act of naming**

*Heather, Linda, Alec and Nadia stand.*
*Heather takes Leila in her arms.*

HEATHER What names do you give this child?

LINDA AND ALEC
    Leila Balfe.

HEATHER Leila, we give you your first name as a beautiful name, a name
from the cradle of the world; an Arabic name meaning 'night',
and a name for you to fill with meaning by the living of your own
days.

    Let night be the place from which you come and the peace to
which you shall return, and the borders of every shining day.

LINDA AND ALEC
    We name you Leila:
    Friends, will you name her too?

ALL    We name you Leila.

    *Linda takes Leila in her arms.*

HEATHER Leila Balfe, we give you your surname as a beautiful name, a name
full of history, and a name for you to keep or let go. May you
grow up to be proud of it, with humility; a strong and tender
bearer of your past; and may you always be open to others with
different names and faces and colours and faiths; ready to share
and teach, yet also to learn, let go, and grow.

LINDA AND ALEC
    We name you Leila Balfe:
    Friends, will you name her too?

ALL    We name you Leila Balfe.

*Alec takes Leila in his arms.*

HEATHER Leila, we give you no other names, but acknowledge and affirm your liberty to choose others, or not. If you should seek to follow Christ then we support your choice of a Christian name; and if you should follow some other way then we support that choice and identity too. Whatever you do, may you be happy and strong, never unfree, and capable of saying at the last − 'I have no regrets'.

LINDA AND ALEC
Leila, we name you, ready to let you be and become yourself: Friends, will you name her too?

ALL    Leila Balfe, we name you your own name.

HEATHER We now invite all of the children here today to come forward to receive a small gift and a blessing.

## Blessing

Bless your eyes that you may have
    clarity of vision,
Bless your mouth that you may speak
    the truth,
Bless your ears that you may hear
    all that is spoken to you,
Bless your heart that you may be
    filled with love,
Bless your feet that you may find and walk
    your own true path.

*The children are each given a gift and return to their places. All stand.*

## Hymn *Come, cradle all* (40)

## The Dismissal

HEATHER
O Wisdom,
dwelling in the womb of God,
generating and nurturing the earth
through nights of darkness,
come and cherish in us
the seed of wisdom.

(Jim Cotter)

Deep peace of the running wave to you,
Deep peace of the flowing air to you,
Deep peace of the quiet earth to you,
Deep peace of the shining star to you,
Deep peace of the Son of Peace to you,
Amen.

**Alec Balfe-Mitchell and Linda Balfe**

## 29   *A welcoming and naming ceremony for a new baby*

*The company sits in a circle.[1] A candle is lit in the centre, and another, unlit candle is put beside it.[2]*

### Introduction

*This can be spoken by the mother's best friend, or the grandmother, or whoever has the facilitator's role.*

We are gathered to celebrate the birth of N/M's baby, to welcome *her/him* by name, to rejoice in the beauty and potential of this new life and to offer *her/him* our love and friendship. Let us dance our greeting.

### The Greeting Dance

*Parents and baby move to sit in the centre of the circle, and the company dance a short version of Enas Mythos[3] around them. The symbolism of this very simple dance is: 'I greet you, I give you space, I move on.' The tune is one the company will want to hum as they dance. At the end of the dance the parents and baby join the circle again. All remain standing.*

### The Naming

FACILITATOR
    N and N, what name do you give your baby?
PARENTS
    We name *her/him* N.
FACILITATOR
    *(sings)* Welcome N! *(three times)*
COMPANY
    *(repeats each time, singing)* Welcome N!

## The bringing of gifts

*All sit.*
*In turn members of the company place symbolic objects around the candle*
*with the words:*

I bring this gift as a symbol of . . . May *he/she* know . . . (e.g. love, joy, peace, enlightenment, potential, prosperity, compassion, rootedness etc.).

## Passing the candle

*The second candle is lit and passed around the circle. While holding the*
*candle, whoever wishes may say:*

My vision and hope for N is . . .

## A short guided meditation *(optional but very desirable)*

*E.g. visualizing the baby's growth to maturity, surrounded always with*
*light and love.*

## A blessing

*This is said by all the company.*

Now, may N, *her/his* family, we, *her/his* friends,
   and every living being,
Young or old,
Living near or far,
Known to us or unknown,
Living, departed or yet to be born,
May every living being be full of bliss.
Amen.
                                        (Sakyamuni Buddha (adapted))

**Joan E. James**


*Notes*

1   This simple ceremony can take place in the baby's own home.
2   The candles and some flowers or flowering plant could be on a small, low table.
3   This is Dance No. 2, side 1, of Tape 1, *Beginners' Dances, Dancing Circles,*
    obtainable at The Findhorn Foundation, The Park, Forres, Scotland IV36 0TZ.

**30** *Thanksgiving for the birth of a child*
*of Muslim father and Christian mother*

---

*The celebrant addresses the congregation in these or similar words:*

Dear Friends: The birth of a child is a joyous and solemn occasion in the life
of a family. It is also an occasion for rejoicing in the community. I bid you,
therefore, to join N and N in giving thanks to Almighty God our Heavenly
Father, the Lord of all life, for the gift of N to be their son (daughter) [and
with N (and NN), for a new brother (sister)].

Let us say together:

I love the Lord, because he has heard the voice of my supplication;
because he has inclined his ear to me whenever I called upon him.
Gracious is the Lord and righteous; our God is full of compassion.
How shall I repay the Lord for all the good things he has done for me?
I will lift up the cup of salvation and call upon the name of the Lord,
I will fulfil my vows to the Lord in the presence of all his people,
In the courts of the Lord's House, in your midst, O Jerusalem.
Allelluia!

(Psalm 116)

MINISTER

Let us thank God that in his goodness he has given you this *son*/this
*daughter*.

God our Father, maker of all that is living,
we praise you for the wonder and joy of creation.
We thank you from our hearts
for the life of *this child*,
for a safe delivery,
and for the privilege of parenthood. Amen.           (ASB, adapted)

*The parents of the child may say together:*

God our Father
in giving us this child
you have shown us your love.
Help us to be trustworthy parents.
Make us patient and understanding,
that our *child* may always be sure of our love
and grow up to be happy and responsible;
in the fear and love of the Lord. Amen.            (ASB, adapted)

MINISTER

Almighty God look with favour on *this child*; grant that, being nourished with all goodness, *he* may grow in discipline and grace until *he* comes to the fullness of *his* own faith. Amen.

*There follows the Peace (ASB, p. 128).*

**John Allen**

## 31    *A Celtic baptism*
### The Baptism of Esther Zoe

LEADER When the poor and needy search for water, and none is to be found, and their tongues are parched with thirst then I, their God, will answer them; I will not abandon them. I will make rivers run on barren heights and fountains in the valleys; I will turn the wilderness into a lake and dry land into springs of water.

ALL    **Living Water to all who thirst, in you we live and have our being.**

LEADER Jesus said, 'Whoever drinks the water that I shall give, will never thirst again; for the water that I give will become a spring within, welling up to eternal life.'

ALL    **Living Water to all who thirst, in you we live and have our being.**

LEADER The Lamb at the centre of the throne will be their Shepherd; he will lead them to springs of living water. And God will wipe away every tear from their eyes.

ALL    **Living Water to all who thirst, in you we live and have our being.**

## The baptismal promises

### A mother's prayer before the Baptism

Eternal God, you fill the heights above;
Send down your blessing now.
Remember the child of my body
In the name of the God of peace.
When the minister of your gospel
on Esther sprinkles the water of meaning
Give to her the blessing of the Three
who fill the heights,
The blessing of the Three
who fill the heights.
Sprinkle down upon her your grace,
Give to her virtue and growth,
Give to her strength and guidance,
Give to her faith and purity,
Sense and reason free from bitterness,

The wisdom of the angels in her day,
So that she may stand free of blame
before your throne,
So that she may stand free of blame
before your throne.

(Based on an ancient Celtic prayer, which would be said soon after the delivery of a child, before baptism in the Church, which would follow eight days after the birth.)

## The Baptism

MINISTER

Esther Zoe, I baptize you
in the name of the One True God,
Creator, Saviour and Holy Spirit;
the Eternal Three in One.

Deep peace of the running wave to you.
Deep peace of the flowing air to you.
Deep peace of the quiet earth to you.
Deep peace of the shining stars to you.
Deep peace of the God of peace to you.

ALL     Amen.

Maggie Eldridge-Mrotzek

## 32    *A welcome for Tristan*
### *27 February 1994*

(The following was in the context of a Roman Catholic Rite of Baptism.)

### Hymn *Father hear the prayer we offer*

### Reception of Tristan

PRIEST   What name have you given your child?
PARENTS

Tristan James.

PRIEST   What do you ask of God's Church for Tristan James?
PARENTS

Baptism.

PRIEST   Tristan James, everyone gathered here today welcomes you with great joy. In their name and in the name of the Christian community I give you a kiss of peace and invite your parents and godparents to do the same.

## Readings

1st reading: *Isaiah 12.2–6*
Psalm: *Psalm 16.5–11*
2nd reading: T. S. Eliot, *The Dry Salvages* (from the *Four Quartets*), lines 199–233.
Gospel: *Matthew 17.1–8*

## Homily

## Prayers of Intercession

## Anointing with Oil of Catechumens

PRIEST   We anoint you with the oil of salvation in the name of Christ. May he strengthen you with his power, who lives and reigns for ever.

ALL      Amen.

## Renunciation of evil and proclamation of good

PRIEST   You are here to mark the start of Tristan's spiritual journey in life. Just as he was born from water in the womb, so too will he now be born through water into a life of the spirit.

PRIEST   As parents and godparents you are asked to help Tristan in his journey by declaring your faith now. *(Parents and godparents say 'I do' after each affirmation.)*

PRIEST   Do you reject dualism, the root of all our divisions?

PRIEST   Do you reject the misuse of our creative energies for evil purposes?

PRIEST   Do you reject injustice, intolerance and indifference?

PRIEST   Do you believe in God the father and mother, creator of heaven and earth?

PRIEST   Do you believe in Incarnation, the embodiment of the creative force in our world?

PRIEST   Do you believe in the power of revelation to bring us wisdom and understanding?

## Prayer

## Baptism

PRIEST   I now baptize Tristan James in the name of the Father and of the Son and of the Holy Spirit.

## Anointing with Chrism

PRIEST   As Christ was anointed Priest, Prophet and Royal Person, so shall we anoint you, Tristan, with chrism, that you may build the kingdom here on earth.

ALL   Amen.

## Clothing with a white garment

PRIEST   Just as Jesus' clothes became white as light, we clothe you, Tristan, in this white garment as a manifestation of Christ in you. You too are loved and favoured and we will learn much by listening to you.

ALL   Amen.

Margaret Leicester

## 33   *Ritual to affirm the passage from girlhood to young woman*

*A low table is put in the centre, or a cloth laid on the floor. On it is a candle, water, decanter of red wine and small glasses, red ribbon cut into strips of about 25cm., a basket to receive the gifts of the women as they arrive, and the cake or cakes.*

## Introduction

*The candle is lit and then the young woman is addressed.*

MOTHER OR GRANDMOTHER

N, tonight we have come together to mark an important stage on your life journey.

2ND WOMAN

We have come as women who love you, family and friends, to acknowledge that you have begun the transition from being a young girl to being a young woman.

3RD WOMAN

Each of us has experienced the changes that you are now experiencing.

4TH WOMAN

The flow of blood is a symbol of life.

5TH WOMAN

It is also a symbol of all the creativity that is inside us.

6TH WOMAN

It is also uncomfortable at times, and so it reminds us that life is uncomfortable, difficult to deal with at times.

## Reading *Luke 1.46–55*

1ST WOMAN

Mary was a young woman, perhaps not much older than you. God called her as a young woman. He gave her a specific task to do. Each of us is called by God to live our life to the fullest and to be what God wants us to be in God's world. When you hear this Song of Mary being read in the future, may you be reminded that you are also a strong and creative woman, blessed by God, and because of that, able to bring blessing to others.

## The Blessings

*Each woman present gives a blessing by naming something special about the young woman, things that they value in her. After or while giving her the blessing, the ribbon is tied or draped over her, reminders of each blessing and a symbol that we as women are all part of the same life fabric.*

## The Wine

*All drink a glass of wine together.*

## The Gifts

*Each woman gives a gift-symbol.*

## Close

*Celebrate by eating cake and finishing the wine!*

*Note*

The statements of symbol and experience are made by the older women. The reading could be done by the young woman celebrating her rite of passage, or by any of the women present.

Erice Fairbrother

## 34    *For my daughters, a liturgy for the celebration of your menarche*

### Introduction

c (CELEBRANT)

Today is a day to celebrate, a day of celebration for N. We are to show our love for N and to thank God for her body, its strength, its growth, its beauty and her ripening and passing into young womanhood.

Let us pray.

ALL    Holy Spirit, who lives in each one of us, may N through your indwelling come to know herself and live according to her true nature. Let her discover joy, strength, compassion and love. Through the love of Christ, Amen.

ALL    Hail Mary, full of grace, the Lord is with you,

Blessed are you among women,

Blessed is the fruit of your womb, Jesus.

Holy Mary, Mother of God,

Pray for us now, and at the hour of our death.

Amen.

### The Anointing

c    Today, N, blessed are you among women. I anoint you with the oil of gladness. We pray that you may find passion and joy in loving another and in being loved. We pray that, if you choose it, you may know the glory of pregnancy and childbirth, and delight in nourishing your children. We pray that you may discover the unfolding of your own special creativity. We pray that you grow through any pain you may meet, a wiser, braver and stronger woman. Amen.

ALL    Today, N, blessed are you among women.

## The gifts

c    We offer gifts to N.

*Mother, grandmother, godparents and friends offer gifts.*

MOTHER
N, I give you this sign of the Moon, a waxing Moon to denote your growth towards fullness.

## Reading *Ecclesiasticus 43.6–9, on the glory of God in nature*

*Others may give their gifts and speak their words.*

## The Collect

GRANDMOTHER
God our mother
You hold our life within you,
nourish us at your breast,
and teach us to walk alone.
Help us so to receive your tenderness
and respond to your challenge
that others may draw life from us,
in your name, Amen.                                    (Janet Morley)

## Old Testament reading

*A godmother reads from the Book of Wisdom 7.24–30 and 8.1.*

ALL    Let the Wisdom of God fill our hearts and souls and minds and bodies. Amen.

## New Testament reading

*The young woman chooses someone to read Mark 12.30–1.*

ALL    Thanks be to God.

## Hymn *The river is flowing*

c    Women are invited to join in this part of our celebration, which welcomes N to womanhood.
*Chalice containing red wine is passed round the circle.*

N, I offer you this cup.

ALL    *(In circle holding hands)* Blessed be our wombs. May the blood we shed bring forth new life. Through the love of Christ. Amen.

*(Turning from centre of circle to those outside . . .)*

ALL    May our bodies be blessed and glorified. Through the love of Christ, Amen.

## The Peace

C    *(All slightly extending arms)* We invite you to join with us in sharing a sign of peace.

*Others come into the circle, exchange a sign of peace, and hold hands.*

ALL    We offer our souls and bodies to be a living sacrifice. Send us out into the world in the power of your Spirit to live and work to your praise and glory. Through the love of Christ. Amen.

## Blessing

C    The blessing of the most Holy Trinity
God unbegotten,
God incarnate,
God among us,
Keep us now and evermore,
Amen.

(Liz Campbell, Women's Agape, Greenham Common)

**Sue Newman**

## 35    *A ritual for a sixty-year-old woman*

*Invite the woman's close friends. Prepare the living room of the woman's home, with flowers, candles (unlit), bread, wine and scented oil laid out, along with some object to represent each stage of the woman's life so far: e.g. a photo of her parents in their youth; a child's mug from her home; favourite books of her girlhood and youth; books from her years of study; photos or letters from close friends of her past; something she has made; something she has written; a song on a music stand; a packet of seeds and a seed tray; a large empty scrap book and a rather good quality bound notebook; newly chosen ring to mark the new stage of life she is embarking on.*

*When guests arrive and have been greeted, all sit down together around the table.*

A FRIEND

We keep silent a while to honour the Word who speaks and the words we will speak.

*(Pause)*

*Each in turn then reads something she has brought, in celebration of Wisdom.*

THE WOMAN

*(thanks them after all have read, and then says)* I am here leaving behind all that has been, except what I take with me in memory. How rich is memory!

ALL     How rich is memory!

WOMAN I leave behind the prospects of my ordinary everyday life so far, and I look forward to new ways, the untapped energy of my riper years, the activity that awaits me now, the vision that I can only now embrace. All that is to come, welcome!

ALL     All that is to come, welcome!

WOMAN All my life I have walked and run after wisdom. Now I claim Wisdom's company for the rest of my life. How gracious is Wisdom!

ALL     How gracious is Wisdom!

*The woman lights the first candle, and the friend lights the other candles from it.*

*The friend anoints the brow and hands of the woman; and the woman then anoints the brow and/or hands of the other guests.*

*They sing, or listen to music, and then eat together a meal to which all have contributed. The bread is eaten and the wine drunk with the meal.*

*After the meal, all go out to the theatre or a concert, wearing flowers from those that had been prepared for the occasion.*

Jennifer Wild

## 36     *A retirement service*

Retirement marks an extremely important stage in the lives of many people, bringing with it a second major identity crisis, not so well documented or widely publicized as the adolescent one. As fewer and fewer people are needed to carry out a widening range of work tasks, men and women are likely to find themselves withdrawing from (or being withdrawn from) paid employment at an increasingly early age. In other words, the feeling of loss, of being put on the scrap-heap at the very height of one's powers (having been committed to the job, highly skilled, and free at last from the distractions of establishing a home and building a family) is likely to grow more and more widespread. It is a very disturbing feeling, and many people find that ways of dealing with it, because they depend heavily on the denial of its existence or at least the postponement of acceptance of its real presence, do not prove particularly effective. The feeling seems to be, 'I'm an adult, used to holding down a difficult job with many responsibilities. If I'm old enough to be retired, then I'm definitely old enough to cope with any emotional problems I might have. I don't know what you're talking about, anyway!' But the people close to us do know; and at a deeper level than the immediately apparent, we know, too. This service attempts to bring these things to the surface of the mind. To this extent, it is an exorcism as well as an initiation, as it aims at integrating within consciousness certain elements which we find unacceptable but which are nevertheless necessary for the restoration of our peace of mind: principally unacknowledged fears concerning the presence of chaos. A service which is intended to symbolize retirement is bound to share at least some of the characteristics of a funeral service. If it does not, it will surely have failed in its object.

## Hymn *Fill thou my life, O Lord my God*

MINISTER

May all delightful things be ours, O Lord God: establish firmly all we do.
The Lord be with you.

ALL     And also with you.

MINISTER

Lord of our life and governor of all our days, you have given us a time for work and also a time for rest. If we have completed any task successfully, we have done it because of the help you have given us. You have strengthened us in our weakness and supported us when we have failed. Give us grace, Lord, to continue faithfully and courageously in your service until our lives' end, so that we, with all your saints, may live in your eternal presence. Through Jesus Christ. Amen.

*The one who is retiring reads from a book which has a definite bearing upon or relevance to his or her job, trade or profession. The minister reads an appropriate biblical passage (e.g. Ecclesiastes 3.1–8 'To every thing there is a season, and a time to every purpose under the heaven').*

MINISTER

We have come together in God's presence in order to celebrate an event of great personal importance to one of our friends. This is the point in *his* life when *he* must leave behind the joys and sorrows, satisfactions and responsibilities of a way of daily living which *he* has practised for many years, and must now launch out into a new world of experience. We shall try to understand and appreciate how difficult it is to make this voyage into the future, for we are determined that *he* will not have to face the challenge alone. That is why we are accompanying *him* to the threshold of *his* new life. As *he* lays down one set of responsibilities and takes up another, we shall do our best to share those burdens with *him* in accordance wth Christ's law. [Philip], you have come to this service in order to receive strength and courage for the present and guidance for the future. Are you willing to go forward into this new stage of your life trusting in God to give you all the things that you need for your journey?

PHILIP    I am.

MINISTER

*(to the congregation)* Are you willing to give [Philip] all the help you can, in every way you can?

ALL    We are.

## Hymn *Teach me, my God and King*

*During this hymn, Philip, accompanied by a young representative of his job, trade, profession (perhaps a student or trainee, or someone newly launched on their own career) comes to the front of the congregation. Philip hands over to the young man or woman an implement or an article of clothing associated with the work he has been doing in the past, to be held by them for the rest of the service. Philip then proceeds to the altar and stands silently there for a moment facing away from the congregation, before taking from the altar something that has been placed there to serve as a symbol of his new life; perhaps something that is associated with a skill or an interest to which Philip intends to devote time and effort in the future. Philip moves back towards the congregation, where he is met by a group of friends and/or family members who welcome him into their number. This group now stands in front of the minister.*

GROUP    Father, we ask you to bless [Philip] in *his* new life among us.

MINISTER

[Philip], the love of the Lord Jesus draw you to himself, the power of the Lord Jesus strengthen you in his service, the joy of the Lord Jesus fill your heart; and the blessing of God Almighty, the Father, the Son and the Holy Spirit be with you and remain with you always. Amen.                                                          (ASB)

*The Minister moves forward and shakes Philip's hand and/or embraces him.*

## Hymn *A safe stronghold our God is still*

MINISTER

> In the presence of God, and among his people gathered here, [Philip] has entered on a new stage of *his* journey through life. *He* goes forward from this place confidently and with good courage, for the Lord is with *him* and *his* companions are at *his* side.

MINISTER

> O Lord God, we commend to you our friend [Philip] as *he* sets out once again on his pilgrimage to you. We thank you for the undiscovered opportunities, joys and challenges that you have in store for *him*. May *he* receive from you wisdom and courage to appreciate without striving, and so grow daily in the knowledge of your love. Through Jesus Christ our Lord. Amen.

ALL    Our Father . . . deliver us from evil. Amen.

> *All say Psalm 116.*

MINISTER

> The peace of God which passes all understanding, keep your hearts and minds in the knowledge and love of God, and of his Son, Jesus Christ our Lord; and the blessing of God Almighty, the Father, the Son and the Holy Spirit, be among you and remain with you always. Amen.
>
> The Lord be with you.

ALL    And also with you.

MINISTER

> Behold, the whole country lies before you; go wherever you think best.

**Hymn** *God is working his purpose out*

**Roger Grainger**

## 37   *A children's ritual*
*Welcoming a sibling*

---

Before the baby is born, one of the parents spends time with the child choosing a present for the baby. The gift might be something the baby could use immediately, a rattle, a baby spoon, or a bottle. The child might earn the money to pay for the present so that there is a real sense of ownership in the giving.

The ritual needs to be performed as soon as possible after the infant is brought home.

### Receiving the baby

*The child sits in a chair and the baby is placed in the child's lap for her [him] to hold. The child addresses the baby by name and welcomes her [him].*

CHILD    Welcome N. You are my baby sister [brother]. I promise to love you.

*The child may hold the baby and enjoy the moment. When it seems right to the parents, the baby is held by one of the parents and the child presents her gift. If the child is old enough to hold the baby and a gift at the same time, there is no reason for the baby to be removed from the child's lap.*

CHILD    This is my gift of love.

*The child should then go with the parents to tuck the baby into the crib. Then the family gathers for a party in the baby's honor; the older child is the celebrant, having been the one who officially welcomed the baby into the family.*

**Vienna Cobb Anderson**


## 38    *Bidding prayers for Suzanna's baptism*
### 27 October 1987

The following prayers formed part of the christening of a daughter of parents of different races and cultures.

Let us pray for Suzanna
On this day of her baptism
When we welcome her into the community of the church
And of those who
As her parents and godparents
Have accepted the responsibility
Of bringing her to know the community of justice.

Let us pray that the continuing together
Of her parents, Judith and John,
In the covenant of their marriage
May be a sign of hope for us
In the relationship of Third World and First World.
May their daughter Suzanna be for them and for us
A sign of that hope bearing fruit
In the coming together of their families
And of parents and children, mothers and daughters
Discovering and rediscovering each other
Across the boundaries of nationality and generation.

And may Suzanna
When she becomes a woman
Come to share in their commitment to the poor
And continue their struggle
For a just and peaceful future
For all our children.

Lord, hear us.

Angela West

## 39     *Blessing for a child welcoming*

May the power of air bring you a clear mind to see your way,
May the power of fire bring you strength and passion to go along
    your way,
May the power of water bring you life and sustenance, and the
    courage to feel through your way,
May the power of earth bring you grounding in a strong body, to be
    centred in your way.

Ann Peart

## 40     *The fate of the earth*

Come, cradle all the future generations,
    and guard their right to live upon this earth,
lest human deeds, by stealth or conflagration,
    snuff out all life, and put an end to birth.

Come, contemplate the sadness of extinction:
    a wasted earth, with empty sky and sea,
no mourners to lament its desolation,
    no voice, no words, no thought, no eyes to see.

We cannot stifle knowledge or invention.
    The ways divide, the choice forever clear:
to drift, and be delivered to destruction,
    or wake and work, till trust out-matches fear.

The precious seed of life is in our keeping,
    yet if we plant it, and fulfil our trust,
tomorrow's sun will rise on joy and weeping,
    and shine upon the unjust and the just.

Our calling is to live our human story
   of good and bad, achievement, love and loss,
then hand it on to future shame or glory,
   lit by our hope, and leavened by a cross.

Come, let us guard the gateway to existence,
   that thousands yet may stand where we have stood,
give thanks for life and, praising our persistence,
   enjoy this lovely earth, and call it good.

*Tune: San Carlos*

**Brian Wren**

# 3

## Jesus came from Nazareth . . .
### A celebration of homes for all who live in them

Home is where we start from, and it is the place where we look for stability in a changing world. Yet from the womb onwards our homes are temporary; they are starting-places and yet a startling number of people have bases for living that are at best inadequate and transitory, and at worst degraded by anxiety, ill-feeling and violence. And not a few people are without homes of any sort. Some Christmas cards have fantasy pictures of old-world homes with lighted windows, snug in a snowy setting under starlit skies. Crisis at Christmas tries to help some people face a bleaker reality — and in any case, those who live in houses are not all happy families with children playing round the Christmas tree or singing carols round the piano while the smiling spinster aunt skilfully accompanies them. In our cities today we work hard to make our homes secure against unwanted intruders; all the more important, then, to encourage those who want to make and celebrate their homes as places of warmth and hospitality.

What we have collected here are housewarming ceremonies prepared by people for themselves or their friends; a celebration of homes for all who live in them — single people, friends, couples (with or without children — married and unmarried, straight and gay), grown-up children with elderly parents, communal households. All these and others are the families of our day, and not all such families find support in church or society.

Some of the rituals here presented have been included in the marriage ceremony where one or both parties have children from earlier relationships, so that the marriage is also a celebration of the new family, recognizing and including the children. Obviously, every case is different, with differing needs; but we are grateful to the Revd Roger Coleman for allowing us to reproduce his 'Celebrating the new family', as well as to those others who have offered us the rituals they have devised to recognize new families in a way that is helpful to all involved.

Possibly the most powerful of the rituals here included is the Homelessness Sunday Liturgy, one church community's attempt to remind itself of the other side of the picture, without which our celebrations of home and family are inexcusably introverted and barren.

**41**   *A house-warming celebration*

---

## Opening greeting and prayers

LEADER God be with us.
ALL   Amen.
LEADER The Lord be with you.
ALL   And also with you.

LEADER The Father be with us.
ALL   Amen.
LEADER The Creator be with you.
ALL   And also with you.

LEADER Jesus be with us.
ALL   Amen.
LEADER The Saviour be with you.
ALL   And also with you.

LEADER The Spirit be with us.
ALL   Amen.
LEADER The Strengthener be with you.
ALL   And also with you.

LEADER The Trinity be with us.
ALL   Amen.
LEADER The Sacred Three be over you.
ALL   And also with you.

LEADER God be with us.
ALL   Amen.

(David Adam)

LEADER We have come together
    to celebrate the gift of this home
    and to ask God's blessing on it

    to renew friendship
    and to make festival together

    to dedicate ourselves and this place
    to the pursuit of peace, justice and wholeness
    and to the care of God,
    Creator, Redeemer and Sustainer.

LEADER Unless the Lord builds the house
ALL     They labour in vain who build it.
LEADER Unless the Lord protects the city
ALL     The Watchers guard it in vain.
LEADER Our hope is found in Jesus Christ
ALL     God's stumbling block and corner stone.

(Iona Community)

## Song of blessing

Come host of heaven's high dwelling place,
Come earth's disputed guest:
Find in this house a welcome home
Bide here and take your rest.

Smoor well these walls with faith and love
That through the nights and days
When human tongues from speaking cease
These stones may echo praise.

Bless and inspire those living here
With patience, strength and peace
And all the joys that know the depth
In which all sorrows cease.

Here may the loser find his worth
And stranger find a friend;
Here may the hopeless find a faith
And aimless find an end.

Build from the human fabric signs
Of how your kingdom thrives,
Of how the Holy Spirit changes life
Through changing lives.

So to the Lord whose care enfolds
The world held in his hands
Be glory, honour, love and praise
For which this house now stands.

*Tune: St Columba*

(John L. Bell and Graham Maule)

## Readings

*There will be a series of short readings.*

*A short space of silence will be kept after the readings.*

## Prayers and blessings

LEADER  Let us now bless this house in the name of God and with our love
and prayers.

*A short space of silence is kept during which prayers may be offered in
silence or out loud.*

LEADER  Be present, Spirit of God, within us,
your dwelling place and home,
that this house may be one where
all darkness is penetrated by your light
all troubles calmed by your peace
all evil redeemed by your love
all pain transformed by your suffering
and all dying glorified by your risen life.

ALL     Amen.

(Jim Cotter)

LEADER  May God give blessing
ALL     To this house and all who come here.
LEADER  May Jesus give blessing
ALL     To this house and all who come here.
LEADER  May Spirit give blessing
ALL     To this house and all who come here.
LEADER  May all who come here give blessing
ALL     To this house and to all they meet here.
LEADER  Both crest and frame
ALL     Both stone and beam.
LEADER  Both window and timber
ALL     Both foot and head.
LEADER  Both gate and door
ALL     Both coming and going.
LEADER  Both man and woman
ALL     Both parent and child.
LEADER  Both young and old
ALL     Both wisdom and youth.
LEADER  Both guest and host
ALL     Both stranger and friend.

LEADER Peace on each window that lets in light
ALL     Peace on each corner of the room.
LEADER Peace on each place that ushers sleep
ALL     Peace on each plate that cradles food.
LEADER Peace of the Father, Peace of the Son
ALL     Peace of the Spirit, Peace of the One.

(Iona Community)

ALL     The peace of God, the peace of earth,
        The peace of the Holy Trinity,
        The peace of Mary mild,
        The peace of the loving Christ,
        Be upon each window, upon each door,
        Upon each hole that lets in light,
        Upon the four corners of this house,
        Upon each thing my eye takes in,
        Upon each thing my mouth takes in,
        Upon my body that is of earth,
        And upon my soul that came from on high.

(Traditional Celtic Blessing)

## The Peace

LEADER The Peace of the Lord be with us all.
ALL     Amen.

*We offer each other a sign of peace.*

## The offering of the gifts

*Each person in turn brings their gift to the table, with a short explanation of what their gift represents.*

*After all the gifts are placed on the table, a piece of music will be played. Silence is kept.*

## Concluding prayers and blessing

LEADER Come, Lord Jesus, be our guest.
ALL     Stay with us, for the day is ending.
LEADER Be with friend, with stranger,
ALL     With neighbour and the well known ones.
ALL     For the door of our house we open
        and the doors of our hearts we leave ajar.

(Iona Community)

ALL    Be the eye of God dwelling with us,
The foot of Christ in guidance with us
The shower of the Spirit pouring on us
And be the Sacred Three
To save, to shield, to surround
The hearth, the house, the household,
This eve, this night and every night.
Amen.

(Traditional Celtic prayer)

## Songs of thanksgiving

*Adoramus te Domine (Taizé)*
*The Doxology*
Praise God from whom all blessings flow,
Praise him all creatures here below,
Praise him above ye heavenly hosts,
Praise Father, Son and Holy Ghost.

**Nicola Slee**

# 42    *House blessing*

*Everyone gathers, if possible, in the hall of the house or flat or in the main room.*

LEADER  Early on Sunday morning women discovered that Jesus was risen. They were given a message for his disciples . . . 'he is gone before you to Galilee'. And he goes before us, too, and is here to greet us, to welcome us as host.

*A cross is placed in the middle of the hall or room.*

ALL    Christ is here. God's spirit is with us.

LEADER  This is a place of new beginnings, but time past is a part of time present. In the past lie causes of joy and sorrow. Let us acknowledge the past with thankful hearts.

ALL    This home is a place of welcome, a place of celebration, a place of meeting, a place of joy and sorrow, a place of rest and peace.

*Everyone moves to the kitchen.*

LEADER  What else will this home be?

ALL    This home is a place of work, the work of hands and head.

LEADER  What else is this house/flat?

ALL    This home is part of the Church, the people of God.

*Everyone moves to the dining area.*

LEADER What else is this home?

ALL This home is a place for sharing — in worship, in caring, in learning, in eating.

*Bread and wine are placed on the table.*

LEADER Gracious God, we offer to you ourselves, our minds and bodies, our home and possessions, our strengths and weaknesses, to share in the life and service of your kingdom. We ask your blessing on everyone and everything that passes through this home.

ALL Amen.

*All share a meal.*

Hazel Barkham

## 43 *Celebrating the new family*
### *A ceremony for recognizing children during the wedding ceremony*

### Author's preliminary remarks

With children present, marriage is more than the union of two persons. It is, in fact, the proclaiming of a new family. 'Celebrating the new family' offers a resource for including, in a significant way, the children of those being married in the wedding celebration.

The family medallion, by adding a third circle to the two 'marriage circles', provides a symbol for recognizing family relationships. Its presentation transcends the 'two-ness' language of many ceremonies and offers a unique opportunity to celebrate the family nature of God's creation.

The acknowledgement of children and parental responsibilities naturally follows the pronouncement of union between husband and wife. Additional resources and options are included to assist with adapting this material to meet special family and theological requirements.

**Introduction** (*to follow pronouncement of union between husband and wife*)

OFFICIANT

Often marriage is viewed as the union of two individuals. In reality, however, marriage is much broader.

As we give thanks to God for the love which brings —— and —— together, so, too, we recognize the merging of families taking place and the additional love and responsibility family and friends bring to this relationship.

## The unity of God's family

OFFICIANT

We are, in fact, all members of one family, of God's family, a relationship emphasized in the Scriptures where it is written: 'And it was a happy day for God when we received our new lives, through the truth of God's word, and we became, as it were, the first children in God's new family' *(adapted from James 1.18). (Other biblical passages emphasizing the oneness of God's family include Leviticus 26.4–6, Ezekiel 34.25–9a, Ephesians 2.14 and Galatians 3.28–9.)*

## Recognition of children

OFFICIANT

As part of the family nature of God's creation we recognize —— and the significant role *he/she/they* play(s) in this marriage today celebrated.

*Child or children may be brought forward by grandparents or others if they are too young to stand as members of the wedding party.*

## Optional reading *(for use when young children are involved)*

READER   The love and hope which God sends to us through the gift of each child finds expression in the Gospel of Mark:

And they were bringing children to him, that Jesus might touch them; and the disciples rebuked them. But when Jesus saw it he was indignant, and said to them, 'Let the children come to me, do not hinder them; for to such belongs the Kingdom of God.'

*(An alternative reading is Psalm 127, substituting 'children' for 'sons'.)*

## Presentation of medallions

OFFICIANT

—— and —— present to —— *this/these* Family Medallion(s) created as a symbol for family unity and in recognition of the hope and joy made visible through this marriage.

*The following may be repeated by the person performing the ceremony or by one or both parents.*

In the placing of *this/these* medallion(s) we pledge to you, ——, our continuing love even as we surround you now with our arms of support and protection.

## Reading

READER  Our children are gifts entrusted to us not as objects to be controlled but as human beings, each unique in their own personality, each separate in their own identity. Consider these words from *The Prophet* by Kahlil Gibran:

> You may give them your love but not your thoughts,
>   For they have their own thoughts.
> You may house their bodies but not their souls,
> For they dwell in the house of tomorrow, which you cannot visit
>          not even in your dreams.
> You may strive to be like them, but seek not to make them like you.
>   For life goes not backward nor tarries with yesterday.
>     You are the bows from which your children
>       as living arrows are sent forth.

## Prayer for the family

*(Couple and children as well as congregation may be invited to hold hands.)*

OFFICIANT

Creator God, you have made us in your own image, male and female, that together we may live as members of your one family.

As you surround us with never-ending love, strengthen us that we, too, might reflect your love, becoming ever supportive of one another in times of sorrow, forgiving of one another in times of anger, patient in those moments when we seek to rebuild out of the pain of broken trusts and shattered dreams.

We give thanks, Lord, for the relationship here celebrated. In your presence we are humbled by the recognition that, today, we face a new future, one which love has unfolded and is unfolding before our very eyes.

May we ever respect the sanctity of this gift.

As you have filled our cup with joy, may we share the strength of our deepening love for one another, including, in ever widening circles, those who wait without hope and live without love's shelter. Amen.

## Blessing

OFFICIANT

'For one person to love another — that is perhaps the hardest of all our tasks, the ultimate test and proof, the work for which all other work is but preparation ... [Love] consists of this — that [we] protect and touch and greet each other.'

(Rainer Maria Rilke, adapted)

*(Couple may kiss and then embrace children.)*

OFFICIANT

Go forth joined together by the love of God. Go forth with hope and joy and a heart full of dreams, knowing that God is always with you. Amen.

## Introduction

OFFICIANT

It is my pleasure to present to you —— and —— in their new relationship as husband and wife and their *son/daughter/children* ——.

*or*

Now I present to you the —— family.

Roger Coleman

## 44     *A rite of blessing at adoption*

## Preparation

*Small table set with flowers, candle and Bible. Guitar or taped music. All assemble around table.*

CELEBRANT

In the name of our loving God, we are gathered today to share our joy in the gift of a new child; to present N to the Lord in order to express our faith that *he/she* belongs to him as much as to us; and to entrust N to the care of N and N.

## Readings

Ephesians 3.14–21. *Pause for reflection.*
Magnificat *(read by all)*.
Luke 9.48. *Pause for reflection.*

## Prayers

CELEBRANT

God is the Creator of all life and calls all beings into existence. He brings about the birth of a new member of the human family and of the Church. Let us pray then with confidence to our God.

BIRTH MOTHER

Gracious God, I give thanks and praise for the safe delivery of my child and the joy *she/he* has brought me. I now entrust *her/him* to the loving care of N and N. May they, with your guidance, help N to grow to the full and complete person you want *her/him* to be. Lord, hear us.

ALL     Lord, hear our prayer.

GRANDPARENTS

May N and N be the best parents for N and may *she/he* bring much joy into their lives.
Lord, hear us.

ALL     Lord, hear our prayer.

*Birth mother gives the child to the adopting parents.*

ADOPTING PARENTS

Loving God, we give thanks and praise that this new life has been entrusted to us. We ask you to accompany us on life's journey as we bring N to know you and to love you.
Lord, hear us.

ALL     Lord, hear our prayer.

SOCIAL WORKER

Bless all adopting parents and birth mothers, especially those facing difficulties in their families and in our society.
Lord, hear us.

ALL     Lord, hear our prayer.

CELEBRANT

Our caring God, each day you call us to serve you by loving others. Help (*birth mother*) and (*adopting parents*) to answer your call with courage and faith. You show your love for us in many ways, and so we turn to you and say, 'Our Father . . .'

## Blessing of birth mother

*Celebrant places his hands on the birth mother.*

CELEBRANT

May the blessing of God of all consolation be with you in times of sorrow. May Jesus Christ, who suffered and died for us all, give you his light and his peace. May the Holy Spirit be with you to grant you strength and encouragement in your life.

## Blessing of the adopting parents and children

CELEBRANT

Blessed are you Lord God, Maker of the Universe and Creator of all. You have made us your children, your family, and have invited us to call you Father. You have made us brothers and sisters in Jesus Christ and temples of your Holy Spirit.

*Celebrant places his hands on the parents.*

CELEBRANT

Bless these parents in their love as they welcome N into their family. Fill their home with your peace and lead them always in your love.

*Celebrant now blesses the children of the family.*

Bless (*name children*) in your love and show them your goodness through the love of their parents and of each other.

## Final blessing and dismissal

CELEBRANT

May God the Creator, Redeemer and Holy Spirit bless us all and keep us for ever. Go now to love and serve the Lord.

ALL     Thanks be to God.

**from** *Our baby has died*

## 45     *Becoming a new family*
### *A ritual for children whose mother (or father) has married for a second time*

---

*The child, or children, gathers the newly wed couple in the living room or other place of choice. The child performs a ceremony of her [his] own making. Parental help may be necessary to accomplish this, but the words need to be the child's own. For this reason, only an outline is given here.*

## The people gather

*The children greet each guest whom they have invited and take the guest to the appropriate seat. The children stand at the place of ceremony and the couple comes and stands before them.*
  *One child states the purpose of the gathering.*

*Example* We have gathered to ask God to bless us as a family.

*A prayer may be said.*

*Example*
Bless us, O God,
and help us keep
the promises we make
to be a family.

## A reading from the Bible

*A child reads the passage.*
*Possible selections* Luke 18.15–17 *(Let the children come to me).*
Psalm 23 *(The Lord is my shepherd.)*

## Making vows as a family

*The children ask the parents questions.*

*Example* Do you promise to love us?

*To which each parent in turn answers:* I do.

*Each child makes a promise of her [his] own.*

*Example* I promise to love you Mommy and —— and to help make us a family.

## Prayers and a blessing

*A child invites all to pray.*
*The Lord's Prayer is said.*
*A child reads a prayer asking for God's blessing.*

*Example* Bless us, O God.
        Make us a loving family.
        In Jesus' name we pray.
        Amen.

*The Peace is exchanged with hugs all around.*

CHILD   The peace of God be with you.
RESPONSE
        And also with you.

*The family then has a party or a meal together with the invited guests.*
**Vienna Cobb Anderson**

## 46    *Mothers' Day ceremony*

---

*A child helps to light a large candle.*

*Three mothers come bringing candles. They light them from the large one.*

1ST MOTHER

We are three mothers, come to celebrate motherhood in the presence of God.

I light my candle for all mothers throughout the centuries who have loved and laughed and laboured.

2ND MOTHER

I light my candle for all mothers alive today, who still love and laugh and labour for their children.

3RD MOTHER

I light my candle because Jesus was born of a woman and nurtured in her love, so that in later years he compared himself and his people to a mother hen gathering her chickens under her wings.

1ST MOTHER

*(extinguishing her candle)* But I must put out my candle, because mothers in South America weep and rage for their 'disappeared' sons and daughters. Let us pray for them.
*(Pause)*

2ND MOTHER

I put out my candle because mothers in Africa and India watch their children die of starvation. Let us pray for them.
*(Pause)*

3RD MOTHER

I put out my candle because mothers in Israel and Lebanon, in Northern Ireland and South Africa, mourn their children who are victims of violence. Let us pray for them.
*(Pause)*

1ST MOTHER

Nevertheless there still abide faith, hope and love.

So I relight my candle in the faith that God is present in every mother's suffering and in every mother's joy.

2ND MOTHER

I relight my candle in the hope of a world where all mothers may rear their children in peace and dignity and delight.

3RD MOTHER

I relight my candle because God is love, and as humankind is made in the image of God, so motherhood most fully focuses that image of love.

1ST MOTHER

Now abide faith, hope and love, these three. And the greatest of these is love.

**Anne Ashworth**

## 47   *On Homelessness Sunday*
### *(falling on 7 October)*

*(ASB Rite A except as below.)*

### Opening hymn *We plough the fields and scatter the good seed on the land.*

PRIEST   In the words of St Francis:
All praise be yours, my Lord, through Sister Earth, our mother
Who feeds us in her sovereignty and produces various fruits,
green grass, herbs and flowers of every colour.

ALL   All praise to you O God for Sister Rain and Brother Sun,
For Sister Moon, for stars and constellations.

### The Gloria

DEACON God of all the universe, you are worthy of glory and praise.

ALL   Glory to you for ever.

DEACON At your command all things came to be, the vastness of interstellar space, the galaxies and stars, the planets in their courses, and this fragile earth, our home.

ALL   By your will they were created and have their being.

DEACON From the primal elements you brought forth the human race and blessed us. But we turned against you and against all creation.

ALL   Lord have mercy upon us.

DEACON Fountain of life and source of all goodness, you call upon us to return and to walk in your ways.

ALL   Fill us now with your blessing.

(US Episcopal *Book of Common Prayer*)

### Prayer for the day

O God, Sustainer of all life, Giver of all gifts,
We thank you for all that you have given us;
and we celebrate the inspiring example of your faithful servant, St
    Francis of Assisi.
Fill our hearts with such compassion as was his and with such
    firmness of purpose,
that the compassion of our hearts becomes the action of our lives.
In the name of Jesus, Lover of all creation, Amen.

### First reading from *St Francis of Assisi* by John Moorman

### Gradual hymn *Yours the city, yours the city* (56)

### The Gospel *Mark 8.1–8*

### Lamentation for the homeless and dispossessed throughout the world

(This replaced the sermon, and was introduced by a narrator, with four
readers telling stories of the homeless and dispossessed in their own words;
a chorus led the congregation in responses. Some of the concluding lines are
quoted here. During the Lamentation, the congregation were encouraged to
contribute offerings for a homelessness project in place of the usual harvest
festival fruits etc.)

NARRATOR
This is our only home, God's family our only family.
CHORUS Earth is our home and all creation is our family.
ALL     *(repeat)*

NARRATOR
If Christ was part of nature at his death, then he is also part of
nature now; and if we recognize that Christ is in nature, and that
Christ is within each of us, then the Christ in us working with the
Christ in nature can save this planet our home.
CHORUS Yes! the Christ within us
working with the Christ that is in each part of nature,
can save this planet our home;
and as homecomers we can live
to enjoy the rainbow of God's covenant.
ALL     *(repeat)*

NARRATOR

God's covenant is always there. It is for us to seek and to find the rainbow.

## Intercessions

*Leader explains that the intercessions will be mostly a time of silences.*

LEADER  For the homeless on the streets throughout the world.

*Silence.*

LEADER  O God, fill our hearts with such compassion,

ALL  **That the compassion of our hearts becomes the action of our lives.**

LEADER  For the refugees everywhere.

*Silence.*

LEADER  O God, fill our hearts with such compassion,

ALL  **That the compassion of our hearts becomes the action of our lives.**

LEADER  For the dispossessed in every land.

*Silence.*

LEADER  O God, fill our hearts with such compassion,

ALL  **That the compassion of our hearts becomes the action of our lives.**

LEADER  For all the inhabitants of the rain forest.

*Silence.*

LEADER  O God, fill our hearts with such compassion,

ALL  **That the compassion of our hearts becomes the action of our lives.**

LEADER  For all people suffering under the yoke of the Third World drought.

*Silence.*

LEADER  O God, fill our hearts with such compassion,

ALL  **That the compassion of our hearts becomes the action of our lives.**

LEADER  For our own feeling of homelessness in this world.

*Silence.*

LEADER  Fill our hearts with hope and trust.

ALL  Our hope is in Jesus Christ, our Saviour and our Rainbow.

## The Confession

ALL  O God, Father and Mother of all creation,

we have forgotten that we are part of your family,
and too often have we failed to recognize
our sister- and brotherhood with all your creatures,
the trees, the plants, the other animals
and our fellow human beings.
For the sake of Jesus Christ, our Rainbow Bridge,
forgive us for the wrongs that we have done,
and the hurt that we have caused.
Awaken in us an awareness of our own divinity,
that we may live as true members of the family of God. Amen.

## Post-communion prayer

ALL     Mother and Father of all . . .
         *(Continue as in ASB p.144).*

## Notices

These included an invitation to members of the congregation to take home
one of the newspaper or magazine clippings from which the information
about homelessness had been derived, so that they could continue to pray
for particular concerns and people.

**Final hymn** *All creatures of our God and King*

Jean Gaskin

# 48    *Prayer for dedication of a house*

We dedicate this house to you and your work as the God of Peace.
May it be a place of joy, laughter and freedom,
A place of renewal and refreshment for those who are weary,
A place of hope for those who have become disillusioned,
A place of healing and comfort for those broken and hurt,
A place of forgiveness for those who seek a new way of life,
A place of encouragement for those who hunger and thirst for
     peace and justice,
A place of vision and inspiration for all those who seek a new and
     better way for our country.

**Corrymeela Community**

**49**   *Blessing on a new home*

---

May this home be glowing with warmth in the chill of winter
And a cooling shade in the heat of the summer sun,
May it be a place where one awakes with eagerness,
And a haven from stress, when the work of the day is done.

May God, our Mother, safely cradle this house in her strong arms,
And breathe the comfort of her love through every room.
May God, our Father, fire the minds of those who dwell here with
    hopeful dreams
And give them the strength to make those dreams come true.
May God, our Companion, fill this home with laughter
And weave a satisfying peace in times of solitude.

May the cupboards be forever full,
And the table spread with welcome cheer.
May friends come often through the door,
But yet the need for privacy be respected here.

May the wild beauty of God,
May the indwelling peace of God
May the surprising mystery of God
Inhabit this new home.

**Jean Gaskin**

**50**   *Blessing prayer for the Advent wreath*

---

Lord, Source of all Energy and Light,
    the ancients saw the sun
    as a great fire wheel rolling across the sky.
May our Advent wreath, this small wheel of green,
    be for us a symbol of the sun
    and of the Son of God.
May its ever-greenness
    be a sign of life and of light
    in the midst of the darkness of winter.
May the candles that burn brightly upon it
    remind us of your Son, Jesus,
    who was the light of the world.

Grant, Lord, that this our Advent wreath
   may be for us and for all who visit our home
   a sign of faith in a world grown cold with disbelief,
   a symbol of hope in a time of gloom and despair
   and a flaming image of love
   in a winter of mistrust and hate.

May all who look upon this symbol of Advent
   be encouraged to prepare their hearts
   for the coming of our Saviour, Jesus Christ.
May this green wreath with its bright candles
   help us to prepare for the real Christmas
   which happens within our hearts.
May, then, your blessing — Father of light,
   Son of Glory and Spirit of Love —
   be upon this Advent wreath and upon our home.
Amen.

                                    **Edward Hays**

## 51   *New Year prayer for families*

This year
   we ask God's blessing on the families of the world;
      one-parent families,
      two-parent families,
      foster families and adoptive families,
      families in shacks and families in houses.
   God bless every style of family.

This year
   we ask God's mercy on families which are split
      by the search for work,
      by warfare,
      by the laws of immigration,
      by plain selfishness.
   God hold the hands of all who are vulnerable.

This year
   we tell out our hopes for a world
      where being young and black doesn't make you a victim,
      where old men and women can be at ease on city streets,
      where children can play freely and without malice;
   may these hopes come true in more and more places.

This year
> we nurture Christ within us.
> May we understand
> when he is not confined by our plans and prejudices.

This year
> we give ourselves
> to care for one another
> as Paul cared for his brood the church.
> Living God, show us the greater family
> of all your people on earth,
> and bind us together in love.

Bob Warwicker

## 52   *Parent's remarriage*
### *As part of the marriage ceremony*

---

*During the marriage ceremony, the children join the couple at the time of the blessing. They kneel with the parents, and the priest says the following prayer:*

Bless, O God, this new family especially *[names of the children]*. Surround them with love; give them a secure and stable home and a sense of belonging. Protect them from all danger, support them in times of trouble, and give them peace. Grant them knowledge that —— and ——'s love for one another includes them in that love and that they are an essential part of this family; in the name of Jesus Christ we pray. Amen.

Vienna Cobb Anderson

## 53   *A hymn for Fathers' Day*

---

A father stoops to lift a weary toddler;
His warming hug will drive away the fear;
He can fulfil the needs of growing children;
When danger threatens, he is standing near.

The child grows up and flexes youthful muscles;
The body fills out to maturity;
The father watches firmly on the sidelines,
Delighting in such creativity.

For he has learned the arts of human parents
From God's creating deep at work inside,
Where gentle pity comforts human weakness
And hands of love lie strong and open wide.

May all who choose a way as human parents
Rest in those strength'ning hands that can uphold,
Draw loving from the Source of all creation,
So when that path is rough, they will stay bold.

*Tune: Intercessor*

**June Boyce-Tillman**

## 54     *Hymn for Mothering Sunday*

How great the debt we owe
To those who love us most;
They give us birth, and help us grow,
And rarely count the cost.

To make us feel secure
They lose their life in ours;
And what they mean to us is more
Than we can say with flowers.

How can we measure love?
Yet treasure it we must
For what God gives us from above
Is held by us in trust.

Then let us vow today,
As those who know love's worth,
To love, to worship, and obey
The Lord of all the earth.

*Tune: Franconia*

**Fred Pratt Green**

## 55     *Mothers' Day hymn*

God of Eve and God of Mary,
God of love and mother-earth,

thank you for the ones who with us
shared their life and gave us birth.

As you came to earth in Jesus,
so you come to us today;
you are present in the caring
that prepares us for life's way.

Thank you, that the Church, our Mother,
gives us bread and fills our cup,
and the comfort of the Spirit
warms our hearts and lifts us up.

Thank you for belonging, shelter,
bonds of friendship, ties of blood,
and for those who have no children,
yet are parents under God.

God of Eve and God of Mary,
Christ our Brother, human Son,
Spirit, caring like a Mother,
take our love and make us one!

*Tunes: Sussex or Penhill*

**Fred Kaan**

**56**

---

Yours the city, yours the city,
With no place to lay your head.
Yours the courage, yours the pity,
Yours the life among the dead.
Yours the poor, and yours the beaten,
Struggling to reclaim their rights.
Yours the victimized we threaten,
Seeking allies for their fights.

Yours the claimant, yours the homeless,
Unemployed or underpaid.
Yours the children, desperate, powerless,
Yours the bleeding heart betrayed.
Yours the hopes by cities heightened,
Rastas, pop groups, youth in quest.
Yours the rich, though unenlightened
By the poor you make the blest.

Yours the movement for empowering,
Yours the kingdom, sure and meek,
Yours the banquet for our flowering,
Yours the shalom cities seek.
Ours your faithful love upholding,
Ours your grace outpassing fears,
Ours the mystery unfolding —
Christ who wipes away all tears!

*Tune: Blaenwern*

**John Vincent**

# 4

# This, the first of his miracles ...
## A celebration of relationships

The material collected for this section reminds us to recognize an element of givenness in all human relationships of love and friendship. Our first thought for a chapter heading was the verse in John's Gospel (19.25) where Jesus from the cross entrusts his mother to the care of the beloved disciple — a paradigm of givenness, indeed, but with overtones perhaps more dark than even the difficult task of building good and lasting relationships warrants. In the end we settled for the presence of Jesus at the marriage feast at Cana, the setting of his first sign, and showing of his glory.

Traditional Christian marriage rites assume a heterosexual couple and a vowed lifetime commitment. The material here offered shows the sincere desire of many people now to express commitment that springs from a religious faith (Christian or Jewish), or that looks to some elements of religious faith as a support for the intentions of two people who wish to celebrate and bless their relationship. Some rites here included seek a blessing on a covenant relationship rather than a formal vow. Some are appropriate for a heterosexual or a same-sex couple. Some arise from the couple's desire to acknowledge previous partnerships, and the close involvement of children. (See also chapter 3 on incorporating children into the new family.) We note the different standing in the eyes of church and state of various of these partnerships; but the rituals and liturgies we have found show that these boundaries are crisscrossed by the lives and commitments of many — in other words, the material here collected recognizes diversity of need and of life-style.

It has not been possible, usually, for us to learn the longer-term effect of the liturgies and rituals included in this collection, but the present chapter contains one notable exception: the longer than usual write-up of a Christian–Jewish wedding shows both the process of creating the liturgy and the effect it had on at least one of the families involved: a deepening of faith and widening of horizons.

**57**    *An experimental liturgy for the blessing of a relationship*

### Preface

Most liturgies celebrate relationships with God and with one another. The liturgy for marriage expresses and celebrates a permanent legal and spiritual relationship between a man and a woman. This experimental liturgy is designed to enable two people to express and celebrate a special relationship before God and their friends and family. The relationship is defined by the couple in the course of the liturgy, after which we ask God's blessing and the community's recognition and support of this relationship.

The service may also be adapted for strengthening and building groups and communities. This material is offered as a resource for worship leaders who may not choose to distribute it as complete text. It can be rearranged and photocopied freely.

### Welcome

*One or more of the following is chosen, depending on the experience of the couple and the location of the ceremony.*

*Either:*

Welcome to this place, hallowed by the presence and the prayers of many people. Couples have come here declaring their commitment and their love, seeking God's blessing and asking for God's guidance. N and N, as you join all those who have stood here before you, claim their strength and stand in the company of friends and lovers everywhere.

*Or:*

Welcome to this place, chosen by you to celebrate your love for each other and to ask God's blessing on your life together. By virtue of what happens here among us and before God, this becomes a special place for you, and for all of us who gather to offer our respect and support for what you have found together. In the new journey that goes on from here, may you find strength and joy in recalling this place and all that it comes to mean.

We gather to celebrate before God the bond of love that N and N have found in each other, to show our respect and offer our support, to affirm our faith in them and what they share together. May the words and symbols, the thoughts and prayers we offer here, serve to strengthen the commitment and trust that N and N now know, and may the experience of the love they share grow ever richer and deeper.

## Introduction

*Either:*

We read in the Gospel of the risen Christ meeting his disciples on the road to Emmaus and joining their journey as they walked uncertain and unaware. Later as that same Christ shared their bread, he met them in a moment of clarity and truth, which led them to get up and go out into the night.

Go with us now, companion God, walk with us again, help us to put aside anxiety and our impatience for clarity and certainty. Enable us to respect each other's freedom as we change and grow. You have taught us that your love is ever unfolding, that life in you is ever becoming and renewing. Let us trust who we are and what we have, celebrating each moment now, entrusting ourselves and the outcome of our journey to you.

*Or:*

The Gospels give many pictures of Jesus offering new ways for us to live together. One is an image of new wine, which is not for putting in old wineskins, otherwise the skins burst, the wine is spilled and the skins are destroyed. New wine is put into fresh wineskins, so that both are preserved. Today N and N are committing themselves to a new way of holding and living out their love.

God, who give and refresh all life, you constantly offer opportunities to begin again in love, to mature in knowledge of ourselves and one another. Enable us to leave behind those constraints and memories that hinder us and help us to grow in trust and understanding. Give N and N we pray a sense of new possibilities unfolding. Let them delight in the mystery and beauty they find in each other. Keep us all open to your leading, confident in the presence of the Christ who goes before and beside us. Amen.

*Or:*

Loving God, we commend N and N and the commitment they make to each other before you and before this gathering. Affirm, we pray, the trust they have placed in each other and the hopes they share. Undergird with your love the confidence and strength they find in each other. In your grace, may they keep their covenant of trust.

## Reflection

*Readings, poems, symbols and music chosen by the couple may be shared to recollect, describe and affirm their partnership.*

## Declaration

*The couple now make their own statement to each other and to the gathering about the relationship being celebrated. This statement may include any of the following intentions:*

to be honest and open with each other

to match the intimacy of their love with their care and commitment to each other

to work at deepening their trust in and understanding of each other

to be loyal to each other

to forgive the hurt given to and received from each other

to allow the love they share to grow and change and deepen

to share with others the strength and encouragement they gain from each other.

## Prayers

*The couple may write their own prayers or choose any of the following to bring before God the journey they share.*

*A prayer of thanks for the couple:*

Loving God, in your wisdom you have given us many gifts. Today, we thank you for N and N, for all that they mean to each other and to their friends and families. We thank you for the love that has brought them to this time and place, and for the declarations they have been able to make before you and us. We pray that they will continue to grow in your love and in the use of the talents you have given them.

*A prayer for forgiveness and healing of the ways in which we have failed to love:*

God of love and understanding, we know that it is impossible for people to live together without sometimes causing pain or misunderstanding. Help us to recognize our part in this failure and to know your forgiveness and healing of the past. In particular, we ask that your love may heal any hurtful memories that N and N may bring to this day. May they know your forgiveness and the peace that comes from your presence, now and always.

*A prayer for the couple:*

God, your strength is sufficient for us all. N and N have committed themselves one to the other in your presence and before us, so we pray that you will continue to be with them in the unfolding of their future. Give them strength and courage in times of difficulty, wisdom and love in times of opportunity and challenge, and the sharing of joy in times of happiness and success. May they continue to grow in your love; through the power of Jesus Christ.

*A prayer for family and friends of the couple:*

God of friends and families, we are linked with N and N in a community of friendship and support. We pray for one another (particularly for . . .). We remember those who cannot be with us today (especially . . .). May we all continue to share in your gifts of love, strength, courage and wisdom, and to know your joy. Give us growing understanding, sympathy with each other's difficulties, patience with each other's faults, and grace to walk in your ways.

## Invocation

Companion God, may N and N know your blessing so that in their relationship they are a source of blessing to each other and to all they meet.

*Or:*

God of all times and seasons, in your strength we make new beginnings. As you open the future to N and N may they know your blessing; go with them in all their living and loving; enable them to be a source of joy and blessing to each other and to all whom their lives touch.

## Affirmation

*Parents, family and friends are invited to express their support for N and N by offering personal statements, prayers and good wishes. Symbols or gifts may also be offered.*

## Dismissal

*For the couple:*

N and N, you have brought us together to witness and celebrate your love for each other. Go now with God's blessing and the good wishes of us all. May your partnership mature within God's grace and may God's love surround and sustain you always.

*For the people:*

Now may God the Creator renew us all and give us peace, God the Redeemer renew us all and give us peace, God the Giver of Life renew us all and give us peace, this day and for ever. Amen.

**Anglican Diocese of Christchurch, Aotearoa/New Zealand**

**58**    *A service of blessing*

---

### Welcome

### Introduction *Psalm 23 (Brother James's Air)*

OFFICIANT
Blessed are you God, Ruler of the Universe,
    you have created us according to your desire.

Blessed are you God, Ruler of the Universe,
    you have formed all human beings in your own image.

Blessed are you God, Ruler of the Universe,
    you have made us to love you and to love each other.

Blessed are you God, Ruler of the Universe,
    you sent your Son, Jesus Christ, to reveal yourself in the world.

Blessed are you God, Ruler of the Universe,
    he has redeemed us and given us the gift of eternal life.

Blessed are you God, Ruler of the Universe,
    through your Holy Spirit you give us joy, peace and friendship.

Blessed are you God, Ruler of the Universe,
    you have brought your servants A— and B— together.

Blessed are you God, Ruler of the Universe,
    you give us life and have brought us to this present time.

ALL
Shout to the Holy One all the earth.
Serve such goodness with joy.
Come before God singing.

Know that the Holy One is God.
He made us. We belong to him.
God's own people, the sheep of his pasture.

Indeed, how good is the Lord.
His love is everlasting.
His faithfulness never changes.

*Silence is kept so we may consider our failures to love God and love each
other.*

ALL
Have mercy on me, O God, in your enduring goodness:
according to the fullness of your compassion
    blot out my offences.

Wash me thoroughly from my wickedness:
and cleanse me from my sin.

For I acknowledge my rebellion:
and my sin is ever before me.

Against you only have I sinned
   and done what is evil in your eyes:
so you will be just in your sentence
   and blameless in your judging.

Surely in wickedness I was brought to birth:
and in sin my mother conceived me.

You that desire truth in the inward parts:
O teach me wisdom in the secret places of the heart.

Purge me with hyssop, and I shall be clean:
wash me, and I shall be whiter than snow.

Make me hear of joy and gladness:
let the bones which you have broken rejoice.

Hide your face from my sins:
and blot out all my iniquities.

                                          (Liturgical Psalter)

OFFICIANT

Father, forgive what we have been.
Consecrate what we are.
Order what we shall be.

# The prayer for the day

# A reading from the Gospel of St John

OFFICIANT

How good it is, and how lovely when friends live together as one.
How lovely the home where your presence dwells,
   God of all creation.
Happy the people you have inspired, who journey through life,
   with you in their heart.
Who have known both sadness and tears, and covered them with
   blessings, like springs of water.
They go with strength to strength, until they appear before
   God in Zion.
For God withholds no good from those who walk in honesty.

As a mother hen gathers her chicks, so you keep us safe
under your wings.

A— AND B—

Our hearts and our bodies call out to the living God.
We shall journey in his presence as long as we live.
We shall fulfil our promises to him in the presence of his people.

## The wine

A—    You and I drink from one cup to remember the joys and happiness
we shall continue to share with God's blessing and presence.

B—    Blessed are you, the Eternal, our God who creates the fruit of the
vine.

*They each drink from the cup.*

## The salt

B—    We taste salt to remember the bitter and unhappy times we shall
share together.

A—    Blessed are you, the Eternal, our God who gives us strength for
suffering.

*They each taste the salt.*

## The bread

A—    You and I eat this bread to remember our daily life together. May
God hallow the ordinary things of life through his blessing.

B—    Blessed are you, the Eternal, Our God, who brings forth bread from
the earth.

*They eat bread.*

## Blessing of A— and B—

OFFICIANT

Blessed are those who came together in God's name. May the
Eternal, whose greatness transcends us yet sets within us the power
of his friendship and love, bless your home and these your friends
who are gathered here.

## The blessing of the home

## The prayers

### The greeting of Peace

*A— and B— exchange a gift.*

### Hymn *Come down, O Love divine*

### Offering of bread and wine

A— Blessed are you, Lord God of all creation, through your goodness we have this bread to offer which earth has given and human hands have made. It will become for us the bread of life.

ALL Blessed be God for ever.

B— Blessed are you, Lord God of all creation, through your goodness we have this wine to offer, fruit of the vine and work of human hands. It will become for us our spiritual drink.

ALL Blessed be God for ever.

### The Lord's Prayer

### Breaking of bread

### Communion

### Post-Communion prayer

### Hymn *Thine be the glory, risen conquering Son*

### The Blessing

OFFICIANT
Let us go in peace to love and serve the Lord.

ALL Thanks be to God.

Malcolm Johnson

## 59 *Order of the blessing of a civil marriage*
*In memory of Kathy Keay, who died on the day her marriage to Mike George was to have taken place.*

The following service may be used when a couple have been married in a Registry Office and wish to have a service of blessing on their marriage.

*The husband and wife: before the minister.*
*The minister says:*

We have come together before God
and to ask his blessing
on the marriage of Kathy and Mike.

They have committed themselves to one another,
in faith, hope and love,
and we pray now, that strengthened by God's grace,
they may be enabled to keep the vows they have made,
to be loyal and faithful to each other,
and to support each other throughout their life.

## Reading of Scripture *1 Corinthians 13.4, 8–13*

### Prayer *Big Hearts*

MINISTER
Give us big hearts, dear God;
KATHY  big enough to embrace all our sisters and brothers
especially those in trouble,
whether of their own making or
because of wrongs done to them.

MINISTER
Give us big hearts, dear God;
MIKE  big enough to acknowledge our own weakness
before pointing the finger at others;
big enough to be humble
when blessed with your good gifts denied to so many.

MINISTER
Give us big hearts, dear God;
KATHY AND MIKE
to reach out again and again
to those who cannot help themselves
until hope is restored to them
and we, thorn-beaten and bloodied
allow our loving to become more like yours.

(Kathy Keay)

*The minister says:*

As a sign that you have come together as husband and wife to seek God's
blessing on your marriage, will you now join hands?

*The couple join hands.*

Marriage is a gift of God given so that Kathy and Mike as husband and wife
may support and comfort one another, and live together in unity, in need
and in plenty, in sorrow and in joy.

It is given that in their tenderness towards each other, and care for one
another, they may be joined body, soul and spirit, in life and in love.

It is given that in their life together they may share their love and concern with others.

It is given that Lara may be brought up in love and tenderness and be led to know and worship God, the giver of all good things.

> *All stand.*

> *The minister says to the man:*

Do you, Mike, thankfully acknowledge that marriage is a spiritual gift? Do you promise that, in your marriage to Kathy, you will be faithful in your love, steadfast in your care, and honest and true in all things, until death parts you?

> *The man answers:*

I do.

> *The minister says to the woman:*

Do you, Kathy, thankfully acknowledge that marriage is a gift of God, and strengthened by his grace, do you promise that, in your marriage to Mike, you will be faithful in your love, steadfast in your care, and honest and true in all things, until death parts you?

> *The woman answers:*

I do, with God as my helper.

> *The minister places his right hand on their joined hands, and says:*

The Lord bless you and keep you
the Lord make his face to shine upon you,
and give you peace.

> *Husband and wife respond, saying:*

Amen.

## Prayer
> *A period of silence is observed.*

MIKE    Lead us from death to life, from falsehood to truth.

KATHY   Lead us from despair to hope, from fear to trust.

MIKE    Lead us from hate to love, from war to peace.

KATHY   Let peace fill our hearts, our world, our universe.

KATHY AND MIKE

Let us dream together, pray together, work together, to build one world of peace and justice for all.

(Universal prayer for peace)

KATHY   I believe that God is in me as the sun is in the colour and fragrance of a flower — the Light in my darkness, the Voice in my silence.

(Helen Keller)

*Address and/or presentation of a Bible to the married couple.*

## Hymn

## The Blessing

Deep peace of the running wave to you,
Deep peace of the flowing air to you,
Deep peace of the quiet earth to you,
Deep peace of the shining stars to you,
Deep peace of the Son of peace to you.


May the road rise up to meet you.
May the wind be always at your back.
May the sun shine warm upon your face,
the rain fall soft upon your fields
and until we meet again,
may God hold you in the palm of his hand.

(Traditional Celtic blessing)

**Based on a Presbyterian Church of Wales service
by Gethin Abraham-Williams**

## 60    *A liturgy for the blessing of a couple*

---

## Gathering in God's Name

CELEBRANT

Dear friends and family, we are gathered here in the presence of
God to witness and to bless the covenant and commitment which
—— and —— make this day with one another. Scripture tells us
that we are created in God's image and love and that we are called
to be vehicles of love unto one another. Our Savior Jesus Christ said
to his disciples, 'Love one another, as I have loved you.' Fulfilling
the two commandments for life that he gave us, to love God and
our neighbor, we give praise and glory unto God and enrich the
lives of one another. By the love we show unto others shall we be
known as followers of Christ. God established a covenant relationship with us founded in love, mercy, forgiveness, and faithfulness. —— and —— come here today to commit their lives to a
covenant union with one another, to live together faithfully, in love,
forgiveness, and mercy. Therefore let us rejoice with them and
pledge our love, friendship, and support unto them.

CELEBRANT *(addressing the partners each in turn)*
—— will you promise to live in a covenanted relationship with
——? Will you love *her/him*, comfort *her*, honor and keep *her*, in
sickness and in health, and forsaking all others, be faithful to *her* as
long as you both shall live?

PARTNER
I will.

CELEBRANT *(addressing the congregation)*
Will all you, who witness their vows, do all in your power to
support them in their union; will you share their joys, and comfort
them in their sorrows?

PEOPLE We will.

## Proclaiming God's Word

CELEBRANT
God's love be with you.

PEOPLE And also with you.

CELEBRANT
Let us pray. O gracious and everliving God, you have created us to
be the bearers of your love. Look mercifully upon these two persons
who come seeking your blessing and assist them with your grace,
that with fidelity and lasting love they may honor and keep the
vows and promises which they make; through Jesus Christ our
Savior we pray.
Amen.

*One or more passages from Scripture are read. If there is to be a Eucharist,
then one reading must be from the Gospels.*

Song of Solomon 2.10–13; 8.6–7a *(Many waters cannot quench
love.)*
1 Corinthians 13.1–13 *(Love is patient and kind.)*
Colossians 3.12–17 *(Above all, put on love.)*
1 John 4.7–16 *(Love is of God.)*
Matthew 5.1–10 *(The Beatitudes.)*
John 15.9–12 *(Love one another as I have loved you.)*

*A homily may be preached.*

## The Covenant

*One partner faces the other, holding her/his right hand and says:*

In the name of God, I ——, take you, ——, to be my beloved, to live
together in a covenant of love, mercy, forgiveness, and faithfulness; whether

we are rich or poor, in illness or in health, whether life is desirable or wracked with misery and pain, until we are parted by death. This is my solemn vow.

> *They loose hands, and the second partner takes the first's right hand and says:*

In the name of God, I ——, take you, ——, to be my beloved, to live together in a covenant of love, mercy, forgiveness, and faithfulness; whether we are rich or poor, in illness or in health, whether life is desirable or wracked with misery and pain, until we are parted by death. This is my solemn vow.

> *The celebrant is given the ring/s or other symbol of love to be exchanged and blesses them with these words:*

Bless, O God, these rings (or symbol) to be a sign of the covenant by which these persons have bound themselves to one another.

> *One partner places the ring on the hand of the other and says:*

——, I give you this ring, as a symbol of my promise, and with all that I am and all that I have, I honor you, in the name of God.

> *This vow is repeated by the other partner if two rings, or symbols, are used.*

CELEBRANT

Now that —— and —— have given themselves to each other by solemn vows and the making of a covenant, with the joining of hands and the giving and receiving of rings, I pronounce their love blessed by us and by God's love for us.

## Prayer for the couple and for the world

CELEBRANT

Let us pray together in the words our Savior taught us:

O God in heaven,
you who are Mother and Father to us all,
Holy is your name.
Your reign has come.
Your will be done
on earth as in heaven.
Give us this day
our daily bread.
Forgive us our sin
as we forgive those
who sin against us.
Deliver us from evil.

Save us from the time of trial.
For all time and all space,
all power and all glory are yours,
now and for ever. Amen.

*Friends may read one or more of the following prayers or may offer their hopes and dreams for the couple.*

Eternal God, creator and preserver of all life, author of salvation, and giver of all grace: Look with favor upon the world you have made, and especially upon —— and ——. Amen.

Give them wisdom and devotion in the ordering of their common life, that each may be to the other a strength in need, a counselor in perplexity, a comfort in sorrow, and a companion in joy. Amen.

Grant that their wills may be so knit together in your will, and their spirits in your Spirit, that they may grow in love and peace with you and one another all the days of their life. Amen.

Give them grace, when they hurt each other, to recognize and acknowledge their fault, and to seek each other's forgiveness and yours. Amen.

Make their life together a sign of Christ's love to this sinful and broken world, that unity may overcome estrangement, forgiveness heal guilt, and joy conquer despair. Amen.

Give them such fulfillment of their mutual affection that they may reach out in love and concern for others. Amen.

Grant that the bonds of our common humanity, by which all your children are united to one another, and the living to the dead, may be so transformed by your grace, that your will may be done now and for ever; through Jesus Christ, our Savior. Amen.

(Episcopal *Book of Common Prayer*)

## The Blessing

*The couple kneels.*

CELEBRANT

Most loving God, send your blessing upon these your servants, —— and ——, that they may so love, honor, and cherish each other in faithfulness and patience, in wisdom and true godliness, that their home may be a haven of blessing and peace, through Jesus Christ our Savior, who lives and reigns with you and the Holy Spirit, one God, for ever and ever. Amen.

## Benediction

CELEBRANT

The blessing of God, whose love created all life and brought you to birth, be with you this day.

The blessing of God, whose love transforms our living and reconciles us to the divine and to one another, be with you always.

The blessing of God, whose love inspires your love, fill you with all spiritual benediction and grace, that you may live faithfully together, and in the age to come, have life everlasting. Amen.

*The couple stands.*

## The Peace

CELEBRANT

The grace, peace, and love of God be with you.

PEOPLE And also with you.

*The Eucharist may follow. If not, the couple may embrace and then process out of the room or join their guests.*

**Vienna Cobb Anderson**

## 61  *Blessing prayers for renewing commitment between two persons*

ONE    Holy Creator of Love,
        we celebrate and renew our mutual lives
        that are lived as one.
    We reseal, by this holy prayer,
        our commitment to each other
        to a life of shared dreams, thoughts and feelings.
    We ask your holy help
        so that we may be always awake
        to the needs of each other,
        needs both spoken and unspoken.
    May our two but twin pathways
        lead us to the fullness of life
        and to you.

OTHER  We ask your divine protection
        from the strong tides of daily troubles

that tend to pull us apart from each other.
Shield us from the social sickness of no commitment.
Show us how to rechannel
    the hidden streams of selfishness
    that always threaten to separate us.
Lord, it was said by the ancients
    that from each of us flows a light
    that reaches straight to heaven;
    that when two persons destined to be united
    come together,
    their two streams fuse into a single bright beam
    reaching to heaven
    and giving splendour to all the universe.
We ask that our love for each other
    will shine as a single flame to all.

ONE    We thank you for the gifts of past years
    as we place our hope in the ancient truth
    that whatever is begun here on earth
    will flower to fullness in heaven.
As a sign of our desire to be united,
    today and in the days to follow,
    we join now our glasses as one
    and share a common chalice of our covenant
    with each other and with you, our Lord and God.
Amen.

*Each partner now pours from an individual glass into a third and empty glass. Each then drinks from this one ceremonial glass.*

**Edward Hays**

## 62   *A liturgy of friendship*

---

*Since this liturgy celebrates friendship as an inclusive, non-hierarchical relationship between persons, nations and God, it is important that the lay-out of the room/building reflects this. The most appropriate arrangement is a circle of chairs or cushions, so that every person is equally included and every person is able to have eye-contact with every other person. In the centre of the circle should be placed a lighted candle. Symbols of friendship may also be placed, such as a photograph of friends or a photograph album, a friendship bracelet, a gift given by a friend which has particular significance. (Participants could be asked to bring some such symbol to be placed in the circle.)*

## Opening sentence

LEADER Faithful friends are a sturdy shelter:
whoever finds one has found a treasure.

(Ecclesiasticus 6.14)

## Introduction to the theme

*The leader introduces the theme of friendship with the following words, or*
*words of his/her own choosing.*

Friendship between persons and friendship with God has an honoured place
in scripture and in Christian tradition. Abraham was called the Friend of
God; God spoke to Moses face to face as a person speaks to a friend; the
celebrated friendships of Jonathan and David and Ruth and Naomi speak to
us eloquently of the power of human friendship. Jesus called his disciples his
friends, and commanded them to love one another with the radical freedom
and mutuality of friendship. The mystics down the ages have named God as
friend and sought that free, joyful, trusting relationship with God that
friends enjoy. Yet, despite this honourable tradition, friendship is a relationship much neglected in the Church. Marriage and family life are
celebrated and ritualized, but friendship – one of the most treasured and
enduring of human relationships – is ignored or taken for granted. God is
frequently named Father, Lord, Master, even Lover, but rarely Friend. In
our liturgy today, we seek to reflect on the meaning of friendship in our lives
and to recapture this rich model for speaking about the love and presence of
God in our lives and our world.

## Ministry of the Word

*A selection of biblical and non-biblical readings are suggested below on the*
*theme of friendship. A number of hymns are also provided which can be*
*used in between the readings. Alternatively, the readings might be inter-*
*spersed with a tape-recording of a popular song on friendship; various*
*appropriate songs are suggested.*

*Suggested biblical readings:*

Ecclesiasticus 6.14–17

Exodus 33.7–11

1 Samuel 18.1–5

Ruth 1

Matthew 11.16–19

Luke 11.5–8

John 15.7–17

*Suggested sources for non-biblical readings:*

Eric James: *The House of my Friends* (Christian Action, 1984)

Brian Frost and Pauline Webb (eds): *Celebrating Friendship: An Anthology* (Epworth, 1986)

Sallie McFague: *Models of God: Theology for an Ecological, Nuclear Age* (SCM Press, 1987), pp. 159ff.

Stephen Neill: *A Genuinely Human Existence* (New York: Doubleday, 1959)

Elizabeth Jennings: 'Friendship', *Collected Poems* (Carcanet, 1986)


*Suggested hymns:*

'What a friend we have in Jesus' (J. M. Scriven)

'I've found a friend, O such a friend' (J. G. Small)

'Thou God of truth and love' (Charles Wesley)

'I come with joy to meet my Lord' (Brian Wren)

'Great God, your love has called us here' (Brian Wren)

'Bind us together, Lord' (B. Gillman)


*Popular songs:*

'With a little help from my friends' (the Beatles)

'You've got a friend' (Carole King)

> *During or after the readings and music, a short period of silence is kept for reflection. Alternatively, participants can be invited to offer their own reflections on the readings and music.*

## Celebration of friendship

*The leader explains the next section of the liturgy, which involves passing the lighted candle around the circle and offering a greeting of friendship as the candle is passed from person to person. Individuals may offer their own greetings to their neighbour, or a formalized greeting may be used, such as the following: 'I offer you my friendship in the love of Christ'; 'The friendship and love of God be with you always'; 'May God take our friendship deeper in the love of Christ'. Alternatively, the candle can be passed in silence, and individuals asked to think about and pray for the person to whom they pass the light.*

## Intercessions

*The leader offers brief biddings followed by a period of silence during which prayers are offered, either silently or aloud.*

LEADER Let us give thanks to God for all those who have befriended us throughout our lives, who have helped us to know that we are treasured and loved for no good reason other than being who we are:

*Individuals may name special friends here or pray for their friends.*

LEADER Let us pray for all those who are without a friend, or whose friends have died or deserted them: the lonely, the destitute, the abandoned:

*Individuals may name or offer prayer for those in need.*

LEADER Let us pray for the church, that it may be a community of genuine friendship, welcoming all into the free, joyful love of God, so that all may come to know themselves cherished as friends of God:

*Individuals may name church congregations or pray for particular projects.*

LEADER Let us pray for the nations of the world, that nation may befriend nation and share justly the good things of the earth so that all may come to enjoy the fullness of life which friends desire for one another:

*Individuals may name world causes or peoples or pray for particular situations.*

## Closing prayer

LEADER God of intimacy,
you surround us with friends and family
to cherish and to challenge:

May we so give and receive caring
in the details of our lives
that we also remain faithful
to your greater demands,
through Jesus Christ, Amen.

(Janet Morley)

*All stand and join hands in the circle and say the words of the grace, or
some similar blessing.*

**Nicola Slee and Gwyn Owen**

## 63  *A Jewish–Christian marriage*

The two families concerned had agreed to a Christian marriage service
which would recognize to the utmost the common ground between Jews
and Christians. The Marriage Service in *The Alternative Service Book 1980*
formed the framework for the service, with alterations to recognize the
Jewish faith. The numbers below refer to the sections of the ASB Marriage
Service. Only those parts are given here where the ASB wording was
changed.

### Opening hymn *Lord of all hopefulness*

### 13 The rings

THE PRIEST SAID

Heavenly Father, by your blessing let these rings be to Franklin and
Annette symbols of unending love and faithfulness, to remind them
of the vow and covenant which they have made this day.

*He said to the bride and groom:*

These rings, circles with no beginning and no end, represent your
love for each other, a love which has the potential to be everlasting,
beginning in trust, growing through companionship, and deepening
with understanding. These rings are an outward and visible sign of
an inward and spiritual bond which unites your hearts in love.

*14 The bridegroom placed the ring on the fourth finger of the bride's left
hand and said:*

I give you this ring as a sign of our marriage. With my body I
honour you, all that I am I give to you, and all that I have I share
with you, within the love of God, Father and Holy Spirit.

*16 The bride placed the ring on the fourth finger of the bridegroom's left hand and said:*

I give you this ring as a sign of our marriage. With my body I honour you, all that I am I give to you, and all that I have I share with you, within the love of God, Father, Son and Holy Spirit. (ASB)

## 20 Wine-drinking ceremony *(from the Jewish marriage service)*

THE PRIEST SAID

This cup of wine is symbolic of the cup of life. As you share the one cup of wine, you undertake to share all that the future may bring; all the sweetness life's cup may hold for you should be sweeter because you drink it together. And, as you break the cup, remember that whatever drops of bitterness life may contain should be less bitter because you share them.

As we recite the blessings over the wine, we pray that God will bestow fullness of joy upon you.

Blessed art thou, O Lord our God, Ruler of the Universe, who hast created all things for thy glory.

Blessed art thou, O Lord our God, Ruler of the Universe, Creator of Man.

Blessed art thou, O Lord our God, Ruler of the Universe, who hast fashioned us in thine own image and hast established marriage for the fulfilment and perpetuation of life in accordance with thy holy purpose.

Blessed art thou, O Lord our God, Ruler of the Universe, Creator of the fruit of the vine.

*Annette and Franklin then drank from a single glass of wine. The glass was wrapped in a napkin and stepped on.*

## The Prayers

24–7 omitted.
The Lord's Prayer.

28 Lord, who taught men and women to help and serve each other in marriage, and lead each other into happiness, bless this covenant of affection, these promises of truth. Protect and care for Franklin and Annette as they go through life together. May they be loving companions, secure in their devotion with the passing years. In their respect and honour for each other may they find their peace, and, in their affection and tenderness, their happiness. May your presence be in their home and in their hearts. Amen.

(from the Jewish marriage service)

Our God and God of our Fathers, bestow thy blessings upon Franklin and Annette as they unite their lives in thy name. Cause them to prosper in their life together. Teach them to share life's joys and life's trials and to grow in understanding and devotion. May love and companionship abide within the home they establish. May they grow old together in health and content-ment, ever grateful unto Thee for the union of their lives. Amen.

(from the Jewish marriage service)

To love somebody is not just a strong feeling – it is a decision, it is a judgement, it is a promise. If love were only a feeling, there would be no basis for the promise to love each other for ever. A feeling comes and it may go. How can I judge that it will stay for ever . . . [if] my act does not involve judgement and decision?

(Erich Fromm)

**Hymn** *Thy hand, O God, has guided thy flock from age to age*

**The Blessing and the signing of the register**

*Two years later those concerned say:*

Annette (Bride):
'I was pleased to be able to express to an audience of family and friends that we do believe we can live our lives together with differing religions. There will be hurdles to overcome but the initial promise and understanding are there to put every effort in to making it work and be a success.'

Frank (Groom):
'To have had a straightforward church service would have somehow seemed like a betrayal of my Jewish heritage, despite the fact that I am not a very "observant" Jew. I think there is a sense of pride involved. But it was not until we were back in the UK and involved actively that it really started to have any meaning. I feel the service had more meaning to us than it would to the average couple who are both the same religion. We were forced to question our own beliefs and priorities. We found that not only could we compromise on something as important as our wedding ceremony but actually create something very special, perhaps even beautiful.'

Evan (Annette's father):
'Heather and I are changed. In over thirty years of marriage we have come to understand more about other people but we have never had to move far outside our "culture". We did not dislike Jews (or Arabs) but nor did we see how much they could enrich our lives. Now we understand a little more about what it means for a whole race to suffer.

Certainly I did not realize the extent to which Christians and Jews and Muslims worship the same God.

We are now wanting to explore and adventure outside the security of our present Anglican lives, trusting more in a universal God.'

Evan Adams and Alan Webster

## 64    *A celebration for a Jewish–Christian wedding*

### The Gathering

*Processional: After all members of the wedding party have taken their places under the hoopa, the ceremony begins.*

RABBI    May you who are here be blessed in the name of the Lord.

*If the ceremony takes place in a synagogue, the rabbi adds:*

We bless you from the house of the Lord.

*Otherwise, the rabbi continues,*

May God who is supreme in power, blessing and glory bless this bridegroom and this bride.

RABBI    *(one of the following prayers)*
O God, source of holiness, help us to see the sacred dimensions of all life. Guide this bridegroom and bride to the realization of sanctity and devotion every day as today. Help them to renew their love continually, as you renew creation. May their concern for each other reflect your concern for all; may their loving faithfulness reflect your love. Throughout the years may they hallow life together, that the home they establish become a blessing. May your light illumine their lives. And let us say: Amen.

*or*

In happiness and joy we thank God for the divine blessing of love that we celebrate today, formally consecrating the love of —— and —— for each other. May they always rejoice in their love, graced by delight through their mutual affection. O Lord, our God, source of all blessing, fulfill every worthy wish of their hearts. Open their eyes to the beauty and mystery of the love they hold for each other, every day as today. May their life together embrace and nurture the promise of this moment, so that all who know them will call them truly blessed. And let us say: Amen.

PRIEST   Dearly beloved: We have come together in the presence of God to witness and bless the joining together of this man and this woman in Holy Matrimony. The bond and covenant of marriage was established by God in creation, and Holy Scripture commends it to be honored among all people.

The union of husband and wife in heart, body and mind is intended by God for their mutual joy; for the help and comfort given one another in prosperity and adversity; and, when it is God's will, for the procreation of children and their nurture in the knowledge and love of God. Therefore marriage is not to be entered into unadvisedly or lightly, but reverently, deliberately, and in accordance with the purposes for which it was instituted by God.

Into this holy union

– [*full name*] – and – [*full name*] – now come to be joined.

If any of you can show just cause why they may not lawfully be married, speak now; or else forever hold your peace.

*The priest says to the persons to be married:*

I require and charge you both, here in the presence of God, that if either of you know any reason why you may not be united in marriage lawfully and in accordance with God's Word, you do now confess it.

## The Declaration of Consent

PRIEST   *(to the woman)*
——, will you have this man to be your husband, to live together in the covenant of marriage? Will you love him, comfort him, honor and keep him, in sickness and in health, and, forsaking all others, be faithful to him as long as you both shall live?
WOMAN I will.

PRIEST   *(to the man)*
——, will you have this woman to be your wife, to live together in the covenant of marriage? Will you love her, comfort her, honor and keep her, in sickness and in health, and, forsaking all others, be faithful to her as long as you both shall live?
MAN    I will.

### The blessing of family and friends

PRIEST    *(addresses the congregation)*
It is important to know that in our times of joy and in times of sorrow, our families and friends will be with us to support us and to share our lives. Therefore, I ask you to make a commitment to the bride and groom at this time. Will all you witnessing these promises do all in your power to uphold —— and —— in their marriage?

PEOPLE    We will.

PRIEST    Who from the bride's family blesses this marriage?

*Those speaking for the bride's family answer*

I do.

PRIEST    Who from the groom's family blesses this marriage?

*Those speaking for the groom's family answer*

I do.

PRIEST    Let us pray.
O gracious and everliving God, you have created us male and female in your image: Look mercifully upon —— and —— who come to you seeking your blessing and assist them with your grace, that with true fidelity and steadfast love they may honor and keep the promises and vows they make. Through their love may your name be praised. Amen.

### The proclamation of the Word of God

Genesis 1.26–8, 31a *(God created humankind in the divine image.)*
Song of Solomon 2.10–13; 8.6–7 *(My beloved speaks.)*
Colossians 3.12–17 *(Love binds everything together in harmony.)*
1 Corinthians 13.1–13 *(Love is patient and kind.)*

*The Rabbi reads from Baal Shem Tov*

From every human being there rises a light that reaches straight to heaven. And when two souls that are destined for each other find one another, their streams of light flow together and a single brighter light goes forth from their united being.

*The couple may light a single candle from two candles.*

### The Marriage

*The priest instructs the man to face the woman, take her right hand in his, and repeat after the priest, saying:*

In the name of God, I ——, take you, ——, to be my wife, to have and to hold from this day forward, for better for worse, for richer for poorer, in sickness and in health, to love and to cherish, until we are parted by death. This is my solemn vow.

> *They loose their hands. The woman, facing the man, takes his right hand in hers and, repeating after the priest, says:*

In the name of God, I, ——, take you, ——, to be my husband, to have and to hold from this day forward, for better for worse, for richer for poorer, in sickness and in health, to love and to cherish, until we are parted by death. This is my solemn vow.

> *They loose their hands.*
>
> *The rings are given to the rabbi, who may say a blessing upon them. The rabbi instructs the man to place the ring on the forefinger of the woman and to say:*

By this ring you are consecrated to me as my wife in accordance with the law of Moses and the people of Israel.

> *The rabbi instructs the woman to respond:*

In accepting this ring, I pledge you all my love and devotion.

> *The rabbi instructs the woman to place the ring on the forefinger of the man and to say:*

By this ring you are consecrated to me as my husband in accordance with the law of Moses and the people of Israel.

> *The rabbi instructs the man to respond:*

In accepting this ring, I pledge you all my love and devotion.

## The tying of the knot

> *The priest asks the couple to join right hands and explains to the congregation the meaning of wrapping the stole around the hands, signifying the tying of the knot, a phrase used to mean 'getting married'. The priest then says:*

Now that —— and —— having given themselves to each other by solemn vows, with the joining of hands and the giving and receiving of ring/s, I pronounce they are husband and wife, in the name of God. Those whom God has joined together let no man put asunder.

PEOPLE Amen.

## The drinking of wine

*A cup of wine is shared by the bride and groom. The rabbi or a cantor recites in Hebrew while the couple drinks.*

## The prayers

*The priest or a member of the family or one or more friends lead the prayers.*

Eternal God, creator and preserver of all life, author of salvation, and giver of all grace: Look with favor upon the world you have made, and especially upon —— and ——, whom you make one flesh in Holy Matrimony. Amen.

Give them wisdom and devotion in the ordering of their common life, that each may be to the other a strength in need, a counselor in perplexity, a comfort in sorrow, and a companion in joy. Amen.

Grant that their wills may be so knit together in your will, and their spirits in your Spirit that they may grow in love and peace with you and one another all the days of their life. Amen.

Give them grace when they hurt each other to recognize and acknowledge their fault and to seek each other's forgiveness and yours. Amen.

Make their life together a sign of your love to this sinful and broken world, that unity may overcome estrangement, forgiveness heal guilt, and joy conquer despair. Amen.

Bestow on them, if it is your will, the gift and heritage of children and the grace to bring them up to know you, to love you, and to serve you. Amen.

Give them such fulfillment of their mutual affection that they may reach out in love and concern for others. Amen.

Grant that all married persons who have witnessed these vows may find their lives strengthened and their loyalties confirmed. Amen.

Grant that the bonds of our common humanity, by which all your children are united to one another and the living to the dead, may be so transformed by your grace that your will may be done on earth as it is in heaven, to the glory of your name, now and for ever. Amen.

### The six blessings

*The rabbi or a member of the family reads the blessings.*

1. You abound in blessings, Lord our God, source of all creation, creator of the fruit of the vine, symbol of human joy.

2. You abound in blessings, Lord our God, source of all creation, all of whose creations reflect your glory.

3. You abound in blessings, Lord our God, source of all creation, creator of human beings.

4. You abound in blessings, Lord our God, source of all creation, who created man and woman in your image that they might live, love, and so perpetuate life. You abound in blessings, Lord, creator of human beings.

5. We all rejoice as these two persons, overcoming separateness, unite in joy. You abound in blessings, Lord, permitting us to share in others' joy.

6. May these lovers rejoice as did the first man and woman in the primordial Garden of Eden. You abound in blessings, Lord our God, source of joy for bride and groom.

## The blessing of the marriage

*The rabbi and priest say the blessing from the Book of Deuteronomy, alternating in Hebrew and English.*

May God bless you and guard you.
May God show you favour and be gracious to you.
May God show you kindness and grant you peace. Amen.

## The breaking of the glass

*The rabbi explains the symbolism of the breaking of the glass. A glass is placed on the floor near the man's foot; the man breaks it by stamping on it.*

PEOPLE  Mazeltov!

PRIEST  The peace and love of God be always with you.
PEOPLE  And also with you.

*The couple greet one another with a kiss and then process down the aisle.*

**Vienna Cobb Anderson and Rabbi Harold White**

# 65    *Partnership promises*

---

OFFICIAN

> *N* and *N*, you are about to make a solemn promise. Do you believe God has called you to live together in love?

PARTNERS

> We do believe.

OFFICIANT

> Do you promise to be loyal to each other, never allowing any other relationship to come before the one you are now to affirm?

PARTNERS

> We do promise.

OFFICIANT

> Will you give yourselves wholeheartedly and without reserve?

PARTNERS

> We will.

OFFICIANT

> Will you, under God, recognize each other's freedom to grow as individuals and allow each other time and space to do so?

PARTNERS

> We will.

OFFICIANT

> Will you do all in your power to make your life together a witness to the love of God in the world?

PARTNERS

> We will.

OFFICIANT

> *(To each partner in turn)* N will you give yourself wholly to N, sharing your love and your life, your wholeness and your broken-ness, your joys and sorrows, your health and sickness, your riches and poverty, your success and failure?

PARTNER

> I will.

Jim Cotter

## 66  *Partnership declarations*

We have gathered together today to acknowledge the love which has brought N and N together as being from God and to ask God's blessing upon them as they live together in company with each other. We also seek to give them support as their friends and as members of the Body of Christ, the Church, and to strive for their good now in our prayers and in our future care and concern.

*Each friend repeats the following:* In the presence of God and God's people, I, N, declare my love for you, N, and seek God's blessing on our friendship. I will continue to love you, care for you, and consider you before my own needs, in good times and through periods of difficulty. I will rejoice when you are happy and grieve when you suffer. I will share your interests and hopes for the future. I will try to understand you even when I do not agree with you. I will help you to be your true self – the person God wishes you to be. In all this I ask God's help, now and in the days to come. In the name of Jesus Christ. Amen.

Hazel Barkham

## 67  *On the occasion of a second marriage*

OFFICIANT
> N, you have been married before and your marriage ended in divorce. Have you faced with honesty your part in the breakdown of that relationship?

BRIDE   I have.

OFFICIANT
> Have you allowed that experience to lead you into new life – to a better understanding of yourself and of your hopes and desires for the future?

BRIDE   I have.

OFFICIANT
> N, you have been married before and your marriage ended with your partner's death. Have you reflected on that relationship and faced with honesty your responsibility for both its weaknesses and its strengths?

GROOM   I have.

OFFICIANT

Have you allowed the experience of that marriage to lead you into new life – to a better understanding of yourself and of your hopes and desires for the future?

GROOM  I have.

OFFICIANT

Owning the past, are you N, and you N, each now ready to give yourself fully to the new marriage relationship which you believe God is offering you?

BOTH  I am.

Clare Edwards

## 68    *Proper preface for a marriage eucharist*

---

It is indeed right and fitting, it is our delight and joy,
that we should in this place, as in all places,
offer thanks and praise to you, Source of all Being,
Eternal Word and Holy Spirit.

All thanks to you, God of love,
Creator of the universe,
maker of man and woman in your own image.

All praise to you
for the creation of human relationships,
for courtship and marriage,
  joy and gladness,
  pleasure and delight.

You bless us in your Holy Spirit
  and call us to share in your work of creation;
in marriage, you join man and woman to each other
  to become one flesh,
to be a sign of your steadfast love.

We give thanks for N and N
as they stand before you now
and witness to your living eternal Word
who comes to them, as to us,
in your Son Jesus Christ, the Redeemer,
whose pattern of life we seek to follow.

Peter Kettle

**69**   *And can it be . . .*

Great God, your love has called us here
As we, by love for love were made.
Your living likeness still we bear,
Though marred, dishonoured, disobeyed.
We come, with all our heart and mind
Your call to hear, your love to find.

We come with self-inflicted pains
Of broken trust and chosen wrong,
Half-free, half-bound by inner chains,
By social forces swept along,
By powers and systems close confined,
Yet seeking hope for humankind.

Great God, in Christ you call our name
And then receive us as your own,
Not through some merit, right or claim
But by your gracious love alone.
We strain to glimpse your mercy-seat
And find you kneeling at our feet.

Then take the towel, and break the bread,
And humble us, and call us friends.
Suffer and serve till all are fed,
And show how grandly love intends
To work till all creation sings,
To fill all worlds, to crown all things.

Great God, in Christ you set us free
Your life to live, your joy to share.
Give us your Spirit's liberty
To turn from guilt and dull despair
And offer all that faith can do
While love is making all things new.

*Tune: Abingdon*

**Brian Wren**

**70**     *Wedding carol*

As man and woman we were made
That love be found and life begun
So praise the Lord who made us two
And praise the Lord when two are one:
  Praise for the love that comes to life
  Through child or parent, husband, wife.

Now Jesus lived and gave his love
To make our life and loving new
So celebrate with him today
And drink the joy he offers you
  That makes the simple moment shine
  And changes water into wine.

And Jesus died to live again
So praise the love that, come what may,
Can bring the dawn and clear the skies,
And waits to wipe all tears away
  And let us hope for what shall be
  Believing where we cannot see.

Then spread the table, clear the hall
And celebrate till day is done;
Let peace go deep between us all
And joy be shared by everyone:
  Laugh and make merry with your friends
  And praise the love that never ends!

*Tune: Sussex Carol*

**Brian Wren**

# 5

# *Who touched me?*
## *Healing our wounds*

People need human contact – to be touched lovingly is a human right and is the stuff of many human rites. The touch of hands in ritual action and rites of anointing are ancient Judaeo-Christian practices, and such healing rites are perhaps the best known and most developed in the churches across a vast variety of theological stances.

We have included here some well-known healing rituals (e.g. that from St Marylebone Parish Church, firmly established in the 1980s as a centre for healing ministry), that can be seen as public rites for individuals worshipping together. There are also services where the universal dimension of healing, wholeness or salvation is made clear in issues of social justice.

The title we have chosen for this section reminds us of the sacramental quality of many forms of touch – those who practise physiotherapy, massage, reflexology, aromatherapy, osteopathy and similar treatments are in immediate continuity with healing ministry, even where they do not see their work as having a religious dimension. And the contrary is true: people undergoing forms of therapy that require a certain degree of separation, of physical isolation, as in radiotherapy, need special human support to transcend the barrier of this necessary but often frightening aloneness.

The rites surrounding abortion which we include here serve, we hope, to make clear that the awful ambiguity of abortion needs above all the supporting love of those around the woman or couple concerned.

Some people have been regarded by their societies as untouchable – temporarily or permanently – and a sharp reminder of this has come with the spread of AIDS in recent years to our 'western' world. In the early days we did not know how to treat these bodies of our fellow humans. Living and dead, they were in danger of being literally untouchable. It is not surprising that some of the best insights and liturgical material have been developed among those who have lived with HIV/AIDS or cared for people with AIDS and their friends and families.

Touch, we must not forget, can also be violent and abusive. Many personal and communal rituals for the healing of memories of physical and sexual abuse are being devised and enacted. We have chosen to include these in a later chapter, but mention them here because it is necessary to remember that all touch is not healing. 'Who touched me?' may be heard as a paraphrase of the strong words of judgement in Matthew's great parable: 'Inasmuch as you abused one of the least of these . . . you did it to me.'

## 71     *Service of healing*

### Private preparation before the service

Lord, we remember your presence with us and offer ourselves to you in Faith and Hope and Love.

We believe in your power, both to heal and to save; we pray that your will may be done, in us and through us.

We hope in your promises; we pray that we may be made worthy of them.

We love you and pray that we may love you better, for by your love we are made and sanctified.

We pray for ourselves, for one another and for all mankind, that we may serve you faithfully and in all things seek your glory, through Jesus Christ our Lord. Amen.

*The service will follow the pattern here given but the content of any section may be varied at the discretion of the minister.*

### Welcome

### Sentence

Jesus said, 'Heal the sick and say, "The Kingdom of God has come near to you".'

### Praise

Glory be to God, Creator of heaven and earth,
    for calling the worlds into being
    and bringing order and beauty out of chaos;
    for awakening our desire for him
    and the thirst after truth.
Glory be to God for his mighty acts in the
    redemption of his creation and his children;
    for sending his Son in the fullness of time
    to be born

to live and work
to seek and save the lost,
to suffer and die,
and to rise victorious over death.
Glory be to God for his Holy Spirit, ever working
in the hearts of his people,
to lead us into truth,
to make us whole
and to fill us with love and joy and peace.

*All say together:*

Holy, holy, holy Lord,
God of power and might,
heaven and earth are full of your glory.
Hosanna in the highest.

## Hymn

## Intercession

| | |
|---|---|
| For the whole family of God: | V. Lord in your mercy<br>R. **Hear our prayer.** |
| For all Christian people: | V. Lord in your mercy<br>R. **Hear our prayer.** |
| For the Church in this country: | V. Lord in your mercy<br>R. **Hear our prayer.** |
| For the sick at home or in hospital: | V. Lord in your mercy<br>R. **Hear our prayer.** |
| For ourselves that we may be set free<br>and made whole by the Holy Spirit: | V. Lord in your mercy<br>R. **Hear our prayer.** |

*Then may be said one or more of these prayers:*

O God, you have prepared for those who love you such good things as pass our understanding: pour into our hearts such love towards you, that we, loving you above all things, may obtain your promises, which exceed all that we can desire, through Jesus Christ our Lord.

Defend, O Lord, us your children with your heavenly grace, that we may continue yours for ever, and daily increase in your Holy Spirit more and more until we come to your everlasting kingdom.                    (ASB)

O Thou who art the light of the minds that know thee,
   the joy of the hearts that love thee,
   and the strength of the wills that serve thee:
Help us so to know thee, that we may truly love thee,
   so to love thee that we may fully serve thee,
   whom to serve is perfect freedom;
   through Jesus Christ our Lord. Amen.

## Readings

## Anthem

## Address

*A period of silence.*

## Hymn to the Holy Spirit *(kneeling)*

## Confession of sin and sickness

*A moment of reflection*

*All say together*
God our Father, we acknowledge before you our need of your saving grace.
Forgive and heal us according to your gracious promises, that we may serve
you in newness of life to the glory of your Name, through Jesus Christ our
Lord. Amen.

## The Absolution

Almighty God our heavenly Father who has promised to make whole and
forgive all who are penitent, have mercy upon you, pardon and deliver you
from all your sins; release you from all sickness and infirmity, and fill you
with the grace of his Holy Spirit, through Jesus Christ our Lord. Amen.

## The Laying on of hands with prayer

*All say together*
God our Father, by whom we are called to ventures of which we cannot see
the ending and by paths as yet untrodden:
give us faith to go out always with good courage, knowing that in the power
of your Holy Spirit we are made strong and that your love will never fail us,
in Jesus Christ our Lord. Amen.

Remember, O Lord, what you have wrought in us, and not what we
deserve, and as you have called us to your service, make us worthy of your
calling, through Jesus Christ our Lord. Amen.

**The Lord's Prayer**

**Hymn**

**Prayer and Blessing**

**Final anthem**

St Marylebone Parish Church, London

## 72 *Service of healing*

### The witness

LEADER In Jesus Christ, we hear the Good News
that God is like a mother hen
who shelters her chickens
under her warm wings.
PEOPLE We believe that God is love.

LEADER In Jesus, we see a God
who wept for the people of the world,
PEOPLE and weeps for our wounding.

LEADER In Jesus, we see a God
who reaches out with healing hands,
PEOPLE who sees our pain and makes us whole.

### Confession

LEADER Let us join in our prayers of confession:
O God, you die for us and conquer death for us,
PEOPLE but we find it hard to believe in your love.

LEADER We see your creativity in all the earth,
PEOPLE but fear to ask for our own healing.

ALL Forgive us and bring us to faith.

### Assurance of pardon

LEADER Hear the word to us in Christ:
If we have faith as small as a mustard seed,
God's power is released in us.
Our healing is a gracious gift.

Rise, take up your bed and walk.
Amen.
PEOPLE Amen.

## Ministry of the Word

Old Testament:        Psalm 13

Gospel:               Luke 8.43–8

## The contemporary witness

## Prayers of intercession

LEADER O God, we cry to you in our anger
that people hurt each other.
PEOPLE **Be with us and heal us, O God.**

LEADER We feel the fear and pain
of an innocent and trusting child.
PEOPLE **Be with us and heal us, O God.**

LEADER We carry with us the things
that have been done to us
which hurt and destroy.
PEOPLE **Be with us and heal us, O God.**

LEADER They stand before us
and weigh us down.
They stop us living with joy and hope.
PEOPLE **Be with us and heal us, O God.**

LEADER Lift us up
on the wings of your Spirit.
PEOPLE **Set us free with your peace
and your power.**

LEADER For you are stronger
than all the forces that stand against us.
PEOPLE **Set us free,
heal our wounds,
O God who never leaves us
nor forsakes us.
Amen.**

## The laying on of hands

*(The person seeking healing kneels.)*

MINISTER

We lay our hands upon you
in the name of Jesus Christ,
healer and lover of the world.

*(Silent prayer)*

May the Lord of love,
who is more powerful
than all those who would harm us,
give you healing for all that is past
and peace for all that is to come.

May she surround you
with comfort and warmth
and fill you with life
that is stronger than death.
Amen.

PEOPLE Amen.

## The anointing

MINISTER

Lift your face to the light.
You are beautiful in the sight of God.
The mark of Christ is upon you;
walk free and open your heart to life,
for Christ walks with you
into a new day.
Amen.

PEOPLE Amen.

## Sharing of the common cup

*The cup is passed between the people with the words:*

PEOPLE We share life with you.

*After the cup is shared, the minister says:*

MINISTER

Take this cup as a sign
of our community with you.
Your tears are our tears;

your hope is our hope;
your prayer is our prayer;
you are not alone.

## The Peace

LEADER The peace of God be with you all.
PEOPLE And also with you.

## Blessing and dismissal

ALL      'May the blessing of God
go before you . . .'

(Miriam Therese Winter)

LEADER Go in peace
and may God the Mother keep you safe;
God in Christ take you by the hand;
and God the Spirit cover you
with her warm bright wings.
Amen.
PEOPLE Amen.

**Dorothy McRae-McMahon**

# 73    *A service of healing for a hurting world*

## Silent meditation

As the mountains are round about Jerusalem, so the Lord is round about his people, from this time forth and for evermore.

(Psalm 125.2)

Be ye transformed by the renewing of your mind. God hath not given us the spirit of fear; but of power and of love and of a sound mind.

(Romans 12.2; 2 Timothy 1.7)

## Responsive praise

LEADER How manifold are your works, O Lord!
MEN AND BOYS
In wisdom you have wrought them all – the earth is full of your creatures.

WOMEN AND GIRLS
> The sea also, great and wide, schools without number, living things both small and great.

LEADER God looked at all creation, and found it very good.

ALL     May the glory of the Lord endure for ever.

(Genesis 1.31; Psalm 104.24–5)

**Hymn** *(Select a hymn of creation and praise)*

## Prophetic challenge

LEADER Listen, people of Israel, to this funeral song which I sing over you;
> Virgin Israel has fallen,
> Never to rise again!
> She lies abandoned on the ground,
> And no one helps her up.

MEN AND BOYS
> You people hate anyone who challenges injustice and speaks the whole truth in court.

WOMEN AND GIRLS
> You have oppressed the poor and robbed them of their gain.

MEN AND BOYS
> And so you will not live in the fine stone houses you build or drink wine from the vineyards you plant.

LEADER I know how terrible your sins are and how many crimes you have committed. You persecute good people, take bribes and prevent the poor from getting justice in the courts.

MEN AND BOYS
> The Sovereign Lord says, 'A city in Israel sends out a thousand soldiers,

WOMEN AND GIRLS
> but only a hundred return;

MEN AND BOYS
> Another city sends out a hundred,

WOMEN AND GIRLS
> but only ten come back.'

ALL     The Lord says to the people of Israel, 'Come to me and you will live.'

(Amos 5.14, 10–12)

## Dialogue

*Begin by having eight to ten worshipers stand one at a time to read a current news headline. These headlines should identify suffering in the world in need of God's healing. Ask all to reflect on these headlines and similar ones they themselves have read. Encourage worshipers to write on a 3×5 index card provided for them one or two sentences that reflect their thoughts and concerns. Allow time for participants to share aloud what they have written.*

## Corporate Confession

Lord, we listen to your prophets' words, knowing they are for us. We have misused your world, so perfect at Creation. Land meant to provide for all, provides for only a few. Young men dream of plows and corn, but find instead guns and warplanes. Women who want homes for their children and soup for their pots, pitch refugee tents and boil grass for dinner. Babies born with your promise, die from disease and starvation. In your world of plenty, millions face impossible choices – food or heat, shoes or a coat, electricity or rent.

Lord of Creation, move us from hardness to compassion, from guilt to forgiveness, from apathy to action, from complicity to justice. Heal our brokenness and the wounds of your creation. Amen.

## Words of assurance and forgiveness

'Comfort my people,' says our God. 'Comfort them! Tell them they have suffered long enough and their sins are now forgiven. Come to me and you will live.'

(Isaiah 40.1–2; Amos 5.12)

## Homily or sermon

## Eucharist, Holy Communion, Lord's Supper

*After partaking of the bread and cup according to your tradition, invite worshipers to the altar for special prayers of intercession and healing for our world*

## Period of intercession
*(Gathered at the altar)*

LEADER

We are together here as members of the Body of Christ, called to do his healing work on earth. Let us claim his healing power and know with certainty that that power will flow through us, his channels, to those in need. Let us be assured, too, of the promise made to all intercessors: '. . . whatever you ask in prayer, believe that you receive it, and you will.'

(Mark 11.24)

## Anointing with oil and laying-on-of-hands

*The rituals of anointing with oil and laying-on-of-hands should be incorporated according to your own religious tradition or as you feel appropriate. The following format is but one alternative.*

*As part of the period of intercession, have a bowl of olive oil available. Those who wish may kneel, prayerfully lifting up both the concern written on their cards and their own personal requests for healing that in their lives which prevents them from being fully open channels for God's healing power. The pastor or a team of clergy and lay persons can move from worshiper to worshiper for laying-on-of-hands and anointing with oil. Some worshipers may wish to verbalize their petitions for healing while hands are laid on their heads and the oil is touched to their foreheads. But whether or not petitions are verbalized, repeat together these words for each individual: 'Lord of Creation, Lord of Mercy, bring your healing touch.'*

## The Goods News of deliverance

*(Read in unison)*

ALL The Sovereign Lord has filled me with the spirit.
God has chosen me and sent me to bring good news to the poor,
To heal the broken-hearted,
To announce release to captives
And freedom to those in prison.
God has sent me to proclaim
That the time has come
When the Lord will save all people,
And defeat their enemies.
God has sent me to comfort all who mourn,
To give to those who mourn in Zion
Joy and gladness instead of grief,
A song of praise instead of sorrow.
They will be like trees
That the Lord has planted.
They will do what is right,
And God will be praised for what is done.
They will rebuild cities that have long been in ruins.

(Isaiah 61.1–4)

Hymn of praise and victory

Benediction

*Bread for the World*

## 74    *Healing liturgy*

---

### Opening statement

Today is the day of salvation, alleluia!
Today the loving wisdom of our God
be near us, be within us, be around us,
to heal, to comfort, to cherish,
to renew and restore
our broken lives,
our broken hopes,
our broken world.

### Hymn *In love revealed* (85)

### Prayer for wholeness

O God,
Giver of Life,
Bearer of Pain,
Maker of Love,
you are able to accept in us
what we cannot even acknowledge;
you are able to name in us
what we cannot bear to speak of;
you are able to hold in your memory
what we have tried to forget;
you are able to hold out to us
the glory that we cannot conceive of.
Reconcile us through your cross
to all that we have rejected in our selves,
that we may find no part of your creation
to be alien or strange to us,
and that we ourselves may be made whole.

Through Jesus Christ, our lover and our friend.
Amen.

(Janet Morley)

## Confession

*In silence we call to mind and attention the ways in which we refuse God's healing in our lives and in our world.*

ALL    We grieve and confess
that we hurt and have been hurt,
to the third and fourth generations,
that we are so afraid of pain
that we shield ourselves from being vulnerable to others,
and refuse to be open and trusting as a child . . .

(Jim Cotter)

## Absolution

*In turn, around the circle, we turn to the person on our left and pronounce the words of forgiveness and healing, using a touch or making the sign of the cross on the person's forehead as we do so. The following words may be used:*

God forgives you. Be at peace. Be well.

## Readings

1    Isaiah 61.1–7

2    Psalm
I will praise God, my Beloved,
for she is altogether lovely.

Her presence satisfies my soul;
she fills my senses to overflowing
so that I cannot speak.

Her touch brings me to life;
the warmth of her hands makes me wholly alive.

Her embrace nourishes me, body and spirit;
every part of my being responds to her touch.

The beauty of her face is more than I can bear;
in her gaze I drown.

When she looks upon me
I can withhold nothing;

When she asks for my love all my defences crumble;
my pride and my control are utterly dissolved.

O God, I fear your terrible mercy;
I am afraid to surrender my self.

If I let go into the whirlpool of your love,
shall I survive the embrace?

If I fall into the strong currents of your desire,
shall I escape drowning?

But how shall I refuse my Beloved,
and how can I withdraw from the one my heart yearns for?

On the edge of your abyss I look down and I tremble;
but I will not stand gazing for ever.

Even in chaos you will bear me up;
if the waters go over my head, you will still be holding me.

For the chaos is yours also,
and in the swirling of mighty waters is your presence known.

If I trust her, surely her power will not fail me;
nor will she let me be utterly destroyed.

Though I lose all knowledge and all security,
yet will my God never forsake me;

But she will recreate me, in her steadfast love,
so that I need not be afraid.

Then will I praise my Beloved among the people,
among those who seek to know God.

(Janet Morley)

3    Luke 13.10–17

*Shared reflection*

*A time to reflect on the reading, in silence or aloud.*

## Intercessions

## Hymn *A touching place* (86)

## The Peace

ALL    The Peace and Wholeness of God our Healer be in us and between
us now and for ever.

*We share a sign of peace.*

## The Prayer of Thanksgiving

MINISTER

God is here.

ALL     Her spirit is with us.

MINISTER

Lift up your hearts.

ALL     We lift them up to God.

MINISTER

Let us give thanks and praise.

ALL     It is right to give God thanks and praise.

MINISTER

Eternal Wisdom, source of our being,
and goal of all our longing,
we praise you and give you thanks
because you have created us, women and men,
together in your image
to cherish your world and seek your face.
Divided and disfigured by sin,
while we were yet helpless,
you emptied yourself of power,
and took upon you our unprotected flesh.
You laboured with us upon the cross,
and have brought us forth
to the hope of resurrection.

Therefore with the woman who gave you birth,
the women who befriended you and fed you,
who argued with you and touched you,
the woman who anointed you for death,
the women who met you, risen from the dead,
and with all your lovers throughout the ages,
we praise you saying:

ALL     Holy, holy, holy,
vulnerable God,
heaven and earth are full of your glory;
hosanna in the highest.
Blessed is the one
who comes in the name of God;
hosanna in the highest.

MINISTER

Blessed is our brother Jesus,
who, before his suffering, earnestly desired

to eat with his companions
the passover of liberation;
who, on the night that he was betrayed,
took bread, gave thanks, broke it, and said:
'This is my body, which is for you.
Do this to remember me.'

In the same way also the cup, after supper,
saying:
'This cup is the new covenant in my blood.
Do this, whenever you drink it,
to remember me.'

ALL     Christ has died.
Christ is risen.
Christ will come again.

MINISTER
Therefore, as we eat this bread and drink this cup,
we are proclaiming Christ's death until he comes.
In the body broken and the blood poured out,
we restore to memory and hope
the broken and unremembered victims
of tyranny and sin;
and we long for the bread of tomorrow
and the wine of the age to come.
Come then, life-giving spirit of our God,
brood over these bodily things,
and make us one body with Christ;
that we may labour with creation
to be delivered from its bondage to decay
into the glorious liberty
of all the children of God.

ALL     Amen.

(Janet Morley)

*Silence is kept.*

## The prayer Jesus taught us

ALL     God, lover of us all,
most holy one,
help us to respond to you
to create what you want for us here on earth.
Give us today enough for our needs;

forgive our weak and deliberate offences,
just as we must forgive others
when they hurt us.
Help us to resist evil
and to do what is good;
for we are yours,
endowed with your power
to make our world whole.

(Lala Winkley)

## The Communion

*The bread and wine is passed around the fellowship.*

## After Communion

ALL    God be in my head and in my understanding
God be in my eyes and in my looking
God be in my mouth and in my speaking
God be in my tongue and in my tasting
God be in my lips and in my greeting

God be in my nose and in my smelling
God be in my ears and in my hearing
God be in my neck and in my humbling
God be in my shoulders and in my bearing
God be in my back and in my standing

God be in my arms and in my reaching
God be in my hands and in my working
God be in my legs and in my walking
God be in my feet and in my grounding
God be in my joints and in my relating

God be in my guts and in my feeling
God be in my bowels and in my forgiving
God be in my loins and in my swiving
God be in my lungs and in my breathing
God be in my heart and in my loving

God be in my skin and in my touching
God be in my flesh and in my paining
God be in my blood and in my living
God be in my bones and in my dying
God be at my end and at my reviving

(Jim Cotter)

**Hymn** *Word made Flesh!* **(87)**

(Jim Cotter)

## The Blessing and dismissal *Foot-washing*

*We bless each other and send each other out by washing each other's feet and anointing them with oil.*

Nicola Slee

## 75 *Liturgy at the time of choosing whether or not to have an abortion*

---

### Gathering in God's name

*The woman, family, and friends gather in God's name. This is a very intimate service. It may take place in a home or a chapel in a church. If there is not a sensitive priest known to the woman facing the abortion, then a friend or mother may take the role of the leader.*

LEADER  Blessed are you,
        loving God, Mother of all.

PEOPLE  Holy is your name,
        now and for ever.

LEADER  Eternal Womb
        from whence all came,

PEOPLE  We lift our hearts to you.
        Heal our wounds.

LEADER  Mother of the world,
        bless us.

PEOPLE  Hear our cries
        and grant us peace.

LEADER  Let us pray.
        Loving God, all hearts are open to you, all desires known, and from you, no secrets are hid. Cleanse the thoughts of our hearts that we may love you, and praise your holy name with our acts this day and for evermore. Amen.

### The Word of God proclaimed

*One of the following readings from Scripture is read as well as any passage that is particularly meaningful to the woman.*

Revelation 21.1–5 *(Behold, I make all things new.)*

Mark 14.1–9 *(She has done what she could.)*
John 1.1–5 *(In the beginning was the Word. An inclusive-language text is essential.)*

*Response to God's Word*

> *If the woman has chosen to have an abortion, a letter to the dead child written by the mother may be read by her or by someone of her choosing. The letter may express her feelings, her thoughts about the abortion, what she would have liked to say to the child.*
> *If the woman has chosen not to have an abortion and to keep her child, a letter expressing her hopes and dreams for her child may be read.*

## Prayers for one another

LEADER Mother of all,
we ask your blessing upon ——
PEOPLE Hear our prayer, O God our Mother.

LEADER Bless all who face the choice of abortion. Grant them wisdom to make their choice, courage to act upon it, and the knowledge of your love.
PEOPLE Hear our prayer, O God our Mother.

LEADER Grant unto all women the support and love that we offer unto ——
this day and always. Bind us close in your love and keep us faithful in our friendships.
PEOPLE Hear our prayer, O God our Mother.

LEADER Let us ask God's mercy and forgiveness upon all our lives.

*Confession*

Hear our prayer, O God our Mother. Forgive us our sins as we forgive those who have sinned against us. Forgive us our passivity, our doubts, our guilt, and our shame. Empower us to forgive ourselves that we may receive the fullness of your forgiveness and grace; in Jesus Christ's name we pray. Amen.

*Absolution*

Loving God, you have given power to your priests to pronounce absolution; give to this your daughter ——, your love to absolve her guilt, remove her fear, heal her wounds, and make whole her body, that she may live her life reconciled to you and to her child, with the opportunity to begin a new life sustained by your Holy Spirit, now and for ever. Amen.

## Act of dedication

*The mother makes a dedication in the name of the child and asks for the community's support to keep her vow. The promise should be personal, specific, and attainable.*

*Example:*
*'In the name of my child, I promise I will give $— every month for the coming year to support a homeless child . . .'*

*'In the name of my child, I promise I will plant a garden on the street where all who pass by may see the abundance of God's grace.'*

## The laying on of hands

PEOPLE   We lay our hands upon you in the name of our Savior, Jesus Christ, beseeching God to uphold you and to fill you with grace, that you may know the healing power of God's divine love. We give you our love, promising to stand by you through this decision and in the days to come. Amen.

## The Peace

LEADER
The peace and love of God be with you this day.
PEOPLE   And also with you.

*The people exchange the Peace with hugs. It may take as long as necessary.*

*If the woman has chosen to have an abortion, it is suggested that the letter that she has written be burned and the ashes buried in a suitable place. This helps to give a tangible sense of letting go and of burial.*

*The service may conclude here or the people may make Eucharist. It is appropriate to use homemade bread. If the Eucharist is celebrated, the following prayer may be used afterward.*

## Post-Communion prayer

PEOPLE   Most loving God, you are the source of life and our defender in the hour of death. We thank you for feeding us with the spiritual food of the body and blood of Jesus Christ. May we be strengthened to meet the days ahead with hope and newness of life. Grant that we may serve others in your name and to your glory. Bless our sister, ——, and her child; give to them peace in the unity of your love. All this we ask through Jesus Christ. Amen.

## Benediction

CELEBRANT

The blessing of God,
the creator of life
be with you this day.

The blessing of God,
the redeemer of abundant love
be with you always.

The blessing of God,
the sanctifier of all,
send you as a blessing to others.

ALL   So be it.
Alleluia.
Amen.

**Vienna Cobb Anderson**

## 76   *Rituals for abortion*

There are three parts to this ritual:

Before: Preparation; the need for courage
During: Friend; the need for support
After:   Guilt; the need for forgiveness

## Before

*Friends gather with the woman at her home prior to the abortion. It could be the night, or the morning, before the surgery. They share a simple meal together as a sign of friendship.*
*After the meal the friends gather in a circle around the woman and lay hands upon her. They may express their feelings and prayers in their own words or say the following together:*

We lay our hands upon you in the name of our Savior, Jesus Christ, beseeching God to uphold you and to fill you with grace, that you may know the healing power of God's divine love. We ask God to fill your heart with strength and courage and we give you our love, promising to stand by you through this decision and in the days to come. Amen.

*The friends then greet one another with hugs.*

## During

*A friend goes with the woman to the place of abortion and stays with her as long as is permitted. Prior to leaving, the friend takes oil, which she has brought with her, and anoints the woman.*

*On the head, saying:* We support your decision.

*On the hands, saying:* We hold your hands in solidarity and love.

*On the womb, saying:* We bless you.

*The two women hug as a sign of peace between them and all the friends who gathered earlier.*

## After

*Friends gather once again with the woman at the time of her choosing. They gather in a circle.*

*Water is poured from a pitcher into a bowl in front of the woman.*

FRIEND  We wash you with water as a symbol of the tears of mourning, the forgiveness of guilt, and the beginning of a new life for you.

*One by one the friends come to the woman, put their hand in the water and place water on her head, her hands, her face, or her feet.*

*At the end the friends greet one another with hugs, the sign of friendship and peace.*

Vienna Cobb Anderson

## 77   *A litany of healing*

God of grace, you nurture us with a love deeper than we know, and your will for us is healing and salvation;
   *We praise and thank you, O God.*

God of love, you enter into our lives, our pain and our brokenness, and you stretch out your healing hands to us wherever we are;
   *We praise and thank you, O God.*

God of strength, you fill us with your presence and send us forth in love and healing among those we meet;
   *We praise and thank you, O God.*

Touch and heal our bodies suffering from sickness, injury and disability, and make us whole again;
   *Hear us, O God of life.*

Touch and heal our minds from darkness, confusion and doubt, and fill them with your light;
   *Hear us, O God of life.*

Touch and heal our hearts burdened by anguish, despair and isolation, and set us free in love;
   *Hear us, O God of life.*

Break the bonds of our imprisonment to fear, compulsion and addiction;
   *Come with your healing power, O God.*

Give us liberty from old hurts and painful memories;
   *Come with your healing power, O God.*

Fill us with peace in our grief from separation and loss;
   *Come with your healing power, O God.*

Take our hands in dying, and bring us through death into your loving presence;
   *Come with your healing power, O God.*

Work through all who share in your ministry of healing, and renew us in compassion and strength;
   *Come with your healing power, O God.*

Restore to wholeness all that has been broken by our sin;
   *Come with your healing power, O God.*

We lift before you all who have died from HIV disease;

*(A time is provided for names to be offered either silently or aloud.)*

Receive them more and more into your joyful presence.

Rejoicing in the communion of [the ever-blessed Virgin Mary, (blessed ——,) and] all the saints, we entrust ourselves, and one another,
   *And all our life to Christ our God.*

Let us pray.
O God, in you all darkness is turned to light and all brokenness is made whole: Look with compassion on us and those for whom we pray, that we may be recreated in our Savior Jesus Christ. *Amen.*

**Marilyn Geist** (adapted and revised)

# 78    *Like drops of water*

Extract from a liturgy of healing for survivors of domestic violence, rape, date rape, marital rape, incest, sexual abuse.

## Litany of healing

*We begin a litany of healing by saying together the words 'in the beginning' and then listening for the response.*

ALL    In the beginning . . .
LEADER There was only pain and anger.

ALL    In the beginning . . .
LEADER There was only denial and humiliation.

ALL    In the beginning . . .
LEADER There was only loneliness and destruction.

ALL    In the beginning . . .
LEADER What else was there? Tell us and we will listen.

ALL    In the beginning . . .

## The stone ritual

*(The leader picks up the rock and shows it to those gathered.)*

LEADER The stone symbolizes a release from pain and renewal of loving, healing energy. As we sit in this circle together, let us relax and focus on the stone. *(pause)* Let us pass the stone around the circle. As you receive the stone, hold it, imagine that you are pouring your pain into it, and then pass the stone to the next person.

*(When each woman has filled the stone with her pain, the leader puts the stone in a bowl of water, washes it, and dries it with a towel.)*

Let us pass the stone around the circle again. This time when you receive it, hold it and fill it with loving energy.

*(When each person has filled the stone with loving energy, place it in the centre of the circle.)*

## Litany of healing

ALL    In the new beginning . . .
LEADER There is the support of community.

ALL   In the new beginning . . .
LEADER There is courage to speak truth to power.

ALL   In the new beginning . . .
LEADER There is the compassion of friendship.

ALL   In the new beginning . . .
LEADER What else is there? Tell us and we will support you.

ALL   In the new beginning . . .

Diann L. Neu

## 79  *The shadow of the dove*

(Written August 1992 after seeing a banner with the shadows of the dove in Brechin Cathedral)

Let us pray:

When the dawn's ribbon of glory around the world returns
and the earth emerges from sleep –

May the shadow of the dove be seen,
as she flits across moor and city.
Over the warm breast of the earth she flies, her
shadow falling on the watcher in the tower
the refugee in the ditch,
the weary soldier at the gate.

May the shadow of peace
fall across the all night sitting of a council;
across the tense negotiators around the table.

May the shadow of hope
be cast across the bars of a hostage cell
filling with momentary light,
rooms tense with conflict, bringing a brief respite:
a slither of gold across the dark.

May she fly untiring across flooded fields:
across a city divided by hate and fear,
across a town wreathed in smoke.

May the shadow of reconciliation,
the dove of peace with healing in her wings,

be felt and seen and turned towards
as she makes righteousness shine like the dawn;
the justice of her cause like the noonday sun.

(Psalm 37.6)

v     Holy Spirit of love
r     Bring healing, bring peace.

**Kate McIlhagga**

## 80     *Litany for AIDS Sunday*

LEADER Gracious God,
You are merciful and loving,
Hear our prayers
on behalf of all who suffer with AIDS:

For all who live in fear of the disease,
PEOPLE Grant them peace in their hearts,
Wisdom in the choices they make,
And courage to face the days ahead.

*The congregation may offer petitions for persons for whom prayers are
desired.*

LEADER For all who live with the disease of AIDS,
PEOPLE Grant them the gift of your love,
hope for the future,
friends to comfort and sustain them,
the will to live,
and faith that resurrection is a promise for *now*
as well as for eternal life.

*The congregation may offer petitions for persons for whom prayers are
desired.*

LEADER For all who minister to the needs of persons with AIDS,
PEOPLE Grant them compassionate hearts,
tenderness and patience in their daily tasks,
and dedication in their ministry to all who suffer.

*The congregation may offer petitions for persons for whom prayers are
desired.*

LEADER For all whose loved ones are affected by AIDS,
PEOPLE Grant them hope each day,
an awareness that love is forever binding,

the knowledge that Christ shares their suffering.

*The congregation may offer petitions for persons for whom prayers are desired.*

LEADER For all who have died of AIDS,
PEOPLE Grant them rest eternal;
may light perpetual shine upon them,
may we always remember them in our hearts.

*The congregation may offer petitions for persons for whom prayers are desired.*

CELEBRANT

O God of love, whose mercy has always included those whom we have forgotten, those whom we have isolated, and those who suffer: bless we beseech you all who are afflicted with AIDS.

Comfort them in their pain, sustain them by your Holy Spirit in their days of hopelessness that they may engage in living. Receive them into the arms of your mercy in their dying.

Open our hearts to provide for their needs, to take away their isolation, to share their journey of suffering and sorrow as well as hope and joy, and to be present with them in their dying, that no one need suffer or die alone.

Strengthen all who care for those who are ill, that their service may be filled with the tenderness of your compassion and the fullness of your love, that their words and deeds may make your presence a living reality for those whom they serve.

Bless those who mourn the death of thir friends and lovers, that they may not be overwhelmed by death but may receive comfort and strength to meet the days ahead with trust and hope in your goodness and mercy; in Jesus' name we pray.
PEOPLE Amen.

Vienna Cobb Anderson

## 81 *Collect for the disunity of men and women*

God of wholeness,
Have compassion on the weariness of women,
who have toiled too long in the shadow;
and look mercifully on the fearfulness of men,
who have closed their eyes in the light of the sun.

Stretch forth your hands
to save us from the shifting sands
of dividedness;
and draw us together,
that we may build your commonwealth
in this fragmented world.

**Jean Gaskin**

## 82    *Christ our health*

Christ our health and Christ our healing,
hear our brothers', sisters' plea.
Firm us up in faith and feeling,
set our bodies, spirits free.
Luster to all flesh revealing,
Christ our sure immunity.

Yea, though pain and plague afflict us,
death surround us like a shroud,
Christ and Christ alone infect us
till our lives be Christ endowed.
From our fears now resurrect us,
Lead us forth in fire and cloud.

Take our bodies, bruised and broken,
break them as thy living bread.
Make of passion wounds a token,
cleansed and filled with wine instead.
In this Sacrament be spoken
words of solace still unsaid.

Speak of love that dares be nameless,
Love that calls us to this place.
Nor shall fever still inflame us,
save the ardor of thy grace.
Christ, thy paths are pure and blameless,
Peace attend us all our days.

Christ for now and Christ for ages,
Christ who lives in plague and pain,
Christ upon a cross courageous,
Christ who died shall ever reign.
Christ alive and Christ contagious,
Christ, Omega, come again.

Christ our health and Christ our healing,
Christ our struggle yet to be,
Christ our font of faith and feeling,
Christ our final victory.
Christ our love to life appealing,
Christ our sure immunity.

*Tune: Westminster Abbey*

**Edward J. Moran**

## 83 *Love's energy*

**With vigour**

1. Deep in cre - a - tion's heart an e - ner-gy
Calls to us but leaves us free,
Dance with that u - ni - ver - sal e - ner-gy
Ce - le - brate life's mys - te - ry.

Deep in creation's heart an energy
Calls to us but leaves us free.
Dance with that universal energy,
Celebrate life's mystery.

Hold out your hands, embrace that energy,
Love that will not let us go.
Let loose the bonds that bind that energy,
Let the streams of mercy flow.

Watch how the world takes up that energy;
Season's change in rhythmic dance.
Ebbing and flowing, tidal energy,
Love in weariness enhance.

Boundless supplies there are of energy
Strength'ning us in loving ways.
Changeless, dynamic, vital energy,
Dance within us all our days.

*Tune: Max (June Boyce-Tillman)*

**June Boyce-Tillman**


## 84    *A song of peace*

(Written (for a dance) on the day of the IRA ceasefire, 31 August 1994, on Rathlin Island, off the North Antrim coast)

Peace flowing outward and peace flowing in,
Draw peace from the centre in which we begin;
Find peace in the ending, the close of the day,
Let peace in the heart wipe the evil away.

Strength flowing outward and strength flowing in,
Draw strength from the centre in which we begin;
Find strength in the ending, the close of the day;
Let strength in the heart wipe the evil away.

Hope flowing outward . . .

Joy flowing outward . . .

Love flowing outward . . .

*Tune: Slane*

**June Boyce-Tillman**


## 85    *In love revealed*

The busy crowd was thronging round;
A frightened woman, cursed for years,
Pushed through the throng and, trembling still,
Reached out and found you through her tears;
She touched your hem, and she was healed,
Behold, God's grace in love revealed.

The little girl was fading fast,
Her father dragged you to his door,
You banished those who wept and wailed,
She rose up, live and whole once more;
You kissed her cheek, and she was healed,
Behold, God's grace in love revealed.

They brought her to you to be stoned,
The woman caught in act of shame,
You turned their judgement into care,
And gave forgiveness, took her blame;
You touched her heart, and she was healed,
Behold, God's grace in love revealed.

The woman of the streets broke in,
Where upright men made you their guest,
She poured her ointment on your feet,
You blessed her, laid her sins to rest;
She wiped your feet, and she was healed,
Behold, God's grace in love revealed.

The women, weeping, found the tomb,
Your body gone, the stone laid by,
You bade them tell the brothers how
Your love in death could never die;
They told the news, and all were healed,
Behold, God's grace in love revealed.

Through centuries of scorn and shame,
Your love has named us as your own,
Through poverty, despair and fear,
Our faith and hopefulness have grown;
You touch us all and we are healed,
Behold, God's grace in love revealed.

*Tunes: Surrey, Sagina, St Chrysostom, etc.*

**Anna Briggs**

## 86    *A touching place*

Christ's is the world in which we move,
Christ's are the folk we're summoned to love,
Christ's is the voice which calls us to care
And Christ is the one who meets us here.

*Chorus*
To the lost
  Christ shows his face
To the unloved
  He gives his embrace
To those who cry
  In pain or disgrace
Christ makes, with his friends,
  A touching place.

Feel for the people we most avoid –
Strange or bereaved or never employed;
Feel for the women and feel for the men
Who fear that their living is all in vain.

Feel for the parents who've lost their child,
Feel for the women whom men have defiled,
Feel for the baby for whom there's no breast
And feel for the weary who find no rest.

Feel for the lives by life confused,
Riddled with doubt, in loving abused;
Feel for the lonely heart, conscious of sin,
Which longs to be pure but fears to begin.

*Tune: Dream Angus (Scots traditional)*
**John L. Bell and Graham Maule**

## 87    *Word made flesh!*

---

Word made Flesh! We see Christ Jesus
  Sharing our humanity,
Loving, graceful, always truthful,
  Close to others bodily,
Full of passion, full of healing,
  Touch of God to set them free.

Wonderful are these our bodies,
  Flesh and blood to touch and see,
Place of pain and contradiction,
  Yet of joy and ecstasy,
Place of passion, place of healing,
  Touched by God who sets us free.

O how glorious and resplendent,
  Fragile body you shall be,
When endued with so much beauty,
  Full of life and strong and free,
Full of vigour, full of pleasure,
  That shall last eternally.

Glory give to God the Lover,
  Grateful hearts to the Beloved,
Blessed be the Love between them,
  Overflowing to our good;
Praise and worship, praise and worship,
  To the God whose Name is Love.

The third verse is late 15th century, tr. J. M. Neale, and found as part of the hymn,
'Light's abode, celestial Salem', *New English Hymnal*, 401, to the tune *Regent
Square*.

**Jim Cotter**

## 88    *A blessing*

---

God of love,
As we touch each other,
May we receive your gentle, powerful and healing touch,
The bearer of pain,
And giver of life,
Now and always. Amen.

# 6

## *Unless I go away . . .*
### Separations and goodbyes

As the chapter title suggests, every new beginning has an ending; to arrive, we must first leave. If Jesus is to lead us into all life, we must first let him die. Despite this truth at the heart of the Christian gospel, the churches are not very good at endings – with the exception, of course, of funerals. Other than life itself, it is as if things are not supposed to end: marriages, jobs, buildings, neighbourhoods are not often formally recognized as dying.

A number of us have, however, had to face a loss and let go of something previously held dear before being able to move into the future. Many people have experienced this in divorce and it is probably increasingly common for clergy to be asked for some sort of ritual in this context. Several of the pieces in this chapter mark endings of relationships, whether marriages or other forms of partnership.

There are additional kinds of loss which we experience when we are suddenly parted from something we have valued very much, even if we were not aware of its value until it wasn't there any more. This was perhaps the case for many who mourned the loss of the Holbeck Hall Hotel in Scarborough. Until it was irretrievably damaged in a cliff landslide, the Holbeck Hall Hotel had been a popular venue for all those important family occasions – parties for weddings, christenings, silver wedding anniversaries, eighteenth birthdays. We include the liturgy compiled by the local Anglican vicar which enabled the community to say farewell to this place of happy memories, and also to find some meaning amidst the chaos, mess and anxiety caused by the building's (and the land's) destruction. Obviously, this was a unique event, but we hope the inclusion of this service will inspire others to commemorate their own local losses and endings, recognizing in particular how important buildings are to a community.

Other material has been written around separations from home, country, community and job – and here again some of the examples (leaving the Baptist ministry) are included to suggest that the idea is adaptable to other situations. The 'Agape on letting go and entering the darkness' conveys the sense of God's invisible but encompassing presence, and reminds us of the need to sit lightly to all our images of God.

## 89 *Service of thanksgiving for the Holbeck Hall Hotel*

### A reading

I would have liked an hotel on the seafront, but none was available. However, there was a fine property on the southern end of the Esplanade; a large house on the edge of the cliff surrounded by a few acres of garden, with no public road between it and the sea. We bought it and I set about conversion. Making it into a country house type of hotel took two years, and when it was completed we named it Holbeck Hall.

(Tom Laughton: *Pavilions of the Sea*)

### Processional hymn *O worship the King*

### Bidding Prayer

We have come together in this place, united in our concern for the Holbeck Hall Hotel. We have come to declare our sorrow at its passing, our anxiety for the future but most of all, we have come to express our gratitude to God for the hospitality displayed in the life and service of a much-loved hotel.

Pavilions may rise and fall, yet in our concern we draw close to the Eternal God whose generosity knows no bounds and who gave us the words of his own prayer.

### The Lord's Prayer

### The Litany of Sorrow

*Sung by the choir. Members of the congregation are invited to join in the refrain:*

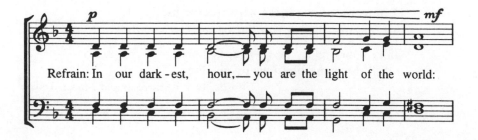

Refrain: In our dark-est, hour,— you are the light of the world:

Com -fort, strength, sup - port you give us by your Spi-rit's

power.

(Music: Martin Dales)

*Refrain:*
**In our darkest hour, you are the light of the world;**
**Comfort, strength, support you give us by your Spirit's power.**

Lord be merciful unto us when we are in need;
for your love is greater than our understanding:

You give, Lord, and you take away;
help us in our loss to bless your holy name:

When we are so full of anger that our hearts would burst;
calm us and let your voice be heard:

Lighten the darkness of our bewilderment, O Lord;
and by your great mercy, defend us from all perils and dangers of
this life:

From poverty, greed and exploitation;
save us and help us we humbly beseech you, O Lord:

Help us to forgive those who trouble us;
that we may find in you the renewal of our lives:

Glory, glory, glory be to you, O Lord;
for all the many blessings of our life:

(Words: C. J. Armstrong and Martin Dales)

**Hymn** *Father, hear the prayer we offer*

## A Procession of History

*during which articles symbolizing the life of the hotel are carried by staff to the altar:*

Tiles from the central fire place
The hotel diaries
The Christmas folder, 1992
Chef's knives
A bottle of Louis XIII brandy

## Prayer

VICAR  Almighty God, you bestow on us the skills and industry for human joy and satisfaction. You did not lose them in the giving and we will not forget them by their return if they are spent in your service.

Help us to order our lives that our joy may be in the welfare of others and to your praise and glory. Amen.

**Reading** *1 Peter 4.7–11*

**Hymn** *All my hope on God is founded*

## A Collage of Gratitude

*read by hotel staff and chosen from the many appreciative letters received from members of the public.*

**Hymn** *Ye holy angels bright*

## Address

**Hymn** *Praise to the Lord, the Almighty, the King of creation*

## Prayers

## The Blessing

**Final hymn** *O Praise ye the Lord! Praise him in the height*

**Christopher Armstrong**

**90**    *A service for a family who are emigrating*

This, of course, is a pre-liminal rite. The post-liminal one would be for an immigrant family in this country, or for this family on arrival at its destination. The chaos in between setting off and arriving would of course be un-ritualized (although people who find themselves involved in this kind of upheaval often remark upon a strange, dream-like quality associated with some parts of the experience). It is a rite of passage in a literal sense, in which ideas of movement and progression correspond to the prospect of a real departure, journey and arrival. Such an undertaking deserves to be properly celebrated, because of the courage and determination required from those taking part. The service is one way, and a good one, of giving shape to thoughts and feelings which are still not properly assimilated, but demand our attention, and whose urgency and lack of organization inhibits us from making the effort to get to grips with them. At another level, the idea of travelling 'overseas' has very powerful implications of existential change because of its association with water, which is recognized, either consciously or unconsciously (or both!) as the natural symbol of new life, and of form and direction emerging out of chaos. The briefest examination of the imagery of initiation ceremonies throughout the world should convince the most sceptical that this is not so far-fetched as it sounds! (Perhaps this motif could be brought out more clearly in the middle section, if appropriate.)

### Hymn *Guide me, O thou great Redeemer*

MINISTER

Surely your goodness and loving kindness will follow me all the days of my life; and I shall dwell in the house of the Lord for ever. The Lord be with you.

ALL    And also with you.

MINISTER

O Lord God you have made men and women to be pilgrims upon earth. As we move onwards upon our journey, discovering new people, new things, new places, new ways of looking at life, our hearts and minds find strength and refreshment from your eternal presence, your changeless love. You give us comfort when we are weary, and the courage needed to undertake new ventures. We praise your holy name, O Loving Lord. Amen.

*Each member of the family shares in reading a passage from the Old Testament followed by one from the New Testament (e.g. Psalm 114:*

*'When Israel came out of Egypt'; Matthew 6.19–34: 'Do not be anxious about tomorrow; tomorrow will look after itself', etc.)*

MINISTER

The Davis family are on the threshold of a new life in another country. In some ways this will really be a new life, although they will be the same people who go on living it. There will be a lot of things they will have to leave behind, and a lot of new things to be got used to. And not only things, of course, but people – which is perhaps harder, and certainly more important. This is a time for farewells, a difficult, sad time: but it is also a time for getting started, getting established upon their chosen course. We have gathered here in church to help them do this by bidding them farewell, and Godspeed. Members of the Davis family, we wish you every blessing in your new life, and Godspeed upon your journey!

*The members of the family come to the front of the church and shake hands with the Minister, one by one.*

## Hymns *Who would true valour see*
## *Great is thy faithfulness*

*During these hymns (and others if required) the family move round the church, shaking hands or embracing everybody. At the end of the hymns, they stand in line facing the congregation and waving to them. The minister goes and stands among the congregation.*

MINISTER

To God's gracious protection we commit you. May the Lord bless you and watch over you. May he make his face shine upon you and be gracious to you. May he look kindly upon you and give you peace; and the blessing of God Almighty, the Father, Son and Holy Spirit, be among you and remain with you always. Amen.

## Hymn *Lead us, heavenly Father, lead us*

*During this hymn the family return to their seats.*

MINISTER

In the Name of Christ, and in the presence of this congregation, we have said farewell to our friends; Jane and Tony, Samantha and Gary (etc.), we shall not forget you, and we ask you not to forget us. You will always be part of our fellowship here for there are no beginnings and endings in Christ, who is all in all. Let us say the Lord's Prayer together for the last time in this place.

ALL  Our Father . . . for ever and ever. Amen.

ALL    *Psalm 23*
       *During this psalm, the family process to the altar, and place a gift on it. On*
       *their way back to their seats, the minister or a member of the congregation*
       *stops them, and gives them a parting gift from the church. This is done in*
       *silence.*

MINISTER
       Go forth in peace and serve the Lord.
ALL    In the name of Christ, Amen.
ALL    The grace of our Lord Jesus Christ, and the love of God, and the
       fellowship of the Holy Spirit, be with you always. Amen.

**Hymn** *Eternal Father, strong to save*

**Roger Grainger**

## 91    *A service signifying the end of a close relationship*

The intention of this service is not to celebrate the breakdown of a
relationship, but to help people to come to terms with one which has
radically changed. For example, it might perhaps be used when a marriage
has ended in divorce – when the two people immediately concerned still love
and care for one another, but not in the same way. Never in the same way
again. It would also be appropriate for a relationship which both parties
had intended should lead eventually to marriage, but which somehow had
not developed in that way, although both are still friends and wish to
remain so. To face facts like this, and to help others to face them too, is not
simply to make the best of a bad job. Indeed it can be a life-saving
operation, for nothing can survive destruction which has not been consciously allowed to die, and things cannot be lived which dare not even be
thought of. Inevitably, it is rather a sad service; it is certainly a penitential
one, and, as such, requires a good deal of courage and resolution on the part
of the two people undertaking it. However it is offered in the belief that the
acceptance of human failure can itself be a kind of success, in that it
provides us with a foundation for new beginnings. This is particularly so in
the context of the rite's ability to transform private intention into public
reality. In this case public will probably mean a rather restricted congregation, perhaps one that consists of a few relatives and friends; it is not to be
expected that a service of this kind will ever really become popular – no one
likes to admit failure (the church less than most!). However I believe that
there are times when it could prove useful . . .

MINISTER

God shows his love for us in that while we were still sinners Christ died for us.

## Hymn *Just as I am, without one plea*

ALL   Almighty God, to whom all hearts are open, all desires known, and from whom no secrets are hidden: cleanse the thoughts of our hearts by the inspiration of your Holy Spirit, that we may perfectly love you, and worthily magnify your holy name; through Christ our Lord. Amen.

(ASB)

MINISTER

Lord Jesus Christ, you said to your apostles: I leave you peace, my peace I give you, Look not on our sins, but on the faith of your Church, and grant us the peace and unity of your kingdom, where you live for ever and ever. Amen.

(Roman Missal)

*Two readings, one chosen by the two people themselves, and one by the minister. The circumstances of the occasion may suggest a particular text, but 1 Corinthians 13 would be suitable here.*

MINISTER

Thomas and Sylvia have come here together today for a special reason and with a particular intention. Their coming marks the end of a precious relationship between them. *(At this point the minister may add, if appropriate,* 'one which began with a solemn pledge undertaken before God', *or some suitable phrase.)* They share a common burden of promises broken, hopes left unfulfilled, and trust betrayed. They ask God's forgiveness for all these things. At the same time, however, they want to thank him for many blessings bestowed on them together and particularly, for a new kind of love which he is fostering between them – different perhaps, but no less real. This is the love which exists between friends. Such a love lays no claim to total involvement with the other person. Nevertheless it is a love which often gives more than it owes. We ask God to bless them both.

## Hymn *(chosen by the two friends)*

*At the end of the hymn, Thomas and Sylvia move to the front of the church, side by side but without touching each other or holding hands. They kneel down facing one another.*

MINISTER

Let us all kneel in silence and confess our sins to God.

*After a pause, the minister moves to the altar, where there is a bowl of water.*

MINISTER

God our Father, your gift of water is always bringing new life to the earth. We ask you to bless this water as a symbol of your cleansing grace. Accept the prayers we offer in Christ Jesus' name and send your Holy Spirit to sanctify a new relationship between these two people.

*He takes the water and sprinkles a few drops over them. Others in the congregation may come forward and kneel down with them to be sprinkled with the water.*

MINISTER

The God of all grace who called you to his eternal glory in Christ Jesus, establish, strengthen and settle you in faith; and the blessing of God Almighty, the Father, the Son, and the Holy Spirit, be among you and remain with you always. Amen.

(ASB)

*The minister gives out the hymn, during which those kneeling return to their seats.*

## Hymn *Gracious Spirit, Holy Ghost*

MINISTER

Sylvia and Thomas have made a solemn act of penitence. They have brought their new relationship before God. As fellow members of Christ's Body, we have asked God to bless them in both these things.

Lord God Almighty, in your Son Jesus Christ you have redeemed the life we live towards one another. There is no shadow of turning in you. Hold our variable natures within your everlasting embrace. Give us stability and constancy, so that we may accept each other as we are, and go forward in the new way you open before us. Through Jesus Christ our Lord. Amen.

ALL      I lift up mine eyes to the hills . . .                    (Psalm 121)

ALL      Our Father . . . for ever and ever. Amen.

MINISTER

Now to him who is able to do immeasurably more than all we can ask or conceive, by the power which is at work amongst us, to him be glory in the Church and in Christ Jesus throughout all ages. Amen.

(ASB)

### Hymn *Souls of men, why will ye scatter*

MINISTER
Let us depart in peace.

ALL In the name of the Lord. Amen.

Roger Grainger

## 92 *Praying our farewells*

This office may be used when anyone is departing from the local community. It may be adapted according to circumstances, including the absence of the person leaving.

*To symbolize unending love, the group may gather in a circle.*

*The Officiant begins:*
God of our beginnings and endings,
we celebrate all we have shared with N and N
and ask your blessing as *they* continue on *their* journey.
May the love that is in our hearts
be a bond that unites us for ever,
wherever we may be.
May the power of your presence
bless this moment of our leave-taking;
this we ask for the sake of Jesus Christ, our Redeemer. Amen.

*Then may follow either the following psalmody or some other.*

1 You, O God, will guard us from all evil:
 you will protect our lives.

2 You will protect our going out and our coming in:
 both now and for ever.

3 Where can I flee from your Spirit:
 or where can I flee from your presence?

4 If I climb to heaven, you are there:
 if I lie in the grave, you are there also.

5  If I take the wings of the morning;
   and dwell in the depths of the sea,

6  Even there, your hand shall lead me:
   your hand shall hold me fast.

(From Pss 121 and 139)

Glory . . .

*Any of the following readings may be used.*

I thank my God, every time I remember you, constantly praying with joy for all of you, because of your sharing in the gospel. And this is my prayer, that love may overflow more and more with knowledge and full insight to help to determine what is best, so that in the day of Christ we may be pure and blameless, having produced the harvest of righteousness that comes through Jesus Christ for the glory and praise of God. (*Philippians 1.3, 4, 9*)

*Exodus 13.21–2; John 3.5–8; John 16.21–4; 2 Corinthians 4.7–9.*

*The following response may be said. The community may say their words together or different individuals take a particular part.*

COMMUNITY (1)

As you journey onward,
we ask forgiveness where we have failed you;
we give thanks for all you have given us;
we assure you of our love and prayers.

THOSE LEAVING

As I leave, I ask forgiveness where I have failed you;
I give thanks for all that you have given to me;
I assure you of my love and prayers.

COMMUNITY (2)

As you experience the pain of change,
and the insecurity of moving on,
we pray that you may also experience
the blessing of inner growth.

THOSE LEAVING

I know that God goes with me.

COMMUNITY (3)

As you meet the poor, the pained,
   and the stranger on the Way,
we pray that you may see in each one
the face of Christ

THOSE LEAVING

I know that God goes with me.

COMMUNITY (4)
>As you walk through the good times and the bad,
>we pray that you may never lose sight
>of the shelter of God's loving arms.

THOSE LEAVING
>I know that God goes with me.

COMMUNITY (5)
>As you ponder your decisions
>and wonder over the fruits of your choice,
>we pray that the peace of Christ
>may reign in your heart.

THOSE LEAVING
>I know that God goes with me.

>*The Officiant then says,*

>We praise and thank you, God of the journey,
>for our *brothers and sisters* who *are* soon to leave us.
>We entrust *them* into your loving care,
>knowing that you are always the faithful traveller
>    and companion on the Way.
>Shelter and protect *them* from all harm and anxiety.
>Grant *them* the courage to meet the future,
>and grace to let go into new life;
>through Jesus Christ our Saviour. Amen.

>*N* and *N*, may God bless you. Amen.

>*Then each person present may make the sign of the cross on the forehead of those leaving, saying,*

>Go in peace, for our God goes with you.

>*and the Kiss of Peace may be exchanged.*
>>**Celebrating Common Prayer: The Daily Office SSF**

## 93  *A liturgy for the leave-taking of a house after separation or divorce*

*The family, community members and celebrant stand in a circle around a plain candle in a plain candle-holder.*

CELEBRANT
>We have come here today, to be with [*parent*] and [*children*] as they

leave this house which was their home for — years.

Let us pray: God of all goodness, we stand before you, our hearts full of memories, of joy and of sadness, as [*parent*] and [*children*] leave this house and all it has meant to them. We ask that you who brought them here be with them now in their leave-taking.

RESPONSE

O Lord, hear our prayer.

CELEBRANT

[*Parent*], as Sarah went with Abraham as he answered God's call on his life, so you travelled with [*separated spouse*] to this house, bringing your children [*name them*] to be a family and to make a home in this community.

[*Children*], you lived here and played here. This was the place you relaxed in, argued in, laughed in, worried in and had good times together in. It was a place you brought your friends, it has been a place where you have had times with your extended family. It has been your home.

And you, who have made up this community, you have been friends and neighbours. You have shared hospitality and conversation here.

Together, you all have shared God's goodness.

RESPONSE

In God was our hope and our trust.

CELEBRANT

Let us remember the past.

*Here follows a time of remembering by members of the family. Each person begins: 'I remember . . .'*

*After each memory, the response is: 'In God was our hope and trust'.*

CELEBRANT

Let us hold those memories, and all that is in the past, before God.

*A time of silence is kept.*

These things, this house, and its time as a home for [*parent*] and [*children*] has come to an end.

*The parent picks up the candle, and holding it, reads:*

It is stripped bare:
none of our things are here any more,
the garden is overgrown with weeds,

where we laughed there is silence,
where there was growing and development, there is space,
where there was togetherness, there is emptiness.

*The parent puts out the candle, and continues:*

The light that was in this home,
the hope in which we trusted,
    is gone out.
There is no place for us here any more.

RESPONSE
What was, is no more. Let it be.

## Reading *Romans 8.35, 37–9: Who shall separate us from the love of Christ?*

CELEBRANT
Those who put their trust in God are not fogotten,
God who made us knows us in our darkest moments,
knows us when we feel most abandoned,
unloved, confused and cut off.

RESPONSE
God's love is steadfast.

CELEBRANT
The God who prepared a home for you here
will restore you and lead you –
you will not want.

RESPONSE
God's love is faithful.

CELEBRANT
The God who gave you a place,
a family and a community,
will fill your cup
and comfort you.

RESPONSE
God's love is everlasting.

*The prayer of the Parent:*

In you, O God, I have always believed.
You were with me here,
You were with me when I left,
although I could not see you
and you seemed far off.

Be with me now and with the children
  as we look for a new house
  and begin a new way of living
  and find a new understanding of home.

*The affirmation and prayer by the Community:*

We are your friends
  our friendship and support continues
  wherever God may lead you,
  and we will pray for you all,
  asking that God will grant you your heart's desire
  and fulfil all your plans.

*Parent's prayer of thanks:*

God of friendship and steadfast love,
I thank you that you have not left us;
that you have surrounded us with love,
that you have given us friends and support,
and that when we have needed help
it has been there for us.
I will never cease to trust in your goodness.

CELEBRANT

Loving God, we thank you
that you are a God of comfort and healing.
Keep us under the shadow of your wings,
parents, children, neighbours and friends,
so that we may dwell in love and safety,
and praise you in all that we do. Amen.

## Hymn *Will you let me be your servant?*

## Blessing

May the light that once brightly shone here
continue to shine on your path.
May the God that brought you here and kept you
go with you now to enfold and protect you.
And may we all, wherever we may go, find in God
our true dwelling place and home,
now and always. Amen.

Erice Fairbrother

# 94    *Coming out of the Baptist ministry*

The author writes:
In September 1993 I resigned from the Accredited List of Ministers of the
Baptist Union, in protest at their guidelines on sexuality which I held to be
theologically, pastorally and personally unacceptable. This liturgy, celebrated with friends who had shared in the decision-making process with me,
marked both that resignation and my commitment to a continuing ministry.

## Introduction

## Song *Praise to God the world's creator*

OFFICIANT
        We are here to recognize your work as a minister in Tameside,
        Manchester and Sheffield
            the celebration of word and sacrament
            the touching and healing of mutual caring
            the spark of shared exploration.
ALL     We give thanks for what is past;
        We trust what is to come.

OFFICIANT
        We are here to rage with you at the recognition of injustice within
        the church
            the oppression practised in the name of a God of freedom
            the concealment and compromise demanded in the name of the
            Gospel of truth
            the exclusion and denial of human worth in the name of the
            creator of all.
ALL     We release what is past;
        we trust what is to come.

OFFICIANT
        We are here to share your pain as you leave the structures of the
        church which have given shape to your work
            the accreditation of your ministry by the Baptist denomination
            the status which comes from the church's recognition of your
            vocation
            the nurture and support of the tradition in which you found
            faith.
ALL     We grieve for what is past;
        We trust what is to come.

OFFICIANT
> We are here to offer you our support and friendship as you travel on in faith
>> in the loneliness and joy of an unknown stage of your journey
>> into an exploration of the sacred with new names and forms
>> in the empowering search for a spirituality of freedom and integrity.

ALL    We let go of all that is past;
we trust what is to come.

## An act of anger and penitence

*With each phrase, a stone is placed in a bowl in the centre of the room.*

For structures and teachings which deny the beauty and mystery of love
**God of love, forgive us.**

For collusion with 'lies, secrets and silence' which conceal our reality and smother our joy
**God of truth, forgive us.**

For failing to live and move and speak and touch in the full power of all that we may be
**God of freedom, forgive us.**

*You are invited to place stones in the bowl, either silently, or with whatever words you choose.*

THE PERSON LEAVING THE MINISTRY
> Water is a sign of forgiveness and cleansing; we pour water over these rocks as a sign of the washing away of the pain of anger and injustice.

## Solo *The rock will wear away*

(Meg Christian)

## Reading from *Our Passion for Justice*

(Carter Heyward)

## Prayers

## Song *Take this moment, sign and space*

(Iona Community)

## Act of commitment and affirmation

OFFICIANT
> [*Name*] you have chosen to leave the ministry of the Baptist denomination, and to relinquish the formal recognition of your

ministry. (*The candle is extinguished.*) What are you choosing for your future way?

RESPONSE

I am choosing a continuing exploration into woman-centred faith and spirituality.

I am choosing work that is healing and empowering of women and men.

I am choosing to share with others the struggle for justice and wholeness.

ALL    In the name of all that is loving,
In the name of all that is holy and just,
In the name of all that moves towards freedom,
We honour the choices you have made.

RESPONSE

You have all been part of the journey that has brought me to this point, and I thank you for all that your love and friendship and faith in me have meant to me. Do you continue to offer me that support and friendship as I continue my journey?

ALL    In the name of all that is loving,
In the name of all that is holy and just,
In the name of all that moves towards freedom,
We offer friendship, support and companionship along the way.

## Litany of blessing for women taking authority

(Janet Morley, *All Desires Known*, p. 62)

*Please join in the response after each clause:*
**Blessed are you among women.**

## Sharing a wilderness meal

When the way means leaving
with the cords of shared struggles
dreams and joys
holding us in love to friends
**Be our strength and joy**
**Be our hope for the way.**

When the way means searching
for hidden water running underground
seeking the secret place
where a fresh spring rises,

bubbling to the surface
**Be our strength and joy**
**Be our hope for the way.**

When the way means trudging
with loving friends and food for sharing
quietly persisting in the work of living
trusting that our truth will become clear
**Be our strength and joy**
**Be our hope for the way.**

When the way means dancing
in spirals of joy and love
hands joined, feet stepping out proudly
and heads held high in power and delight
**Be our strength and joy**
**Be our hope for the way.**

*Sharing of milk and honey.*

To a world where all are valued for themselves,
where no one is exploited or abused,
where all can stand proud and strong,
**We say yes.**

To a church where healing and love embrace all,
where there is acceptance of dissent and difference,
where conformity gives way to the spirit of freedom,
**We say yes.**

To lives grounded in peace and justice,
where struggle and self-acceptance walk in joy,
where strength and tenderness join hands,
**We say yes.**

**Song** *I will be gentle with myself*

(Libana)

**Close**

We go forward on the journey
rejoicing in all that we have
and open in trust and faithfulness
to all that is to come.

**Jan Berry**

**95**   *A liturgy for release from marriage vows*

---

A liturgy such as this needs an introduction to clearly explain the ground, for there will be those who will find it strange that the Church should embrace such a rite.

The Church remains committed to marriage as 'a life-long union in which a man and a woman are called so to give themselves in body, mind and spirit, and so to respond that from their union will grow a deepening knowledge and love of each other' (*An Australian Prayer Book,* p. 560).

This ideal of marriage has to be lived out in an imperfect world, and where there is a failure of the marriage relationship to provide a deepening knowledge and love of each other this has left people entrapped in inhuman prisons of mutually destructive relationships.

In our own age there has been a significant rise in divorce, and this has often left people uncertain, and sometimes with a sense of guilt and failure before God. We have always understood that where one partner died the other was free. This liturgy seeks to enable that same freedom for people where it is the relationship rather than the partner which is dead.

This liturgy should only proceed after the priest has consulted with the Bishop. Some inquiry should also be made to ensure that responsibilities incurred in the relationship and which are ongoing, especially those involving children, are being honoured. Whilst this liturgy seeks to set people free from their marriage vows, it does not intend to excuse people from those responsibilities.

It would seem right that the liturgy happen in church; though it may be fairly private, the person may value the support of a few close friends. The service does stand on its own. If it is to happen in the eucharist then only the Release and the Commitment will be needed.

### The Welcome

*The priest greets the people and says:*

Blessed be God
**who is creating the heavens and the earth.**

We are here to remember the grace of God in the midst of the brokenness of our world and of our lives.

We acknowledge that a relationship has ended and that in God N is freed for a new beginning.

Loving God,
thank you for all that is good,
for our creation and our humanity,
for the gifts of life and of one another,
for your love which is unbounded and eternal.

We come together in your presence,
conscious of the great hopes you have for us,
conscious of our own limitations and knowing that you love us still.

*(A New Zealand Prayer Book)*

*A silence is kept for reflection.*

We need your healing, merciful God:
give us true repentance.
Some sins are plain to us;
some escape us,
some we cannot face.
Forgive us;
set us free to hear your word to us;
set us free to serve you.

*(A New Zealand Prayer Book)*

*The priest says:*

God forgives you.
Forgive others – forgive yourself.

*(A New Zealand Prayer Book)*

*Silence for reflection.*

Through Christ, God has put away your sin:
Approach your God in peace.

Let us also offer one another a sign of peace.

*A psalm may be said.*

*A passage of scripture is read. (Suggested passages of scripture: Matthew 11.28–30; John 6.25–34; 1 Corinthians 13.)*

## The Release

*The priest says:*

God is with us.
In Christ we find new life.

*The priest turns to the person seeking release:*

PRIEST  N, marriage is a gift from God.
Are you ready to be released from your marriage vows?

N  I come before God who is my freedom.
My marriage is over,
and I seek God's blessing that I may go from here
to live in the liberty of Christ.

PRIEST  Christ died and rose again:
the Christian life is marked by forgiveness and new beginnings.

N  I promised before God that which I am no longer able to keep.
I seek God's forgiveness and freedom.

PRIEST  Jesus gave authority to the Church to bind and to loose.
By the authority of Christ committed to me
I loose you from your marriage vows,
in the name of the Father, and of the Son and of the Holy Spirit;
Creator, Redeemer and Giver of Life. Amen.

## The Commitment

PRIEST  Having been set free,
will you, with God's help, strive to know God's holy will for your
life, keep the commandments and serve God faithfully?

N  I will.

PRIEST  God calls us to freedom and light:
Live in freedom, live in light.

ALL  Shine as a light in the world
to the glory of God.

*As a symbol of the light by which we walk, the priest may give the person a
lighted candle and pray:*

O God, the source of all life and love, watch over us all
and keep us safe in your care
for all our hope is in you,
through Jesus Christ our Lord. Amen.

## The Blessing and Dismissal

*The priest gives the blessing:*

To God's gracious mercy and protection we commit you:
The Lord bless you and keep you,
The Lord make his face to shine on you

and be gracious to you,
The Lord lift up his countenance on you
and give you peace,
both now and evermore. Amen.

*The final grace may be used:*

ALL    The grace of our Lord Jesus Christ, and the love of God and the
fellowship of the Holy Spirit be with us now and evermore. Amen.

**Roger Herft**

# 96    *Service of new start*

## Call

Grace to you and peace from God our Father and the Lord Jesus Christ.

### Scripture sentences

OFFICIANT

Let us worship God.
He has shown you, O Humanity, what is good;
And what does the Lord require of you
But to do justice, to love kindness,
And to walk humbly with your God?

### Purpose of service

OFFICIANT

We are gathered here in the presence of God to end N's marriage,
to celebrate the beginning of a new phase in her life,
and to support her with our prayers.

We are here to confess our sins to God
in the joyful confidence of forgiveness
through the death on the cross of the risen Lord.

We are here to rededicate our lives to God,
asking that he will guard and guide us.

### Prayer of approach

OFFICIANT

> Almighty God, you know us through and through;
> you know us far better than we know ourselves.
> Help us to look into ourselves with fresh understanding
> that we may see into areas previously in darkness
> and so enter into the light of the children of God.
> Through Jesus Christ our Lord, Amen.

### Reading *John 8.1–11*

### Prayer of confession

I confess to God Almighty and in the presence of all God's people that I have sinned in thought, word, and deed.

I confess that the marriage vows made before you have been broken, that the marriage relationship has ceased, and that I bear some of the responsibility for this failure.

I confess that I have taken upon myself the sins of others and have failed to lay the burden at the foot of the cross.

I confess that I have seen the wonder of your creation in others but have resolutely refused to see it in myself.

I confess that I have been afraid to accept the healing which you have poured out on me.

I pray God Almighty to have mercy on me, pardon and deliver me from my sins, and give me time to amend my life. Amen.

### Prayer of assurance

OFFICIANT

> God of love, ever gracious and ever kind,
> we pray for N as she ends this chapter of her life
> and begins a new chapter.
> In repentance and faith may she know you
> as a God of mercy and new beginnings,
> who forgives our failures,
> restores our wholeness,
> and renews our hope.
> We ask your blessing on her children,
> the offspring of the marriage,
> that their lives may be rich and full.
> We pray that they also will be healed,

and enabled to form adult relationships
untainted by past hurts.
May your presence surround them,
your faithfulness encourage them,
and your spirit strengthen and guide them:
through Jesus Christ our Lord. Amen.

## Statement

Your marriage is ended.
Go in peace to start afresh.

## Blessing

May God, the source and giver of love,
fill you with all joy and peace,
that in Christ your love may be complete.
And the blessing of God Almighty,
Father, Son, and Spirit,
be with you always. Amen.

**Lesley McNeil**

## 97    *Liturgy for divorce*

### The gathering of the people

Dearly beloved: We have come together in the presence of God to witness
and bless the separation of this man and this woman who have been bonded
in the covenant of marriage. The courts have acknowledged their divorce
and we, this day, gather to support them as they give their blessing to one
another as each seeks a new life.

In creation, God made the cycle of life to be birth, life, and death; and
God has given us the hope of new life through the Resurrection of Jesus
Christ, our Savior. The Church recognizes that relationships follow this
pattern. While the couple have promised in good faith to love until parted
by death, in some marriages the love between a wife and a husband comes
to an end sooner. Love dies, and when that happens we recognize that the
bonds of marriage, based on love, also may be ended.

God calls us to right relationships based on love, compassion, mutuality,
and justice. Whenever any of these elements is absent from a marital
relationship, then that partnership no longer reflects the intentionality of
God.

The Good News of the Gospel of Jesus Christ is that we are forgiven our sins and our failures, we are raised from the dead and restored to a new life. The death of love, like the death of the grave, has no power to rob us of the life that is intended for the people of God.

Thus we gather this day to support and bless —— and —— as they confess their brokenness, forgive one another for their transgressions, receive God's blessing, celebrate the new growth that has occurred in each of them, and make commitments for a new life.

## The Declaration of Consent

CELEBRANT *(to the man)*

——, do you enter into this parting of your own free will; do you confess before God, ——, and the Church that you repent your brokenness that kept you in a destructive relationship? Do you seek forgiveness for the mutual respect and justice that you have failed to give and set your spouse free of this relationship, that you and she may receive from God and from one another the gift of new life and move toward health and wholeness once again?

MAN   I do.

CELEBRANT *(to the woman)*

——, do you enter into this parting of your own free will; do you confess before God, ——, and the Church that you repent your brokenness that kept you in a destructive relationship? Do you seek forgiveness for the mutual respect and justice that you have failed to give and set your spouse free of this relationship, that you and he may receive from God and from one another the gift of new life and move toward health and wholeness once again?

WOMAN I do.

## The Ministry of the Word

CELEBRANT

The Lord be with you.

PEOPLE And also with you.

CELEBRANT

Let us pray.

O gracious and ever-living God, you have created us male and female in your image: Look mercifully upon —— and ——, who come to you seeking your blessing. Forgive them for forsaking their vows, and for the pain that they have caused one another. Restore each of them by your grace to a new life of hope, renewal, and growth, and keep them ever in the love of your mercy, through Jesus Christ our Savior. Amen.

*A reading from Scripture*

*Luke 15.1–7 (Repentance and forgiveness)*
*Luke 9.42b–48 (Your faith has made you well)*
*Psalm 55.12–23 (Women who feel rejected)*

> *The choice of a reading depends upon the individuals' need, whether for forgiveness or wholeness, or both.*

## The Undoing of the Vows

> *The man faces the woman, takes her right hand, and says:*

In the name of God, I ——, release you, ——, from your vow to be my wife. I thank you for the love and support you have given me. I ask your forgiveness for my part in the failure of our marriage.

> *The woman faces the man, takes his right hand, and says:*

In the name of God, I ——, release you, ——, from your vow to be my husband. I thank you for the love and support you have given me. I ask your forgiveness for my part in the failure of our marriage.

> *The celebrant asks each in turn to return their rings:*

——, I give you this ring, which you gave me as a symbol of our marriage. In returning it, I set you free. I pray you will find peace and joy in your new life.

> *The rings are given to the celebrant, who places them upon the altar, or the man and woman may place the rings there themselves.*

> *The celebrant says:*

I place these rings upon the altar to symbolize that your lives are lived in the mercy and love of God.

> *Or, if the couple choose to place their own rings on the altar, the celebrant may say:*

These rings are placed upon the altar to symbolize that your lives are lived in the mercy and love of God.

## The Prayers
*The Lord's Prayer*

O God in heaven,
You who are Mother and Father
to us all,
Holy is your name.
Your reign has come.
Your will be done,
on earth as it is in heaven.
Give us today our daily bread.
Forgive us our sin
as we forgive those
who sin against us.
Deliver us from evil.
Save us from the time of trial.
For all time and all space,
all power and all glory are yours;
now and for ever. Amen.

Let us pray.

Eternal God, creator and preserver of all life, author of salvation and giver of grace: Look with favor upon the world you have made and for which your Son gave his life, and especially upon —— and ——, who come to you seeking your blessing. Grant unto them grace in moving from the old ways and wisdom in the ordering of their new lives. Amen.

Grant that each may know the power of your love to transform death into life and to bring forth the discovery of new identity out of pain. Teach them to trust once again and restore their hope, that once more they may view the world through love-filled eyes. Amen.

Bestow on them your Spirit, that —— and —— may be guided and sustained by you in the choices they individually make. Inspire the service they offer to the world that it may be distinguished by compassion for all. By your grace, may each become a witness to your forgiving and healing love as they reach out to care for the needs of others. Amen.

Make their individual lives a sign of Christ's love to this sinful and broken world, that forgiveness may heal guilt, joy conquer despair, and trust be forever placed in you. Amen.

*The man and woman kneel.*

Most gracious God, we give you thanks for your tender love in sending Jesus Christ to come among us, to be born of a human mother, and to make the way of the cross to be the way of life. Defend —— and —— from every enemy. Lead them both into all peace, to a renewal of life, and the hope of wholeness and love. Bless them in their separate lives, in their work, in their rest, and in their play, in their joys and in their sorrows, in their life and in their death. Finally, in your mercy, bring each to that table where your saints feast forever in the blessing of your presence and love, through Jesus Christ, who with you and the Holy Spirit, lives and reigns, One God, for ever and ever. Amen.

(cf. *The Book of Common Prayer* (USA),
'The Celebration and Blessing of a Marriage')

*Benediction*

> The blessing of God whose breath gives life
> be with you always.
>
> The blessing of God whose
> love is forgiving
> set you free from guilt and despair.
>
> The blessing of God
> who sanctifies your living
> be with you this day,
> to lead you to a new life
> of hope, peace, love, and service.
>
> May God be praised and glorified through your lives,
> now and for ever. Amen.

**Vienna Cobb Anderson**

## 98    *At the time of divorce: a children's liturgy*

---

*This ritual needs to occur in a place that is 'holy' for the family; that may be in a church, the family's dining-room table, or at a favorite outdoor location. It is possible to do this in conjunction with the Ritual of Divorce. The parents make a pledge to the children and give them a gift as a symbol of their vow. The parents may speak in their own words or use the ones below.*

### Making vows to the children

*The mother takes the child [children] by the hand or in her arms and says:*

I promise that I will love you always whether we are together or apart. I will care about everything that happens to you. I will try to help you feel secure when you are afraid, to give you comfort when you are hurt, and to protect you from all harm.

> *The mother gives the child a gift, saying:*

This gift is a symbol of what I have promised to you. Whenever you see it, remember my love.

> *The father takes the child by the hand or in his arms and says:*

I promise that I will love you always whether we are together or apart. I will care about everything that happens to you. I will try to help you feel secure when you are afraid, to give you comfort when you are hurt, and to protect you from all harm.

> *The father gives the child a gift, saying:*

This gift is a symbol of what I have promised to you. Whenever you see it, remember my love.

### Praying together

> *The family may kneel together or hold hands as the parents pray:*

Bless us, O God, as we who once lived together now are separated and live apart. Bless our children. Keep them safe from all harm, give them courage to face the pain of this division, and the knowledge that our brokenness is not their fault. Help us to keep the promises we made to them; let us not fail them again; in the name of Jesus Christ we pray. Amen.

### Blessing the family

> *If this ritual is done in a church in the presence of a priest, the priest then offers them a blessing.*

PRIEST  The blessing of God,
whose love gives you life,
forgives mistakes,
and heals brokenness,
be with you now and always.

ALL  Amen.

**Vienna Cobb Anderson**

## 99    *Separation*
*A ritual used within a small act of worship*

I first used this with a mother who wanted help from a worshipping group to let go her intense bonding with her daughter, after the child's long illness. I have used it subsequently for other sorts of separation rituals.

*The gathered folk sit in the round. A plant with a blossom and a bud is on the altar, on a paper, out of its pot.*

*After thanksgiving worship, the mother and a small group of close friends come together in the centre of the circle and hug. The daughter is not present. The minister invites the mother to come to the altar.*

MINISTER
N1 and N2 as mother and daughter have blossomed from the same life-giving root for some time. It is now time for them to separate and to grow from their own rootedness.

N1, is this what you want?

N1    Yes, it is time for us to separate.

MINISTER
Help me separate this plant so that we can put it on the altar in two parts. One is to show that you are in God's keeping and the other is to show that N2 has her own life in God's love.

*Together they separate the plant and place it on the altar in two parts.*

MINISTER
In the Name of God, Creator, Christ and Holy Spirit, N1 and N2 have their separate being in Love that is eternal and that will hold them now and always. Amen. So be it.

*Minister leads N1 back to her friends who hold out their hands to her and guide her back to her place.*

**Mary Robins**

## 100    *Agape on letting go and entering the darkness*

*The role of READER can be passed round the circle with each person taking it in turn to read.*

### Coming together body prayer

*All stand in a circle.*

FACILITATOR

We have come to this place, each of us bringing with us the dust, the noise, the clamour and the irritations of our day – let us be like children and imagine that we are trees – our arms are branches, reaching out and upwards to the sky, touching as trees touch in a forest glade – swaying a little in the gentle breeze. It is autumn – as the wind blows, our leaves are letting go from us and falling to the ground. Think of the falling leaves as the noise, the clamour and the irritations, dropping away from us – maybe there are a few droplets of rain to wash away the dust and tiredness as well.

*All sit.*

READER 'There is in God, some say, a deep and dazzling darkness.'

(Henry Vaughan)

ALL Therefore, why should we fear darkness – for darkness is of God?

READER In the beginning, 'darkness was on the face of the deep', and out of this darkness God created everything.

ALL Out of this darkness we were created.

READER Before we were born we were safe in the dark warmth of our mother's womb.

ALL Before it is a tree, a seed grows in the damp darkness of the earth.

READER God's darkness is a superessential darkness.

(Eckhart)

ALL A mystery behind mystery, a mystery within mystery that no light has ever penetrated.

(Eckhart)

READER God spoke to the assembled Israelites out of the midst of the fire, the cloud and the thick darkness with a loud voice.

(Deuteronomy 5.22)

ALL And after the mighty wind, the earthquake and the fire,
God murmured to Elijah in a still small voice.

READER In my distress I called upon God.
He came swiftly on the wings of the wind,
Thick darkness under his feet
 and darkness a covering around him.

(from Psalm 18)

ALL Every day I call upon thee, O God;
And spread out my hands to thee.
O God, why dost thou cast me off?
Why dost thou hide thy face from me?

(from Psalm 88)

READER How can we think about this God of contradictions
who helps one and not another?

ALL     What is this God who shouts from the dark centre of a fire,
but then disdains the fire, wind and earthquake
to whisper in a still small voice?

READER But now you put a question to me asking, 'How shall I think about
God, and what is God?' And to this I can only answer you, 'I do not
know.'

*(The Cloud of Unknowing)*

ALL     With your question you brought me into that same darkness and
into that same cloud of unknowing.

*(Cloud)*

READER God is neither this nor that. As one saint says, 'If anyone imagines
that he knows God and his knowledge takes form, then he may
know something but it is not God.

(Eckhart)

ALL     God is neither this thing or that thing that we can express.

(Eckhart)

READER God cannot be gendered; nor anthropomorphically conceived.

(Daphne Hampson)

ALL     Love God as God is: a not-God – a not-mind – a not-person – a
not-image.

(Eckhart)

READER God is nothing – No thing.
God is nothingness and yet God is something.

(Eckhart)

ALL     Religion is powerful. When our symbols are wrong we distort
human relations.

(Hampson)

READER God is not found in the soul by adding anything, but by a process of
subtraction.

(Eckhart)

ALL     Rather pause ... become still ... be patient ... love yourself ...
lay on one side all self-hatred ...

(Monica Furlong)

READER For the intellect to be free, it must become naked and empty by
letting go to return to its prime origin.

(Eckhart)

ALL     We become a pure nothing by an unknowing knowledge which is emptiness – and darkness – and being still.

        (Eckhart)

READER  Think of the soul as a vortex or a whirlpool and you will understand how we are to sink eternally from negation to negation into the One.

        (Eckhart)

ALL     And how we are to sink eternally from letting go to letting go into God.

        (Eckhart)

READER  The highest and loftiest thing that one can let go of is to let go of God – for the sake of God.

        (Eckhart)

ALL     I pray God to rid me of God.

        (Eckhart)

## The meditation

*Theme:* Whatever image of God comes to mind I consider it with love, I recall how it has helped me, and I thank that image for its help – then I put it away.

READER  God's exit is God's entrance.

        (Eckhart)

ALL     God's exit is God's entrance.

READER  God says: Now is the time to tell you where I am and where I will be. I am in Myself, in all places, in all things as I have ever been – without beginning.

        (Mechtild of Magdeburg)

ALL     To see God aright is to know him alike in everything.
          For God is equally near to everything and every place.

        (Eckhart)

READER  God must be envisaged to be that which promotes our full humanity.

        (Hampson)

ALL     God enables our wholeness.

        (Hampson)

READER  God may be reached and held close by means of love –

        (*Cloud*)

ALL     Therefore strike that thick cloud of unknowing with a sharp dart of longing love.

(*Cloud*)

READER     God is that love and power, that healing and strength, which we find to be abroad in the world.

(Hampson)

## Intercessions

READER     Out of the dark and dazzling centre of God wells a stream of living water, giving life, hope, consolation and healing.

ALL     From the dark and dazzling stream of God's love flows our compassion and the trust we have in each other.

READER     We each have a leaf-shaped piece of paper on which to write our intercessions – instead of lighting a candle we are going to pass our written intercessions to the person on our right, saying the intercession aloud if one wishes, or silently, but passing the paper-leaf with the words: 'I entrust this prayer to your safe keeping.'

ALL     Truth seeth God, and wisdom beholdeth God, and of these two cometh the third: that is, a holy marvellous delight in God, which is Love.

(Julian of Norwich)

## Sharing the Agape

ALL     As we share this bread and wine, bread baked in the darkness of the oven and wine matured in the darkness of a barrel, we remember how Jesus, our teacher, gave bread and wine to his friends.

*The Agape is followed by a time of silence to consider what we have shared.*

## Song *The Rose*                                    (Amanda McBroom)

## Preparing to leave

READER     Before we go out into the darkness, let us go from one to another and bless each other in the name of the hidden God.

ALL     The God of darkness and mystery in whom we are bathed, in whom we are enveloped, in whom we dwell.

*All bless each other separately.*

Jean Gaskin

## 101    *Space is a kind of time*

Space is a kind of time
and time is a kind of space.
And we can use them.
At first it looks as if they are the masters.
But we can use them.

We are about to create new spaces,
spaces between us
part of the rhythm of life.
We embrace,
and then we stand apart.

A space between us can be a lovely thing,
neither to be feared nor to be filled.
Did you ever just stand back
from someone or something?
Did you ever just stand back
and cherish the other?
Did you ever just stand back
to look, to love, to savour, to appreciate?
Can we draw from this leavetaking
whatever good may lie in separation?

## 102    *Prayer for the Sunday after Easter*

The excitement is over,
the balloons are burst and the Easter Garden cleared away.
We are in a time of anti-climax
and our hearts feel as empty as the empty tomb.
O God, help us to endure the emptiness
when a beloved friend has gone away.

Sharer of our sorrows,
help us to share each other's grief.

Christ is risen!
He is risen indeed!

**Jean Gaskin**

**103**  *Hymn for people seeking release from broken relationships and forgiveness for having failed others*

God! When human bonds are broken
and we lack the love or skill
to restore the hope of healing,
give us grace and make us still.

Through that stillness, with your Spirit
come into our world of stress,
for the sake of Christ forgiving
all the failures we confess.

You in us are bruised and broken:
hear us as we seek release
from the pain of earlier living;
set us free and grant us peace.

Send us, God of new beginnings,
humbly hopeful into life.
Use us as a means of blessing:
make us stronger, give us faith.

Give us faith to be more faithful,
give us hope to be more true,
give us love to go on learning:
God! encourage and renew!

*Tune: Laus Deo (Redhead No. 36)*

**Fred Kaan**

# 7

## *Into your hands . . .*
### *Dying, death and bereavement*

The helplessness and dependence of Jesus dying on the cross is repeated in some way in every dying. Dying is often a very long process, an enormous and very slow turning. Such a dying has room for many ritual moments, for which Christian tradition has supplied rites of confession, anointing, last communion and so on. Without prejudice to these, the material in this section points to the opportunities that can be found for the dying person and those nearest to him or her to make use of the simplest acts of love that enrich the process both of dying and of bereavement. Contributors encourage the sharing of memories, hopes and pleasures, the comfort of touching, and of presence – basic human acts which people are often somehow inhibited from doing or allowing, but which are irreplaceably part of this process of letting go of this life and of each other.

When it comes to preparing the funeral, it is important to have the service fit the person. Every funeral should be special and personal – and this depends a great deal more on the family and friends having thought about it beforehand, rather than on a member of the clergy having a magical awareness of what is appropriate in this particular case. So we have included some components of funeral rites worked out for parents and older family members – one does not have to be an ordained minister to make a collection of material that appeals to one for possible use. And this does not have to be a morbid preoccupation – the remembrance of death can serve to remind us of what is of lasting value to us in our own lives and in the lives of those we love.

Most of the liturgies included here were written in response to 'untimely' deaths – the deaths of the very young, or of those who have died unexpectedly or in accidents. Not all bereaved parents of young children are able to articulate their grief in a ritual context, but the funeral of Nicholas, a two-day-old baby, is a moving testimony to the human capacity to experience and express love, bewilderment, pain and grief.

In the case of accidental death it may be necessary to work out how to express ritually the anger that surges up on such occasions. Such deaths touch an anxiety that is in us all – 'it could happen to anyone at any time' – and perhaps it is this anger that is worked out with such ferocity against the person, if any, who caused the accident, and thereby the death of a beloved person. When there is no human to blame, then God is the object of our rage. Even people who say that their faith in God has been destroyed by such an event, still seem to need a God to hate. The liturgy to commemorate victims and survivors of road deaths (see chapter 8), while lacking the particularity of an individual's funeral rite, also provides a way of dealing with this shocking experience of grief.

## 104     *Preparing for death*

These rituals may be performed in many ways. Choose the ones most comfortable and appropriate to you and your loved one. There are endless possibilities that will come to your mind as you reflect upon these. The order of the rituals may be varied and repeated according to your needs.

### Expressing love

- *Conversations.*
- *Touching (massage; holding hands; embracing).*
- *Sharing favorite things (playing music; reading; walks; picking flowers; collecting leaves).*

*Prayer:*

Bless our love, O God the source of love. Help us to share the depth of our love with each other in the last days. Give us the grace to be tender and kind in the midst of stress and the fear of death and loss. Grant that the little things we do together may be signs of the power of love to make us whole and to bond us for ever; in the name of Jesus Christ we pray. Amen.

### Remembering the blessings of your lives and giving thanks

- *Naming what has been of value to the dying person.*
- *Naming what you'll always remember and value.*
- *Naming what's been important to each of you.*
- *Giving thanks for these blessings you have known (talking about them together; writing them down in a letter or booklet; making something together, if possible, e.g., bread, a favorite dish, a scrapbook).*

*Prayer:*

Receive our thanks, O God of love, for this wonderful relationship that we have shared. You have blessed us with commitment, fidelity (friendship), trust, and abiding love. These we have known and expressed in large and small ways. Our lives have been enriched by each of them. Let your continued blessings be upon us, binding us in love when we are no longer together, that those things that we remember in the days to come may continue the joy we have shared; in Jesus Christ's name we pray. Amen.

## Sharing special moments

- *Things you've always wanted to do but have not done.*
- *Just being together in stillness, conversation, or activity.*
- *Enjoying simple things: sunsets, birthdays, etc.*
- *Naming events to anticipate and live for.*

*Prayer:*

We thank you, O God of love, for the time to engage in special moments that will enrich our memories of love. We thank you for the opportunity to wonder and reflect on the meaning of our love. We thank you for the blessing our relationship has been to our lives. May these moments we have shared be the basis of sharing the love we have known with those in need of such blessing in their lives; in the name of Jesus Christ we pray. Amen.

## Doing practical things

- *Writing a will.*
- *Preparing a living will.*
- *Planning one's funeral (with the family if possible; leave room for others' plans and needs).*
- *Discussing how and where to die.*

*Prayer:*

Direct us with your grace, O God of love, as we prepare to do the difficult task of planning the practical things we need to do. Strengthen us to say the words so hard to name. Let these objectives draw us deeper in trust and love; in the name of Jesus Christ we pray. Amen.

**Vienna Cobb Anderson**

# 105    *At the time of death*

## Crying and talking

Too often we hide our tears from one another in order 'to protect' the other person. Tears are a sign of love, of how much we shall miss our beloved. Let them flow.

*Prayer:*

Let our tears of love flow as your love flows over us, O merciful God. Hold us close in your love as we face our parting; in the name of Christ we pray. Amen.

## Saying good-bye

Those who are dying often need the permission of the living to die. When it is given it makes it easier to let go of life. The dying is more peaceful and less of a struggle. Sometimes it's possible for a family member to do this and some just can't do it. If the latter is true for you, ask a priest, minister, or someone close to you to help.

*Formally:*

- *Saying prayers or a litany.*
- *Making Eucharist together.*
- *Having a priest give the commendation.*

> Depart, O Christian soul, out of this world;
> In the name of God, who created you;
> In the name of Jesus Christ, who sets you free;
> In the name of the Holy Spirit, who sanctifies you now and
>     for ever.
> May you rest in peace in the love of God.
> Amen.

*Informally:*

- 'It's okay to go.'
- 'You can go on your journey.'
- 'If it's time for you to die, it's all right.'
- 'You can go now, —— I'll always love you.'
- *Whatever words feel most appropriate to you are always the best.*

*Singing:*

Singing helps us to relax, for it reminds us of being sung to sleep as a child, or of favorite memories. Music eases pain. To sing someone into their dying, if appropriate to the person and circumstance, is a lovely gift. It helps bond two people when there is nothing the living can 'do' and when often the dying can no longer respond.

*Prayer:*

As you have blessed us in our loving, bless us in our parting, O God. As nothing can separate us from your love, so let ours be bonded for ever; in the name of Christ we pray. Amen.

## Washing the body

This is the last direct act of love we have the opportunity to share. It is an intimate act. For some too painful to do, for others it is the perfect act for saying good-bye. Choose what is right for you; trust your feelings and instinct to know what to do.

- *Have someone read psalms while the washing is done in silence.*
- *Use this opportunity to share last words.*
- *Just touching and being quiet and private is fine.*
- *The body may be wrapped in a sheet or dressed.*

*Prayer:*

As Jesus' feet were washed in an act of love and in preparation for his burial, so too do we bathe our beloved. Grant to her [him] the joy and peace of salvation; in the name of Jesus Christ we pray. Amen.

## When you're not there at the time of death or for the funeral

- *Say a prayer or read the burial office at the same hour as the funeral.*
- *Get out a photo and cry and talk to the one you love.*
- *Light a candle at a church or at home.*
- *Share stories with friends.*
- *Create a ritual of good-bye of your own.*
- *Read old letters.*
- *All the above.*

*Prayer:*

Unto God's mercy, protection, and love I commit you, ——. I give thanks for the blessings and love we have shared. May you dwell in peace and in the light of God now and for ever. I shall not forget you, I promise; in Christ's name I pray. Amen.

## A wake

The need to cry is often stifled by being 'in public' at a funeral. A wake is a more intimate and private gathering that permits us to express our grief openly in the company of others who are grieving as well. The sooner we can be in touch with our feelings, the better it is for our grieving process; thus a wake can be helpful.

- *Tell stories with friends.*
- *Share food and drink.*
- *Look at pictures.*
- *Comfort one another.*

*Prayer:*

Receive our prayers for ——, O God of love. Grant her [him] rest, peace, and the joy of your presence. Bless —— and all of us who mourn. Let us not hide from this pain in words or busy actions. Keep us open to the depths of love and our need for one another; in the name of Jesus Christ our Savior we pray. Amen.

## Funeral ritual

- *Set the context in which you wish all that's said to be heard and understood. This may be done by readings, a family statement, or a homily.*
- *Name and remember what you will always cherish.*
- *Express belief in what comes next for your loved one and for you.*
- *Commit the person you love to God, the earth, and the future.*
- *Say good-bye (place a flower in the grave; put earth into the grave; stand in silence at the grave and listen to your heart).*

*Prayer:*

Hear our prayers for ——, O God of love. You made us of the dust of the earth, and we have returned her [him] to the earth, to your creation, and committed her to your love. Bless —— in death as you have been faithful to her in her living. Comfort us who mourn and empower us to commit our short and fragile lives to do your will on earth; in the name of our Savior, Jesus Christ, we pray. Amen.

**Vienna Cobb Anderson**

## 106 *As death nears*

In the name of God: Creator, Redeemer and Sanctifier.

As Jesus taught us, so we pray:

Our Father, who art in heaven . . .

O God, who brought us to birth,
and in whose arms we die:
we entrust to your embrace
our beloved *sister/brother*.
Give *her/him* release from *her/his* pain,
courage to meet the darkness,
and grace to let go into new life,
through Jesus Christ, Amen.

(Janet Morley)

God of the dark night
you were with Jesus praying in the garden,
you were with Jesus all the way to the Cross
and through to the resurrection.
Help us to recognize you now, as we watch with [N]
and wait for what must happen;
help us through any bitterness and despair,
help us to accept our sadness,
help us to remember that you care for us
and that in your will is our peace. Amen.

(*A New Zealand Prayer Book*)

God be your comfort, your strength;
God be your hope and support;
God be your light and your way;
and may God: Creator, Redeemer and Sustainer,
bless you and remain with you
now and for ever. Amen.

(*A New Zealand Prayer Book*, adapted)

**Joyce Yarrow** CSF

**107** *Prayers at death*

---

In the name of God: Creator, Redeemer and Sanctifier.

Jesus, remember us in your kingdom and teach us to pray:

Our Father, who art in heaven . . .

Neither death, nor life, nor angels, nor rulers,
nor things present, nor things to come, nor
powers, nor height, nor depth, nor anything else
in all creation, will be able to separate us from
the love of God in Christ Jesus our Lord.

(Romans 8.38–9 NRSV)

God of mercy
into whose hands your Son Jesus Christ
commended his spirit at his last hour;
into those same hands
we now commend your servant N,
that death may be for *her/him* the gate to life
and to eternal fellowship with you;
through Jesus Christ our Lord. Amen
(*Celebrating Common Prayer: The Daily Office SSF*, adapted)

Go forth, N, upon your journey from this world;
in the love of God the Life-Giver who created you;
in the mercy of Jesus the Redeemer who suffered death for you;
in the power of the Holy Spirit who strengthens you;
in communion with all the blessed saints;
with the angels and archangels and all the heavenly host;
May your rest this day be in peace
and your dwelling in the city of God.

God of all consolation,
grant to those who grieve
the spirit of faith and courage,
that they may have the strength to meet the days to come
with steadfastness and patience,
not grieving without hope,
but trusting in your goodness;
through him who is the resurrection and the life,
Jesus Christ our Saviour. Amen.

(*A New Zealand Prayer Book*, adapted)

God be your comfort, your strength;
God be your hope and support;
God be your light and your way;
and may God: Creator, Redeemer and Sustainer,
bless you and remain with you
now and for ever. Amen.

(*A New Zealand Prayer Book*, adapted)

**Joyce Yarrow** CSF

## 108   *The blessing of a dead baby*

Let us commend N to the everlasting love of God.

God, our Creator
by your mighty power you gave us life,
and in your love you have given us
new life in Christ Jesus.
Bless this child N
and keep *her/him* in life eternal,
in the faith of Jesus Christ our Saviour,
who died and rose again,
and is now alive and reigns with you
and the Holy Spirit, in glory, for ever. Amen.

(based on ASB)

As Jesus taught us, so we pray:

Our Father, who art in heaven . . .

*If the mother is present*

Gracious God,
in your mercy you have safely brought
your daughter N through childbirth.
Comfort this family,
grieving the loss of their hoped-for child.
Help them to find assurance
that with you nothing is wasted or incomplete,
and uphold them with your love,
through Jesus Christ our Saviour. Amen.

(*A New Zealand Prayer Book*, adapted)

**Joyce Yarrow** CSF

**109**     *On the death of a child*

Creator of all,
we thank you for the gift of life
you gave to N.
In our confusion and grief
help us to remember the joy
which *s/he* brought us
in the short time that *s/he* lived
and guide us through our present darkness
to the light of your unfailing love,
through Jesus Christ our Lord. Amen.

(*A New Zealand Prayer Book*, adapted)

**Joyce Yarrow** CSF

**110**     *Order of service for the funeral of a two-day-old baby*

**Entrance** *All Stand*

**Introduction**

**Hymn** *Now thank we all our God*

*Last verse adapted as follows:*

All praise and thanks to God,
  Creator, now be given,
Saviour and Comforter,
  Who reigns in highest heaven;
The one eternal God,
  Whom earth and heaven adore;
For thus it was, is now,
  And shall be evermore.

**Reading** *Psalm 23 ('The Lord is my shepherd')*

## Extract from a reading: 'To my son'

I woke this morning,
Sad,
But serene,
Reflecting
On your short life.
I am happy that you
Were given –
Through us –
The gift of Life.

Time telescoped;
A whole life
In three days.
A limited life:
A pure one.

You knew no pain.
You did not suffer.
You caused no harm.
You were only loved;
An innocent.

Nadia was born
In sunshine.
You were delivered
In wind and rain.
When the leaves rustle,
Branches bend,
Clouds chase,
Rains lash,
Skies darken
And clear –
I will know you
Are there,
And see
Your spirit
Moving
Freely
In that wind.

But today
All is calm.
You are back inside me.

I am at peace
As you are.
And we are
Going
To give you
Your name.

(Linda Balfe)

(Nicholas Colomb was named and blessed at a service held in St Mary's Hospital on Wednesday 12 June 1991.)

## Reading

Nicky
You blinked at me
when you were born
And then your eyes
never opened again.
But you saw the light
And you felt the warmth
And you heard our tender voices.
Now you are gone
And we are left behind to grieve.
You are at rest, at peace,
At the last,
Already.
And we have still to go where you
have gone ahead of us.
We brought you
But you overtook us.
And the grief over your loss
Overtakes us.

May we do honour to you
Now
And in the future
By remembering you
And following you, too,
To the bitter end.

(Alec Balfe-Mitchell)

## Hymn *Lord of all hopefulness*

**Reading** *Mark 10.13–16 ('The Kingdom of God belongs to such as these')*

**Address**

**Hymn** *How shall I sing to God?* (**125**)

**Prayers**

**The lighting of a candle**
*for the remembrance of Nicholas.*

*Alec and Linda will light a single candle while these words are sung:*
*Ubi caritas et amor, ibi Deus est.*
(Where generous and true love are found, there God is.)

**Words of committal**

**Hymn** *Come, cradle all the future generations* (**40**)

**Blessing and dismissal**

Alec Balfe-Mitchell

## III   *Dedication and funeral of a stillborn baby*

### Dedication

Gracious Father,
in darkness and in light,
in trouble and in joy,
help us to trust your love,
to serve your purpose,
and to honour your name.
Through Jesus Christ our Lord, Amen.

Loving Father, we commend N to your loving care.
By your mighty power you gave us life, and in your love you have given us
new life, in Christ Jesus.
We entrust N to your merciful keeping in the faith of Jesus Christ, your Son
our Lord, who died and rose again to save us, and is now alive and reigns
with you and the Holy Spirit in glory for ever. Amen.

N, I sign you with the cross, the sign of Christ, to show that you belong to him.

Lord, you took children in your arms and blessed them, receive N into your arms that she may know your never failing love and care.

Lord, there is so much that we do not understand at this time, help us to give thanks for N's brief life, a life which we were not to see. We pray for those who mourn, especially . . .; surround them with your love and care that they may be able to give N into your care. And may the blessing of God, Father, Son and Holy Spirit be upon us evermore. Amen.

## Funeral: Opening sentences

The Lamb who is at the throne will be their shepherd and will lead them to springs of living water; and God will wipe away all tears from their eyes. (Revelation 7.17)

The steadfast love of the Lord never ceases, his compassion never fails: every morning they are renewed. (Lamentations 3.22,23)

## Introduction and prayer

Give to those, Lord, who are in the darkness deeper than the womb, the true vision of your light, your strength and your saving grace, through Jesus Christ our Lord. Amen.

## Hymn *The Lord's my shepherd: I'll not want*

## First Reading

The unfinished symphony,
the sculpture
knocked from the pedestal
just before
the final touch . . .

though never come to birth,
never living,
never dies
but continues its creation
in the heart
of its Creator.

and so the symphony,
the masterpiece,

the stillborn child! . . .
lives eternally
in a mother's loving heart;
in the heart
of its Creator.

'I have not lost
any which you gave me.'

(Marjorie Gray)

## Second Reading *Mark 10.13–16*

They brought children for him to touch. The disciples rebuked them, but when Jesus saw this he was indignant, and said to them, 'Let the children come to me; do not try to stop them; for the kingdom of God belongs to such as these; I tell you, whoever does not accept the kingdom of God like a child will never enter it.' And he put his arms round them, laid his hands upon them, and blessed them.

## Address

## Prayers

ALL
God be in my head
and in my understanding.
God be in my eyes
and in my looking.
God be in my mouth
and in my speaking.
God be in my heart
and in my thinking.
God be at my end
and at my departing.

Father in heaven, you gave your Son Jesus Christ to suffering and to death on the cross, and raised him to life in glory. Grant us a patient faith in time of darkness, and strengthen our hearts with the knowledge of your love; through Jesus Christ our Lord. Amen.

Let us commend N
to the love of God our Father.

Heavenly Father, by your mighty power you gave us life, and in your love you have given us new life in Christ Jesus. We entrust N to your merciful keeping, in the faith of Jesus Christ your Son our Lord, who died and rose again to save us, and is now alive and reigns with you and the Holy Spirit, in glory for ever. Amen.

> O God we thank you for the loan of N
> for the joy of her presence in the womb,
> for the privilege of loving and nurturing her.
> Today you share our sorrow,
> help us too, to know your joy
> as her spirit returns into your care.
> Grant strength to her family
> to give N into your care,
> in the sure knowledge,
> that they will be reunited with her
> in that other world, where all your children
> enjoy complete health of body, mind and spirit.
> Deal graciously with all who mourn, those here and
> those unable to come, that they may know the
> consolation of your love;
> through Jesus Christ our Lord. Amen.

*The Lord's Prayer*

## Hymn *Morning has broken like the first morning*

## The Grace

ALL    The grace of our Lord Jesus Christ,
the love of God,
and the fellowship of the Holy Spirit,
be with us all evermore. Amen.

**Clare Edwards**

# 112    *A service of commemoration and healing after abortion*

The service was prepared for a young woman who had chosen to have an abortion after rape by her boyfriend. This incident also brought up issues of earlier abuse for her. The service was held on the day when the baby would have been born.

## Opening sentence

The steadfast love of the Lord never ceases, his compassion never fails;

every morning they are renewed.

(Lamentations 3.22)

We come together today to mark what might have been the birth of ——'s baby, we come to share our love and care for —— and we come trusting in God's steadfast love and his great compassion for all of us.

We want to think about and offer to God more than just today. We bring memories of the difficult last months and we want to look forward with hope to the future.

In the last months, choices have had to be made, choices that have been hard and choices where there was no perfect solution. At times it's easy to think we took the wrong path, but then we remember again all the good reasons that took us that way.

Lord we ask you to honour ——'s decision, a decision made out of great pain, a pain that you know and understand, a pain that you carry with her. Together we come before you as those who have fallen short of the perfect love you made us for, yet trusting that each time we turn, you are there to draw us back to yourself.

And so we pray together,

> Eternal God, giver of light and grace,
> we have sinned against you and against our neighbours,
> in what we have thought,
> in what we have said and done.
> We have wounded your love,
> and marred your image in us.
> We are sorry and ashamed,
> and repent of all our sins.
> For the sake of your Son Jesus Christ,
> who died for us,
> forgive us all that is past;
> and lead us out from darkness
> to walk as children of light. Amen.          (ASB)

Almighty God have mercy upon us, pardon and deliver us from all our sins, and bring us to eternal life, through Jesus Christ our Lord. Amen.

We say together Psalm 23. During this the candle will be lit to remind us of Jesus the shepherd who is also our light.

> *(During the following prayer the young woman laid a single red rose beside the lighted candle.)*

We remember your light and your presence with ——'s baby, a baby given up in love. Lord, as you are the creator of all life so we entrust ——'s baby into your care.

Lord God, by your mighty power you gave us life, and in your love you have given us new life in Christ Jesus. We entrust ——'s baby to your merciful keeping, in the faith of Jesus Christ your Son our Lord, who died and rose again to save us, and is now alive and reigns with you and the Holy Spirit in glory for ever. Amen.

> Gracious God,
> in darkness and in light,
> in trouble and in joy,
> help us to trust your love,
> to serve your purpose,
> and to praise your name;
> through Jesus Christ our Lord. Amen.

God in heaven, you gave your Son Jesus Christ to suffering and to death on the cross, and raised him to life in glory. Grant us a patient faith in time of darkness, and strengthen our hearts with the knowledge of your love; through Jesus Christ our Lord. Amen.

> Lord have mercy upon us.
> Christ have mercy upon us.
> Lord have mercy upon us.

Our Father in heaven . . .

> O God,
> Giver of Life,
> Bearer of Pain,
> Maker of Love,
> you are able to accept in us what we
> cannot even acknowledge;
> you are able to name in us what we
> cannot bear to speak of;
> you are able to hold in your memory
> what we have tried to forget;
> you are able to hold out to us
> the glory that we cannot conceive of.
> Reconcile us through your cross
> to all that we have rejected in our selves,
> that we may find no part of your creation
> to be alien or strange to us,
> and that we ourselves may be made whole.
>
> Through Jesus Christ our lover and our friend.
> Amen.                                            (Janet Morley)

Lord, as we entrust the past into your loving and compassionate hands so we look with you to the future.

### Reading *Jairus' daughter: Mark 5.21a–24 and 35b–43*

### Silence

### Reflection

Our God is one who draws us on out of the painful and death-like experiences. To take his hand is to bring all that the past has made us and step out into his future for us. So he calls each one of us by name, and says, 'Talitha cum', that is, 'Get up my child'.

'. . . and he told them to give her something to eat.' Jesus calls us on into the future and, directly by his love and by the love he gives us through others, he gives us food to enable us to get up and to step out.

*Communion from the reserved sacrament might follow.*

### Final prayer and blessing

May God in his infinite love and mercy bring the whole church, living and departed in the Lord Jesus, to a joyful resurrection and the fulfilment of his eternal kingdom. And the blessing of God Almighty, the Father, the Son and the Holy Spirit, be with us and with all whom we love today and always. Amen.

Clare Edwards

## 113   *Service for a stillborn child*

### Sentence

As one whom a mother comforts, I will comfort you, says the Lord.

OFFICIANT
> We come here to thank God for [*child*];
> to thank God for *his/her* conception,
> to thank God for the months *she/he* was carried
>   in [*mother*]'s womb
>   and in [*father*]'s heart;
> to thank God that in *his/her* short life
>   *she/he* brought joy and laughter,
>   anticipation, and hope for the future.

We gather to share our grief and our anger
that a life promised has been taken;
that hope seems to have been cut off
   and joy destroyed.

We are here to lay our questions
and our anger, our sadness and our fear,
   at the feet of Christ,
who opened his arms to receive
   all who were wounded and distressed.

We are here to acknowledge our feelings of guilt and failure.

Jesus says: 'Those who come to me I will not cast out.'

*Those present are encouraged to verbalize their hopes and fears, their anger, their sadness; to place flowers, poems, gifts, symbols of love and light on the coffin or on a nearby table.*

*A time of silence and letting go.*

## Prayer

ALL     O God, as [*child*]
was cradled in the womb,
cradle *her/him* and hold *her/him*
that as we let *her/him* go,
we may know that *he/she* has gone
from our loving arms into yours for ever.
In Jesus' name we pray. Amen.

Kate McIlhagga

# 114    *Service of healing after a miscarriage (1)*

## Introduction

*When all have gathered, the leader introduces the service in words like:*

- We have come together to mourn the death of our unborn child, a life that had been growing with N for . . . weeks.
- We had looked forward to the day when we would have seen *his/her/this* face and form, with joy and wonder in our hearts.
- But now our child has gone from us; we now look forward to that day, in the kingdom of our loving God, when we will meet for the first time.

'Now we see dimly, then we shall see face to face.'

- Jesus wept at the death of his friend Lazarus. Jesus weeps with us now, sharing the loss of our hopes, the loss of our dreams.

## Readings

*Possible options:* Psalm 139.13–16; Isaiah 43.1–5; 2 Corinthians 5.1; John 14.1–4; Mark 10.13–16; John 7.37–8.

## Homily

This may include teaching on grief and God's love. We acknowledge our fears, anger and frustration. We recognize that in the deepest of our sorrows God stands with us.

The homily is most effective when it is brief, empathetic, personal and reflects the humanity of the speaker.

## Possible symbolic actions

Water is a most powerful symbol to enter into here. It speaks of living-giving and death-dealing; of the birth process and the death process. It also can have a soothing, therapeutic effect.

> *Before the prayers, fill a glass bowl with water, perhaps arranging some greenery around it, and sprinkling a few flower petals on the water. You could also have a candle beside the water. Have a towel handy.*
>
> *When indicated in the service, the couple come to the bowl and 'enter into' the symbol in some way that seems appropriate to them. They may plunge their hands in and hold them under (a death echo) or swirl them about, or cascade the water from their hands (life). They may gently stroke each other's hands under the water, or simply experience its soothing, supporting quality. They may wish to sign themselves with it.*
>
> *While there are some words to accompany these actions, they should not be rushed in any way. It is important for the couple to experience the symbol at their own pace.*
>
> *Others at the service may wish also to share in this symbolic act.*

*Possible words to use during a symbolic action:*

'Whoever is thirsty should come to me and drink. Whoever believes in me, streams of life-giving water will pour out from their hearts' (John 7.38).

*(Revelation 21.1–7 could also be read.)*

Though we are saddened that our unborn child was with us for so short a time, we entrust *him/her* into your loving care with all confidence.

Our miscarried child was a gift from you, hear our prayer and look upon *him/her* with love.

Bless this mother. We thank you for her womanliness, her beauty of form and spirit; may her love for her lost child be her strength.

Bless this father. Comfort him in his sadness and grant him peace in your eternal love.

*Those present may wish to voice their own prayers.*

## Conclusion

We pray now that:
- All who are saddened by the death of this hoped-for child, this couple, their family and friends, may put their hope in Christ and through him and each other, receive comfort, peace and holiness.
  **Lord, hear us.**
- That the power of the Holy Spirit may fill us all with freedom and change our fears into trust.
  **Lord, hear us.**
- We pray too for a blessing on this family if in time other children are entrusted to them.
  **Lord, hear us.**
- And may God who is all loving, all creative and all healing, bless us for ever.

## Burial

*Remains, or ashes of remains, if these are available, may be wrapped in leaves or cloth and buried in the family garden, near a special plant, or a new tree may be planted above them.*

from *Our Baby has Died*

# 115   *Service of healing after a miscarriage (2)*

This may be helpful to parents at a time near when the expected baby would have been born, or at any other appropriate time.

## Introduction

*When the people have gathered, the priest or leader welcomes them and states the purpose of the gathering in words like these:*

My friends, we come together in love for N and N, to be with them as they grieve over a life that has ended.

We come, too, to celebrate God's never-ending love for us; for the tiny life that has now been given over to the tenderness and infinite love of God;

for N [*the mother*], loved in her sadness as Mary was when she stood at the Cross and watched her child die;

for N [*the father*], who has also stood by in helplessness, and is loved as John the disciple was loved when he stood by Mary under the Cross;

for all of us here that we may know God's certain love for us now, in this place and for ever.

Finally, we come to ask this God-who-loves for gifts of healing and strengthening, for understanding and peace.

> *The mother comes to the table where the Book, oil and candle are placed, and prays, using words like:*

Blessed are you, our loving God, giver of all gifts. We thank you for your gift of life to us and for friendship.

> *She now lights the candle while saying:*

We entrust to your tender care the life that you gave us for these/this [*number*] weeks/months/short time.

> *She takes the bowl of oil in her hands:*

And we thank you for this gift of oil. May it bring healing for our hearts and strengthening for our journeys.

> *She places it on the table.*

## Readings

> *The readings have been chosen beforehand and individuals asked to read them. If the mother is to do one, she may commence, otherwise she could now invite the first reader to commence.*

*Some options:* Isaiah 43.1–5; Mark 10.13–16; Psalm 139; John 14.1–3; Romans 8.31–5, 37–9; John 6.37–9; 1 Thessalonians 4.13–18 (or 13–14, 18).

## Response

> *The response to the readings may be a time of quiet reflection or perhaps an appropriate song. After a period of silence, the priest or leader may invite people to share some of their reflections.*

### The ritual action

*When opportune, the leader gathers these reflections together, then introduces the ritual action in words like these:*

We have opened our hearts to God's word to us. Let us pray that the sign of love we are about to share will help us to know that Christ will be our strength. May we learn to follow Christ more nearly, day by day.

*The father now takes the oil and signs the mother on the forehead, gently rubbing the oil in. He then stands, sits or kneels beside her. The mother may sign the father on his forehead also.*

*The leader then takes the candle to them to hold with words like:*

May Christ be light for your journey; may Christ's love warm you and encourage you.

*He invites the others to come round and lay hands on or extend hands over the parent(s), with words like:*

God loves us. Let us ask God now, in our own words, for the gifts we would like given to N and N.

*To conclude the priest or leader may round off all these prayers into a general blessing. Perhaps:*

We thank you loving God for all your gifts to us. Hear these prayers of ours, and those we have still in our hearts, and bless us all, now and always. You who are Creator, Redeemer and the Giver of life. Amen.

*The parents now take the oil and go around the group, signing each on the forehead. They may use words or they may prefer to let the actions and their eyes speak. They may not wish to sign at all.*

*During the signing, an appropriate song may be played or sung.*

### Conclusion

*When this is completed, the leader concludes the ritual by inviting all to join in the Lord's Prayer.*

from *Our Baby has Died*

## 116    *Blessing for a deceased baby*

Baptism is a sacrament of repentance and discipleship, a rite of passage for the living, and most members of the clergy feel it should not be applied to early losses or stillbirths. However, a blessing for a deceased baby can be worded so that the profound imagery of water inherent in baptism is maintained without the actual sacrament being given. This blessing can be combined with a naming ceremony.

*The person officiating can describe the significance of water in this manner while blessing the baby:*

Water, one of the most important elements of creation, is essential for human life in countless ways. In our grief it becomes the symbol of God's cleansing and forgiveness, the power of spiritual renewal, and the flow of life throughout the ages. With water we now bless this child:

> O God of creation,
> Your spirit moved over the waters of the universe
> To create life in its first struggling forms.
> You led your people through the waters of the seas to salvation.
> Your power moves in the waters of the womb to hold and
>     protect us.
> Bless this baby [*name*] in your love. Amen.

We bathe this child in the love of God. We bathe this child in the tears of her parents. We know the power of water to permeate life and hold this child. The water of the womb sustained this child as the water of the universe and the power of God will hold her now. Amen.

(Adapted from *Sister Mary Claire van Orsdal* OSU)

When combined with the naming of the baby, usually by asking the parents 'What name have you given your child?' this can be as powerful and comforting as baptism. The feeling of commitment to the baby can be especially strong if a naming certificate is completed and handed to the parents at the close of the service. Sister Jane Marie Lamb has established the custom of using a small seashell to hold water for blessing or baptizing a baby. When the ceremony is finished, the member of the clergy gives the seashell to the parents as a cherished keepsake.

**Ingrid Kohn and Perry-Lynn Moffitt**

## 117   *Prayers of the people at a funeral*

CELEBRANT
> For our *brother/sister* ——, let us pray to our Lord Jesus Christ who said, 'I am Resurrection and I am Life'.
> Lord, you consoled Martha and Mary in their distress: draw near to us who mourn for ——, and dry the tears of those who weep.

PEOPLE **Hear us, Lord.**

CELEBRANT

You wept at the grave of Lazarus, your friend: comfort us in our sorrow.

PEOPLE **Hear us, Lord.**

CELEBRANT

You raised the dead to life: give our *brother/sister* eternal life.

PEOPLE **Hear us, Lord.**

CELEBRANT

You promised Paradise to the thief who repented: bring our *brother/sister* to the joys of heaven.

PEOPLE **Hear us, Lord.**

CELEBRANT

Our *brother/sister* was washed in baptism and anointed with the Holy Spirit: give *him/her* fellowship with all your saints.

PEOPLE **Hear us, Lord.**

CELEBRANT

*He/she* was nourished with your Body and Blood: grant *him/her* a place at the table in your heavenly Kingdom.

PEOPLE **Hear us, Lord.**

CELEBRANT

Comfort us in our sorrows at the death of our *brother/sister*: let our faith be our consolation, and eternal life our hope.

We remember the healing of your faithful people in time past. Heal us, too, in our present afflictions, especially those suffering from AIDS – men, women, children, straight and gay, believers and nonbelievers – all of your children.

*The congregation is invited to offer names of those for whom they wish prayer.*

We pray for all who have lost loved ones to AIDS and for all who are now afraid to risk loving. We remember those who have died of AIDS. We give thanks for the gift of their lives.

*The congregation is invited to offer names.*

O God, in you all is turned to light and all brokenness is healed. Look with compassion on us and on those for whom we pray that we may be recreated in wholeness, in love, and in compassion one for another. Amen.

## 118  *What is dying?*

What is dying? I am standing on the sea shore. A ship sails and spreads her white sails to the morning breeze and starts for the ocean. She is an object of beauty and I stand watching her till at last she fades on the horizon, and someone at my side says, 'She is gone.' Gone where? Gone from my sight, that is all; she is just as large in the masts, hull and spars as she was when I saw her, and just as able to bear her load of living freight to its destination.

The diminished size and total loss of sight is in me, not in her, and just at the moment when someone at my side says, 'She is gone', there are others who are watching her coming, and other voices take up a glad shout, 'There she comes', and that is DYING.

Bishop C. H. Brent (1862–1929)

## 119  *Death is nothing at all . . .*

Death is nothing at all . . .
I have only slipped away into the next room.
I am I and you are you.
Whatever we were to each other that we are still.
Call me by my old familiar name;
Speak to me in the easy way which you always used.
Put no difference in your tone,
Wear no false air of solemnity or sorrow.
Laugh as we have always laughed at the jokes we
     enjoyed together.

Play, smile, think of me, pray for me.
Let my name be the household word it always was.
Let it be spoken without effort, without the
     ghost of a shadow in it.
Life means all that it ever meant. It is the
     same as it ever was;
There is absolutely unbroken continuity.
What is this death but a negligible accident?
Why should I be out of your mind, because I am
     out of your sight?

I am but waiting for you, for an interval,
 somewhere very near,
Just around the corner.
All is well. Nothing is lost.
One brief moment and all will be as it was before.

Henry Scott Holland (1847–1918)

## 120 *They that love beyond the world . . .*

They that love beyond the world cannot be separated by it. Death cannot kill what never dies. Nor can spirits ever be divided that love and live in the same divine principle; the root and record of their friendship.

If absence be not death, neither is theirs.

Death is but crossing the world, as friends do the seas; they live in one another still. For they must needs be present, that love and live in that which is omnipresent.

This is the comfort of friends, that though they may be said to die, yet their friendship and society are, in the best sense, ever present, because immortal.

We think not a friend lost because he is gone into another room, nor because he is gone into another land; and into another world no man is gone, for that heaven which God created and this world are all one.

William Penn (1644–1718)

## 121 *Prayer of Quaker origin*

We give back to you, O God, those whom you gave us. You did not lose them when you gave them to us, and we do not lose them by their return to you. Your dear son has taught us that life is eternal and love cannot die. So death is only an horizon, and an horizon is only the limit of our sight. Open our eyes to see more clearly, and draw us closer to you that we may know that we are nearer to our loved ones, who are with you. You have told us that you are preparing a place for us: Prepare us also for that happy place, that where you are we may also be always, O Dear Lord of Life and Death.

**122**   *Prayer following pregnancy loss*

May the Holy One who blessed our mothers
Sarah, Rebeccah, Rachel, and Linda,
bless and protect [*mother*].
May the wounds she has suffered,
both physical and emotional,
soon be healed.
May she find comfort in knowing
that you, O God, weep with her.
May the Source of Life,
the Creator of all flesh,
restore her body to its rhythms
and her soul to its songs of joy.
As she and [*husband*] stand before you
help them to move forward
to feel the pain,
acknowledge the loss
and move forward.
May all of us here be committed to living
always aware that we are created in your image,
by caring, supporting, and loving one another
in times of pain as well as in times of joy.
As we have wept together,
so may we soon gather to rejoice together.
And let us all say
Amen.

**Diane Cohen**

**123**   *A psalm for the dying*

Relatives and friends, I am about to leave;
    my last breath does not say 'goodbye',
    for my love for you is truly timeless,
    beyond the touch of boney death.
I leave myself not to the undertaker,
    for the decoration in his house of the dead,
    but to your memory, with love.

I leave my thoughts, my laughter, my dreams
    to you whom I have treasured
    beyond gold and precious gems.
I give you what no thief can steal,
    the memories of our times together:
    the tender, love-filled moments,
    the successes we have shared,
    the hard times that brought us closer together
    and the roads we have walked side by side.

I also leave you a solemn promise
    that after I am home in the bosom of God,
    I will still be present,
    whenever and wherever you call on me.
My energy will be drawn to you
    by the magnet of our love.
Whenever you are in need, call me;
    I will come to you,
    with my arms full of wisdom and light
    to open up your blocked paths,
    to untangle your knots
    and to be your avenue to God.

And all I take with me as I leave
    is your love and the millions of memories
    of all that we have shared.
So I truly enter my new life
    as a millionaire.

Fear not nor grieve at my departure,
    you whom I have loved so much,
    for my roots and yours
    are forever intertwined.

Edward Hays

## 124    *Psalm of grief*

---

God I will curse you, for you are my enemy,
and my heart recoils from your touch.
Your loving kindness is a lie,
and your dealings are without mercy;
for I have seen the dying of my friend,
and I have witnessed the work of your hands upon her.

Daily you broke her body on the rack,
you exposed her skin to be scorched,
and into her belly you have thrust your knives.
You delivered her into the care of fools,
and those who were to heal her, handled her brutally.

In her desolation she prayed to be released,
but you turned your face from her plea.
At the sight of her agony you hardened your heart,
and carried her back from the grave.
You bestowed on her the pain of survival,
you caused her children to hope.

You laid your hand on her a second time,
you crushed her so that she could no more breathe.
You shrivelled up her bones with your fire,
she was dried out like a garment before the wind;
you consumed her flesh while she was yet alive.

How then shall I praise your compassion,
and how can I with integrity bless my God?

For like one who inflicts torture
beyond what her victim can bear,
so untenderly did you give her to death;
and as one who can no longer wrestle for life,
so did she find peace within your arms.

**Janet Morley**

## 125  *How shall I sing to God*

---

How shall I sing to God
when life is filled with gladness,
  loving and birth,
  wonder and worth?
I'll sing from the heart,
  thankfully receiving,
  joyful in believing.
This is my song, I'll sing it with love.

How shall I sing to God
when life is filled with bleakness,
    empty and chill,
    breaking my will?
I'll sing through my pain,
    angrily or aching,
    crying or complaining.
This is my song, I'll sing it with love.

How shall I sing to God
and tell my Saviour's story:
    passover bread,
    life from the dead?
I'll sing with my life,
    witnessing and giving,
    risking and forgiving,
This is my song, I'll sing it with love.

*Tune: Weaver Mill*                                    **Brian Wren**

## 126    *Hymn for William Benjamin Tillman*

We bring our gratitude to you
For guidance in our lives,
For those whose love has touched our hearts
And made our souls revive.

We bring our thanks for caring strength
That holds us on our way,
And brings us closer to your heart,
And drives our fear away.

For human hands can foster hope
And make our pathway clear,
Support us in our weaknesses
And make your Love come near.

We ask your blessing for these souls
As on through death they speed,
And pray that you will bless us too
With all the strength we need.

*Tune: St Anne*

**June Boyce-Tillman.**

# 8

## She stooped to look inside . . .
*Rites of remembrance*

She wept, she stooped, she looked, she saw. Mary of Magdala, apostle to the apostles, reveals the resurrection.

In remembering things painful to us, we weep, we stoop, we look, and we, too, often see resurrection. In getting down and looking into the black places of our lives we sometimes find angels.

This chapter contains first a simple liturgy for All Souls drawn to our attention by the vicar of a small country parish for whose congregation the service was both somewhat adventurous and deeply moving. Other memorial services here have been written when the death has been particularly shocking – the death of a child, or death in an accident.

'The healing of memories' is a phrase that reminds us of the healing power of remembering and some of the memorial liturgies here relate to deaths that occurred some time ago. But the power of remembrance and the need to face the past and let it be past, so as to be free to move into a happier future, is most strongly expressed by the liturgies for survivors of abuse. All the liturgies included here have been compiled by survivors themselves and/or their friends. **It needs to be emphasized that these liturgies, in particular, should take place in the context of, and be surrounded by, supportive and ongoing pastoral care. Jim Cotter has written:**

> Where violence has been done to the boundary between public and private life, particular care needs to be taken with any healing ritual and prayer that there is a secure boundary which cannot be intruded upon. Where that is so, there can be a measure of healing when a particular emotional wound can be exposed for acceptance and binding. Even though a group may be entirely supportive, parts of this process of healing may well need to be undertaken by the person alone or at most with one trusted other. There needs to be sufficient sense of privacy for acknowledgement of the violation and sufficient openness so that the violation may be held and to a degree healed.
>
> The person may already have shared the painful story in a counselling setting. It may be that some of the detail is still too painful to tell out loud. But it may be that the story can be told as part of the ritual, or that it can be written down and presented to the group.

# 127    *All Souls: an evening of remembrance and thanksgiving*

This is held on the Sunday evening nearest to All Souls, around the beginning of November. Those with very large numbers attending may want to use the first Sunday in Lent too. A notice is placed in the parish magazine and all those who we know have suffered a bereavement in the past year get a personal written invitation. This requires a little more co-ordination than just reading the burial register: a list of all cremations has to be kept, including those whilst the Rector was on holiday, and a note of local families who have been bereaved with the funeral service taking place elsewhere.

The invitations are sent out just over a fortnight in advance and include a tear-off slip for the names of those who have died to be included out loud in the prayers. A similar slip is in the magazine (with a note that some prefer to hold a name in silence, so we do both).

We print a special service sheet each time so that those attending have a service which is simple to follow and something to take home. Reading through the hymns at home can be very helpful. Right at the beginning of the service the Rector always tells people they can sit or stand as they feel the need; similarly it is OK to cry – for both men and women.

**Welcome, explanation of service and what to do with candles**

**Introduction**

**Sentence**

**Hymn** *All people that on earth do dwell*

**Confession and absolution**

**Choir hymn or anthem**

**Reading** *e.g. Lamentations 3.22–6, 31–3*

**Hymn** *Tell out my soul*

**Reading** *e.g. 1 Peter 1.3–9*

**Creed, Lord's Prayer and three collects**

**Hymn** *Rock of ages*

**Sermon**

**Hymn** *The Lord's my shepherd*

*At this point the lights are dimmed and the candles with stands, given out on entry, are lit.*

*We keep two minutes silence, standing.*

*Names, sent in, are prayed for aloud. (Alphabetical order helps people focus on 'their' name.)*

*All the candles are brought forward to be placed together around the Easter Candle and others on the nave altar in front of the pulpit.*

*Prayers for all who mourn.*

**Hymn** *Lord of all hopefulness*

**The Blessing**

David Edwards, George Cobb, Geoff Catchpole

## 128    *Remembering the dead*

### Remembering and naming aloud

Anniversaries and birthdays are important to mark; they help us to grieve and to begin the process of letting go of the dead and of reconnecting with the living. Letting go doesn't mean forgetting; we never do. The pain and grief are always there in some degree. Making the grief present may be more healing than hiding it.

- Look at old photos.
- Place a special photo in an important place; put flowers beside it.
- Gather friends and share stories.
- Set a place at the table.
- Light a candle.
- Talk to your loved one. (There's nothing 'crazy' about doing this. It has helped a lot of people cope with the days ahead.)
- Visit the cemetery.
- Place flowers at the grave.
- Give a gift in memory of your loved one. (This is especially good to do when a special occasion arises like a wedding at which the person is not present and is missed. The gift reminds all of the presence of her love in our hearts and acknowledges our remembrance of her on that occasion.)
- Do something for another in the person's name.

*Prayer:*

We remember this day ——, and the love with which you blessed us, O God
of our creation. Grant that our memories of the wonders and joys of life that
we shared may remain clear and as beautiful as they were on the day of their
occurrence. May we be forever bonded in your love; in Christ's name we
pray. Amen.

## Committing to life once again

- Make new relationships; invite others to your home for a meal.
- Discover new involvements; volunteer your time to a worthy cause.
- Learn to live *with* rather than *getting over* grief; talk about the one you
  love.
- Incorporate the deceased person's values into your own living: undertake a special project that your beloved would have done; choose a
  value of hers that you can accept as your own.

*Prayer:*

Hear my prayer, O God of love. Give me the courage to face life again, to
make new friendships, commitments, and to risk loving and losing love.
Embolden me to reach out to others, to try new things and to do them alone.
Let the love that I have known with —— be my surety that you will always
be with me until my life's end. Bless —— with your eternal love; in the name
of Christ I pray. Amen.

**Vienna Cobb Anderson**

## 129 *A service of prayer and remembrance*
### *for all those affected by road deaths and injuries*

Road death services started in Coventry Cathedral in 1992; the hope is to
have the Sunday after Remembrance Sunday observed widely as a day of
remembrance for those who have died on the roads.

City centre services bring together bereaved relatives, drivers, and the
emergency staff who are all deeply affected by a level of road death and
injury that is often taken for granted.

> *At this service there were counsellors at the side of the church – identified
> by a white badge – for anyone who might need someone to talk to
> afterwards.*

**Words of welcome**

**Opening hymn** *Immortal, invisible, God only wise*

**Readings** *Genesis 3.22–4: The first humans learn of knowledge, of good and evil. Proverbs 1.20–5: The call of wisdom.*

**Responsorial psalm** *Psalm 8*

O God our God, how glorious is your name over all the earth!
When I look at your heavens, the work of your hands, the moon and stars which you created –
Who are we that you should be mindful of us, that you should care for us?
Yet you have made us little less than gods, and crowned us with glory and honour.
You have given us rule over the works of your hands, putting all things under our feet:
God, our God, how glorious is your name over all the earth!

**Prayers**

Creator God, we give you thanks for all that you have made, and for the gift of knowledge, enabling us to share in the works of creation.
We thank you for food and shelter, and for the great discoveries made by humankind – for fire, for the wheel, for wood from the forest and minerals from under the earth and sea.
We praise you for the free will which enables us to make choices.
We meditate now on the choices we have made throughout history – we have used the gifts of the earth to make ploughshares and swords – we have used them to travel and enrich our lives, but also to endanger and destroy the lives of ourselves and others.
     **Kyrie eleison (Lord, have mercy).**

We confess that we have turned our back on wisdom, on the discernment which would help us know good from evil.
     **Kyrie eleison (Lord, have mercy).**

We confess that we have created a society in which the freedoms of some are gained at the expense of others, and in which we have fought wars and allowed many to die and be injured to protect those freedoms.
     **Kyrie eleison (Lord, have mercy).**

We confess that we hardly know the soaring face of your justice, and that in our own pale reflection of it we are content to leave many people with a

burning sense of injustice throughout their lives.
**Kyrie eleison (Lord, have mercy).**

Loving and just God, we need your wisdom and compassion. We gather all these prayers for ourselves and our world in the words that Jesus taught us:

ALL    Our Father . . .

## Hymn *Lord of beauty, thine the splendour*

## Readings *Matthew 27.45–6, 50, 55–6: The death of Jesus*

## Response

ALL    Yahweh, hear my prayer;
let my cry for help come to you.
Since I am in trouble,
do not conceal your face from me.
Turn and listen to me.
When I call, respond to me quickly.
For my days are vanishing like smoke,
my bones burn like fire,
my heart withers like scorched grass;
even my appetite is gone.
Yahweh, hear my prayer;
let my cry for help come to you.                    (Psalm 102)

## Prayers

We have come here today, loving God, because we are hurting. We have all been involved in some way in death and injury on the roads.
**Kyrie eleison (Lord, have mercy).**

Many have lost sons and daughters, grandchildren, husbands and wives, mothers, fathers, brothers, sisters and good friends. Their deaths were sudden and violent, or they suffered for hours and days before losing their struggle for life. Their loss has left a great hole in our lives that we feel nothing can fill.
**Kyrie eleison (Lord, have mercy).**

Some are ambulance drivers, policemen and women, doctors and nurses, and ministers, and have to deal with the trauma of responding to emergencies and telling relatives what has happened. Sometimes we find it impossible to live with our memories.
**Kyrie eleison (Lord, have mercy).**

Many are drivers, and some have been behind the wheel when someone was killed or injured. Others know just how close they have come to that nightmare. Many of us cannot sleep or find peace of mind for thinking about what has happened.

> **Kyrie eleison (Lord, have mercy).**

All of us look to you for justice and healing. We cry out for the healing touch of the living to bring us back from the world of the dead – we cry out for the witness of the living to bring justice for those who have died.

> **Kyrie eleison (Lord, have mercy).**

Most of all, we have come to remember. We bring before you, on our own behalf, and on behalf of those who cannot be here through distance, illness, or distress, the names of all those we love who have died on our roads.

(adapted from prayer by Alan Luff)

*Here the names are read out from the Oak Leaves, and the basket of leaves is placed on the communion table.*

### Prayer

God, whose only son was crucified for us, bless us all as we remember these your servants who have died. We commend them, and all those whose names are not known to us, to your eternal care. May our memories of them be joyful ones. May we feel their presence amongst all your saints who witness to you in every age, and may we all at the last be united in your presence.

**Solo** *Pie Iesu, Domine: dona eis requiem – sempiternam requiem. (Holy Jesus, Lord, grant them rest – everlasting rest)*

**Reading** *John 20.25b–27: Jesus entrusts his mother and his friend to each other's love and care*

**Hymn** *We cannot measure how you heal* (**140**)

### The Peace

MINISTER
The peace and love of Christ be with you.

PEOPLE
And also with you.

MINISTER
Let us share Christ's peace with those around us.

*(Those who wish take the hands of those around and offer them the peace of Christ.)*

**Reading** *Romans 8.18–25, 35–9: Paul tells us that nothing, not even death, can separate us from God's love.*

## Sermon

**Hymn** *Now the green blade riseth from the buried grain*

## Prayers

We thank you, God of Love, for bringing us together to worship you today; for the opportunity to lay our grief and pain before you, and to be united with others who have been affected by the same loss and pain.
    **Deo gratias (Thanks be to God).**

We thank you for helping us to understand more about all the gifts of creation, of knowledge, and of wisdom, and about our common responsibility for each other and for the world we share.
    **Deo gratias (Thanks be to God).**

We thank you for offering us, in the face of death, the loving care of the living – for those in the emergency services who have tended our loved ones and shown care and compassion to us, for colleagues who have supported us in our work, for those of our friends and relatives, and also for complete strangers, who have come to our aid in times of great need.
    **Deo gratias (Thanks be to God).**

We thank you, above all things, for the birth and life of Jesus Christ, your Word, your Wisdom made flesh, born as one of us so that all who know him may also know your wisdom as she walks the streets of our world. We thank you for his crucifixion and resurrection, which has bridged the awful chasm between death and new life, and restored to us the hope of life where life has no right to be.
    **Deo gratias (Thanks be to God).**

Cast away from us, God of Light, all the sorrows and shadows of our lives on earth. Where your light seems faint and far off, sustain us in your love; where we see the new dawn of love and justice, bring us to the clear light of day, and where your light is bright for us in this life, bring us to the searing purity of your eternal Light and Life.

## The blessing

God's care and love surround you,
God's promise re-unite you with all those you love,
and God's justice bring all of us to a new

heaven and a new earth,
and may the blessing of God, Creator,
Redeemer, and Sustainer, be with you all,
now and always. Amen.

**Final hymn** *Now is eternal life*

*(Acorns were handed out after the service as a sign of new life.)*

**Anna Briggs**

## 130   *Act of acknowledgement and farewell after an abortion*

It is often not until many years after the event that a woman gets in touch with the sorrow, anger, remorse, etc. associated with having 'solved' the problem of an unwanted pregnancy by means of abortion. Since abortion was in the past, and is still, usually a guilty secret, open mourning is difficult, even when the feelings are finally owned.

The following act of acknowledgement and farewell arose out of such a situation – where it was felt that some form of ritual would help in the healing process. A woman can follow these steps on her own, but it would be preferable to share the proceedings with a sensitive friend or a small supportive group.

> *An intuitive decision is made as to the gender of the foetus (if this is unknown), and a name is chosen.*
>
> *An honest letter is written to the aborted child, explaining the circumstances in which the termination of pregnancy took place (e.g. expressing the pain involved in making such a decision). Feelings at the present time may also be expressed.*
>
> *A 'place of remembrance' is chosen in which to say goodbye. A decision is taken as to whether – in this place – a tree should be planted, a cairn built, a small cross erected, petals scattered . . . or similar. The appropriate preparations are made.*
>
> *The woman goes to the place of remembrance soon after dawn (a clear sunny day helps greatly . . .), and slowly offers these words and actions:*
>
> *(Kneel, sit, stand, or whatever feels comfortable. It may be appropriate to touch the womb area.)*

I name you ——, and in naming you, I acknowledge that you were a potential human being, a child of the universe of God.

I choose this place in which to make memorial to you, and I ask for God's presence and blessing here. *(Slowly and with reverence, plant tree, build cairn – or similar.)*

In this place, I ask God's forgiveness – and yours – for withholding my love from you, for reacting to your presence in my body – and thus surrounding you – with fear/loathing/terror/dread . . . and for giving you no experience of human caring to remember now. And I ask forgiveness for denying you the pathway to life, for putting others into the position of doing violence to you, and for giving you no dignity in death.

Now I offer you my love and my sorrow.

And I commit you to the loving mother arms of God, in the faith that all fear and hurt and loneliness have passed for you now, that in God your potential is realized – and that you have found the wholeness and happiness held out to us all by the Love at the heart of life.

And although I will not forget you, I let you go. *(The letter to the child may now be burned, or torn up and buried. Or a balloon, kite or small downy feather may be released.)*

I ask God's healing for myself and all whom I involved in your death.

May peace come to us all.

Kate Compston

## 131     *A litany of remembrance*

---

In the rising of the sun
and in its going down,
we remember them.

In the blowing of the wind
and in the chill of winter,
we remember them.

In the blueness of the sky
and in the warmth of summer,
we remember them.

In the rustling of leaves
and in the beauty of autumn,
we remember them.

In the beginning of the year
and when it ends,
we remember them.

When we are lost
and sick at heart,
we remember them.

When we have joys
we yearn to share,
we remember them.

So long as we live,
they too shall live,
for they are part of us,
and we remember them.

All humankind are one vast family,
this world our home.
We sleep beneath one roof,
the starry sky.
We warm ourselves before one hearth,
the blazing sun.
Upon one floor of soil we stand,
and breath one air,
and drink one water,
and walk the night
beneath one luminescent moon.
The children of one God we are,
brothers and sisters of one blood,
and members in one worldwide
family of God.

From the Book of Remembrance:
Cathedral of St Paul the Apostle, Los Angeles, California

## 132  *The Eucharist for the abused*

### Opening sentence

PRESIDENT 1   I am come that you may have life, life in all its fullness.

**Hymn** *All shall be well, in love enclosed* (**143**)

## Bidding

PRESIDENT 1

We are here to celebrate the Eucharist for the abused. We shall offer by name those known to us. We shall grieve with those who still weep and share the confusion of those who do not yet know the source of their dispossession. We shall mourn their loss of innocence, understand their sense of powerlessness and accept their anger. We believe in the power of the Eucharist to transform the ties that bind people to their past and we shall celebrate this act on behalf of those who cannot yet do it for themselves.

We shall bring into the open love of God the fearful, guilty secrets of a society that exploits and violates vulnerability and sexuality, still twisting love into the shape of a crucified stranger. We believe that naming abuse destroys the evil power of secrecy and makes it easier for others to speak out, be heard and be made whole.

We do this in the power of God, the vulnerable Lover. We call now on the angels to come close to us, surround us and protect us while we centre ourselves in that love.

After Janet Morley's poem there will be five minutes of silence in the darkness. If this is done with the eyes open it may help to keep us aware of the presence of others.

## Poem

READER 1

and you held me and there were no words
and there was no time and you held me
and there was only wanting and
being held and being filled with wanting
and I was nothing but letting go
and being held
and there were no words and there
needed to be no words
and there was no terror      only stillness
and I was wanting nothing and
it was fullness and it was like aching for God
and it was touch and warmth and
darkness and no time and no words and we flowed
and I flowed and I was not empty

and I was given up to the dark and
in the darkness      I was not lost
and the wanting was like fullness and I could
hardly hold it and I was held and
you were dark and warm and without time and
without words and you held me

(Janet Morley)

*Five minutes' silence. At the end, subdued lights.*

## The healing

PRESIDENT 2

With us today is ——; her (*his*) body, her (*his*) feelings and her (*his*) spirit have been injured. We are here to mourn with her (*him*), cry out in anger with her (*him*) and bring her (*him*) into God's healing power.

We love and affirm ——. Although s/he has been injured, s/he is not destroyed. Although s/he has been humiliated, s/he has not lost her integrity. Although love for her (*him*) was violated, s/he has not lost her capacity to love.

We affirm her (*his*) wholeness, her (*his*) goodness, her (*his*) truthfulness, her (*his*) integrity, her (*his*) ability to love.

We dispel the forces of destruction and the abuse of trust and power which seek to make her (*him*) a victim.

## Speaking out

THE SURVIVOR

*The person/people who have been abused may speak, if they wish, about what has happened – maybe from a prepared statement if that is easier.*

## Preparing the oil

Some of you have been given small bottles containing the essences of various fragrances. Will you each in turn put drops of the essence in the bowl of oil in the middle, where they will be mixed. They have been specially chosen for the healing of ——, for the healing of her (*his*) deepest wounds. During it a song taken from a Celtic source will be sung.

*During the following which is sung as a solo, each of the seven people places two drops of the fragrance in the bowl where it is mixed.*

## Song *Give thou to me, O God* (**142**)

## The Anointing

*One of those present lights a central candle.*

PRESIDENT 2

We light this candle as we go down with —— into the depths of her being to meet the hidden things, the creatures of her dreams, the storehouse of forgotten memories, hurts and strengths.

——, listen to the pain of your wounds and live from the depths of them, making them the source of your creating. Meet the wounded, frightened child within, with adult, caring strength. She will give you a precious gift.

Recall the words of God that are never spoken without achieving the task for which they were given:

PRESIDENT 2

I am the ground of your beseeching.

*The anointer touches the base of the spine with these words:*

From violence to your humanity, may you be healed.

ALL    **May you be healed.**

PRESIDENT 2

I will hold you in the hollow of my hand.

*The anointer touches the abdomen with the words:*

From violence to your sexuality, may you be healed.

ALL    **May you be healed.**

PRESIDENT 2

You are called by my name; you are mine.

*The anointer touches the solar plexus with the words:*

From violence to your identity, may you be healed.

ALL    **May you be healed.**

PRESIDENT 2

I have loved you with an everlasting love and with loving kindness have I drawn you.

*The anointer touches the heart and says:*

From violence to your feelings, may you be healed.

ALL    **May you be healed.**

PRESIDENT 2

All power in heaven and earth is given to me . . . And lo, I am with you always.

*The anointer touches the throat and says:*

From violence to your ability to speak out with confidence, may you be healed.

ALL    **May you be healed.**

PRESIDENT 2

You will know the truth and the truth will set you free.

*The anointer touches the forehead and says:*

From violence to your mind, may you be healed.

ALL    **May you be healed.**

PRESIDENT 2

To the one who overcometh, I will give a crown of life.

*The anointer touches the crown of the head and says:*

From violence to your spirit, may you be healed.

ALL    **May you be healed.**

PRESIDENT 2

The Creator Spirit surrounds you, upholds you on all sides, flows around you, caresses you, loves you and wills you to be whole.

Love your body, for it is the temple of the whole-making Spirit and the only means of expression it has.

Love your mind, for it will give you the understanding to discern the wisdom required to endure.

Love your spirit, for it will help you to grasp and retain the eternal values.

## The oblation and absolution

THE SURVIVOR

*She picks up the central candle and places it in a sand bowl on the altar with the words:*

I place this candle on the altar as an offering of myself.

Next to it I place these for those who have abused me.

*She names them one by one. There is a short silence.*

PRESIDENT 2

The Lord hears our prayer.

ALL    Thanks be to God.

PRESIDENT 2

Please add to these, candles for anyone known to you who has been abused. Feel free to name them and talk about them if you wish. Feel free also to stay silent. After each there will be a short period of silence and then the versicle and response:

PRESIDENT 2
> The Lord hears our prayer.

ALL
> Thanks be to God.

THE SURVIVOR
> There is one more task for these candles to do. On these flames of love I place the account of my abuse and its legacy – suicidal despair, various forms of self abuse, bitterness, violence, hatred, cynicism and a crude desperate search for a loving attention which alienated people from me and drove away the very affection for which I sought. May they be consumed by love.

> *The paper is burned. The full lighting is switched on.*

ALL
> We are the body of Christ. May our only wounds be these:
> the wound that we cannot avoid because we belong to each other,
>     and feel and hear the murmur of the world's pain;
> the wound of a sense of compassion for others;
> the wound of a deep longing for God, the source of life and love,
>     deep within us and far beyond us.

PRESIDENT 2
> Let us offer one another absolution, turning to our neighbour and saying: *God forgives you. Forgive others. Forgive yourself.*

> *The mutual absolution.*

## The Ministry of the Word

PRESIDENT
> Let us say together the Collect for Purity.

ALL
> Almighty God, unto whom all hearts be open . . .

READER 2
> A reading from the Lady Julian of Norwich:
> And in this he showed me something small, no bigger than a hazelnut, lying in the palm of my hand, as it seemed to me, and it was round as a ball. I looked at it with the eye of my understanding and thought: What can this be? I was amazed that it could last, for I thought that because of its littleness it would suddenly have fallen into nothing. And I was answered in my understanding: It lasts and always will, because God loves it; and thus everything has being through the love of God.

### Psalm 126

*Antiphon: Yea, the Lord hath done great things for us already: whereof we rejoice.*

1. When the Lord turned again the captivity of Sion: then were we like unto them that dream.
2. Then was our mouth filled with laughter: and our tongue with joy.
3. Then said they among the heathen: the Lord hath done great things for them.
4. Yea, the Lord hath done great things for us already: whereof we rejoice.
5. Turn our captivity, O Lord: as the rivers in the south.
6. They that sow in tears: shall reap in joy.
7. They that now go on their way weeping, and bear forth good seed: shall doubtless come again with joy and bring their sheaves with them.

   Glory be to the Father and to the Son; and to the Holy Ghost. As it was in the beginning, is now and ever shall be. World without end. Amen. (BCP)

## The New Testament reading *Revelation 21.1–7: 'The one that overcometh shall inherit all things'* (Reader 3)

## The Gospel *John 15.1–3: 'I am the true vine'* (Reader 4)

## The Sermon

## The Offertory

*The bread is brought to the altar with the words: The bread of suffering.*
*The wine is brought to the altar with the words: The wine of celebration.*

## The Eucharistic Prayer

*(Third Eucharistic Prayer, Rite A, ASB)*

PRESIDENT 3

*Preface*
And now we give you thanks that through your Incarnation you entered our human vulnerability and that through your violent death and glorious resurrection showed us the redemptive power of suffering, opening up a vision of hope to all survivors of abuse.

*Silence will be kept.*

PRESIDENT 3
As our Saviour taught us, so we pray:
ALL    Our Father . . .
PRESIDENT 3
We break this bread to share in the body of Christ.

ALL    Though we are many, we are one body, because we all share in one bread.

Lamb of God . . .

PRESIDENT 3
We shall each serve the other with the words:
The bread of life.
The cup of salvation.

*The elements are passed around.*

## Post-Communion sentence

PRESIDENT 4
I am the way, the truth and the life.

ALL    We praise you, O God: we acknowledge that you are our Sustainer.
All the cosmos worships you: Everlasting Source of all things.
All the angels sing aloud to you, so do the heavens and all their powers: Cherubim and Seraphim continually do cry:
Holy, holy, holy is the great Mystery that draws all things within Itself: Heaven and earth are full of the majesty of your glory.
The glorious followers of Ancient Wisdom: praise you.
The dancing chorus of the Joyful Ones: praises you.
The holy community of those who suffer: praises you.
The blessed Household of those of integrity throughout the world: praises you.
The regenerative cycle of the natural world: praises you.
The ordered splendour of the universe: praises you.
The Author: of all-encompassing Goodness.
And your Child, Jesus: who is called Emmanuel.
And also the Holy Spirit: who renews and restores us.
You are clothed in glory, O Christ: You are the everlasting Child of the Eternal Family.
Thanks to Mary's willingness: you were born as a baby here on earth.
By undergoing the sharpness of death: you opened up the possibility of heaven to all believers.
We believe: that you are the One to whom we are ultimately answerable.
We, therefore, pray you to be with us in our vulnerability: and show us the possibility of its redemption through your own death and resurrection.
Make us to be included in the merry company of your Saints: in everlasting glory.

Lover of all, be with us: for we belong to you.

Sustain us: and keep the vision of hope alive in us.

Day by day: we magnify you.

And we shall continually worship your Being: to the end of time.

Be true to your promise as the One who watches over us: to protect us from evil this night.

O Lamb of God, be merciful to us: be gentle with us.

O Maker of all things, let your joy gladden our hearts: for we have faith in you.

O Faithful One, it is in you that I have trusted: please do not let me down.

(Version of the *Te Deum* by June Boyce-Tillman)

## Blessing

PRESIDENT 4

Fall in love with living,
Wrestling with the chaos and the pain
Within yourself and within the world.
Join the celebration of life,
Dancing with the angels and the clowns.
And may the God of peace and joy,
Who is continually making all things new,
Embrace you
As a partner
In the divine creating.

Let us offer one another a sign of peace.

*The kiss of peace is exchanged.*

## Closing hymn *We shall go out, with hope of resurrection* (**141**)

## Dismissal

PRESIDENT 4

Go in the peace of Christ

ALL    Thanks be to God.

**June Boyce-Tillman** (with acknowledgements to Janet Morley, Jim Cotter, Rosemary Radford Reuther and Teresa Parker)

# 133 *Liturgy for a hard journey*

## Introduction

This service was prepared for someone dealing in a painful way with abuse in her early life.

### Greeting

LEADER
   Life is a journey on many different roads
PEOPLE **but God is always with us.**

LEADER Sometimes we lift our faces to the sun
PEOPLE **and God is with us.**

LEADER But then there is the hard journey
   through pathways of pain
   and fears in dark places.
PEOPLE **But God is with us.**
   **Nothing can separate us**
   **from the love of God in Christ Jesus.**

## Who we are on the journey

LEADER O God who travels with us in the shadows,
   you know who we are.
   We long for life which is full and free.
   We long to know the truth
   and we want to leave behind us
   all the things which hold us back.

   *(Silent reflection)*

   We want to move forward in faith
   but the way seems so dangerous
   and we stand in helpless fear
   before the hiddenness in our past
   and in our future.

   *(Silent reflection)*

LEADER Stand beside us, gentle Christ.
PEOPLE Walk before us, brave Jesus.
   Call us on into life, Holy Spirit.
   Amen.

## We are not alone

LEADER Hear the Word to us in Jesus Christ:
I will never leave you nor forsake you,
even to the end of time.
I will walk with you
down the pathways of death
and lead you to eternal life.
Amen.

PEOPLE Amen.

## The Word *Isaiah 43.1–5; 49.13–16(a)*

## Lighting of the candle

LEADER The candle is the sign of the light, warmth and power of the Holy Spirit.

*(The candle is lit and the person on the hard journey is asked to come near to the candle.)*

LEADER See the light for your journey
and believe that the Spirit always
moves ahead of you.

Stretch out your hands
and feel the warmth of the flame.
It is the warmth of the love of God for you
and our love for you.
That love will surround you wherever you go.

Take into yourself the power of the Holy Spirit
that you may be given courage
for the next step on the journey.

*(The person on the journey kneels and those present gather around for the anointing and the laying on of hands.)*

LEADER We are the Body of Christ for you.
As our hands are upon you
so you are one with Jesus Christ
who heals us
comforts us
protects us
and lifts us up to walk forward again.
As we anoint you with the sign of the cross,
we claim the power
of God the loving parent

God in Jesus Christ
and God the Holy Spirit for you.
Receive all these gifts
and claim the life that is before you.

### Prayers of intercession
*for the particular person.*
*(The candle is given to the person.)*

### The Blessing Song

ALL    'May the blessing of God
go before you . . .'

(Miriam Therese Winter)

**Dorothy McRae-McMahon**

## 134    *Liturgy of healing from sexual abuse*

---

The setting for this liturgy is not a group meeting. It has been included as a resource – something that can be adapted to each person's needs. It is a guideline, to be shared with the person concerned, who should make the final decisions. It is offered in love from one woman to another.

The material has been gathered from the sharing of women who have been victims both in Aotearoa New Zealand and beyond.

Physical setting: A place that seems safe *to the abused person* must be chosen.

Consider also the use of some of the following: the altar, or table with white cloth; candles, flowers, a cross, the Bible, icons, earth, oil, salt, incense or pot-pourri, music, water, vestments, white veil, personal symbols.

Music, silence, poetry, shared actions and/or words can be used.

It needs to have a time of letting go (which may or may not include confession and forgiveness).

It may include the ritual of laying-on of hands, symbolic washing, anointing, dance, or the Eucharist.

### Prelude *Quiet music, especially chosen.*

### Greetings and prayer

VOICE 1 God be with you.
ALL    And also with you.

VOICE 1 Let us pray:

Creating God, who formed us in our mother's womb
and called us by name:
breathe into us your living Spirit
and pour forth the waters of your healing.
Embrace N in your delighted, fearless love,
that she and all who gather here may claim the gift
you gave us at our birth — our humanness.

Walk with us on the journey to freedom, we pray,
for the sake of the world you love.

ALL     Amen.

### Readings *(any or all of the following)*

*Biblical: 2 Samuel 13.1–20 (selected verses); Romans 8.35–9*

*By his wounds you have been healed*

O God,
through the image of a woman
crucified on a cross*
I understand at last.
For over half my life
I have been ashamed
of the scars I bear.
These scars tell an ugly story,
a common story,
about a girl who is the victim
when a man acts out his fantasies.

In the warmth, peace and sunlight
of your presence I was able to
uncurl the tightly clenched fists.
For the first time
I felt your suffering presence
with me in that event.
I have known you as a vulnerable baby,
as a brother, and as a father.
Now I know you as a woman.
You were there with me
as the violated girl
caught in helpless suffering.

The chains of shame and fear
no longer bind my heart and body.

A slow fire of compassion and forgiveness
is kindled.
My tears fall now
for man as well as woman.

You, God,
can make our violated bodies
vessels of love and comfort
to such a desperate man.
I am honoured
to carry this womanly power
within my body and soul.

You were not ashamed of your wounds.
You showed them to Thomas
as marks of your ordeal and death.
I will no longer be ashamed of mine.
I will bear them gracefully.
They tell a resurrection story.

(Anonymous)

* 'Crucified Woman', a seven-foot high bronze by Almuth Lutkenhaus, is hung at the entrance
of Emmanuel College in Toronto, Canada.

### Shedding: Psalm of a rape survivor

God, this is serious:
This is the worst thing that has ever happened to me.
I am torn and sore, I am violated, I have suffered an outrage:
I am reduced to my elements.
I am stripped of courtesy, social graces, theory, conscience,
    the oughts of a lifetime:
I am shattered by grief at the loss of myself
And nothing can ever be the same again.

*God, in my grief and loss I do not know what Wholeness means:
Show me the way forward.*

God, contain my fear:
For I have been very frightened, and I am still afraid.
In the middle of the night I wake up trembling:
My dreams are full of menace.
Some days the good light of your beautiful world is
    suddenly dimmed by the colour of terror.
There are times when I cannot bear to be alone:
Yet I no longer know whom I can trust.

I mourn the enjoyment of solitude, God:
I grieve for my self-assurance:
I mourn the death of my confidence in the good will of men.

*God, in my fear I do not know what Trust means:*
*Show me the way forward.*

God, license my anger:
For I am your perfect creation, and I have been broken.
Do not stifle my cries of rage and pain:
For they are my rallying-cry to my shattered self.
Do not let me deny my anger to meet the requirements of others,
   however distressed they may be, or however dear:
I need all my own resources for my own re-assembly.
Do not burden me with those who would frown on my want
   of ladylike self-control:
For I am not ready, yet, for good manners;
Keep away from me those who, for their own comfort,
   would urge on me the beauty of fairness and tolerance:
For I am not ready, yet, to be fair;
Do not let me be distracted by those who would soothe me too
   early:
For I am not ready, yet, to be calm;
Nor by those who would counsel forgiveness too soon:
For I am not ready, yet, to forgive.
You and I, God, have first a repair job to hand:
Into that work I would channel the energy born of my anger.

*God, in my rage I do not know what Forgiveness means:*
*Show me the way forward.*

Indwelling God, work with me now:
For we are collaborators in my healing.
I am made to your plan, this vivid spirit, this good body:
Skin and striped muscle, bone, hair, blood,
The chambers of heart and cochlea, the labyrinth of lungs.
Smooth moistness of eyes and orifices, tough lacy net of nerves:
I am indeed most fearfully and wonderfully made!
And nor am I made once for all:
I am not made quiescent, I am constantly renewed.
Beneath my bruised skin, my mind's agony,
Are vast, deep regions unaware of torment:
Where, cell by cell, our unceasing work of repair and renewal goes
   on.
Even as I cry to you, God, for healing

Even as I shed terror, tears, laments, grief and loud anger
The bruises fade, the fabric of my good body is renewed –
Hair, skin, the delicate soft membrane of unseen inner fastnesses –
And the heavy load of violation shrinks:
The cells that knew the outrage live out their time and fall away,
    their history expunged.
And the thing that I know was done to me is shed:
Cell following neutral cell, in passionless tiny death.
Back to the common storehouse of your endless re-creation.
I am made new when I am ready to be new.

*God, if in remembering too much, I do not know what Healing*
    *means:*
*Show me the way forward.*

Generous God, who made me your perfect creation,
Who programmed my good body for self-renewal.
Thank you for giving me the gift of shedding.
I know I can never forget what happened to me:
But I know that, with your help, I will get well.

*Show me the way forward.*

(P. A. Sandle)

*A time follows when N will share if she wishes.*

## Community lament

VOICE 1
My sister, you have been injured; your body, your feelings, your
spirit have been wounded.
VOICE 2 We mourn with you. We lament with you. We cry out in anger. We
are filled with grief.

## Affirmation

VOICE 1 We love and affirm you.
VOICE 2 You have been injured, but not destroyed.
You have been demeaned
but you have not lost your dignity.
You have been subjected to ugliness
but you are beautiful.
Evil has gripped you but you are good.
The lie was all around you in the silence,
but you are truthful.

We affirm you, N, to be whole.

*Using a sprig of rosemary or other greenery, water may be sprinkled over N and then around the room and over others present. As this happens, the following could be read:*

N, with this water we commit you to that journey into freedom, the washing away of all evils which stain our human story.

We send you forth to claim the promise of new life; to reclaim God's original blessing, and to live again in harmony with all creation.

*If anointing is to take place, it can be done in silence, or the words from A New Zealand Prayerbook – He Karakia Mihinare o Aotearoa p. 743 could be used.*

*N comes forward and as friends surround her the time together is completed with these words of blessing:*

The blessing of God, the source of love,
of the Anointed One, love in human flesh,
and of the Holy Spirit, love's power,
be upon you this day and for ever. Amen.

Dorothy Brooker and others

## 135 *Prayer of thanksgiving*

LEADER   We take apples, symbol of the fruitfulness of creation,
RESPONSE   God's creativity in the world.

L.   We will cut into the fruit because Christ, the source of life was wounded and bruised, so that we might understand the nature of suffering,

R.   The wounds of creation.

L.   We take honey, symbol of all that is sweet and pleasant in life,

R.   Joy at the heart of creation.

L.   We will savour the sharpness and the sweetness because pain and joy are closely interwoven in a pattern that is difficult to comprehend or separate,

R.   The warp and the weft of living.

L.   The Spirit of God be with you;

R.   And with your spirit.

L.   Lift up your hearts;

R.   We lift them up to God.

L.   Let us give thanks to God;
R.   It is right to offer thanks and praise.

L.   For the story of creation,
     For the inner energy of life,
     Crying out to be born and struggling to maturity,
R.   Thanks be to God.

L.   For those who have laboured to see justice and truth prevail,
     For the prophets who have struggled within themselves and the world,
R.   Thanks be to God.

L.   For Jesus of Nazareth, who is called Christ,
     Living out the truth of God
     And bringing Good News to the poor and oppressed
     Of his day
     And our day,
R.   Thanks be to God.

L.   For the Spirit of God, who moves in our hearts,
     Blending the grieving with the joy,
     Helping us to discern truth from falsehood,
     And keeping hope alive in the midst of despair,
R.   Thanks be to God.

L.   And so, with all the cosmos,
     The natural world with all its creative splendour,
     Our forebears who have helped to fashion and shape
     That world and our lives,
     The angels and archangels who continually hold
     All things in loving truth,
     With all who, now and in the future,
     Yearn for justice and truth, we worship:

R.   Holy, holy, holy, God of power and strength,
     Heaven and earth are full of your glory,
     Hosanna in the highest.

     Blessed are those who come in God's truth,
     Hosanna in the highest.

L.   We belong to one another and all creation
     And, through this bond
     To Jesus,
     Who, on the day before he was handed over to those who would abuse
         him,

Had a meal with his friends,
Eating and drinking with them.

And so we eat together,
As a symbol of our sharing a common humanity
Which is a mixture of sorrow and joy
And binds us all together.

R. We celebrate the grief, born of dying,
We proclaim the possibility of new life,
We declare our intention to live in that hope.

L. So, we are joined together, women and men of faith,
With all who seek to live in God's truth.
We live and work together in a shared vision
Of a cosmos, filled with peace and justice.
We keep alive the memory of the crucifixion of Jesus
Together with his resurrection
And root the possibility of our own new life
Within this hope.

R. Strengthening God,
Take away all that prevents us from achieving this end.
Strengthening God,
Take away all that prevents us from achieving this end.
Strengthening God,
Give us true peace.

L. We pray that we will be made new to live our life to the full
And make this vision a reality.

We cut this fruit to recall
The sharpness of the wounds of God
We dip it into the honey to recall
The sweetness of God.

We offer it to one another with the words:
The sharpness of God
And the sweetness of God.

**June Boyce-Tillman**

# 136    *Meditation on the Collect for Purity*

Lord, hear our prayer
   and let our cry
     come to you.

Lord, I was too small to pray.
   Why did my cry
     not come to you?

ALMIGHTY GOD

   I didn't know you
   you were so insignificant
   compared with him
   the one who abused me . . .

   He was almighty
   he held the power
   over me – he was
   so much bigger
   you see.

   You may have
   created but
   he destroyed
   my world.

TO WHOM ALL HEARTS ARE OPEN

   How vulnerable you made me
   wide open in my deepest self
   yet you did not give me any safety strategies
   through your blindness to the realities
   of your world
   my heart was ripped open
   before it was full grown
   and was it divine arrogance
   that kept you from intervening
   from owning me
   at the point of violation?

ALL DESIRES KNOWN

   But there was no desiring
   only repulsion and shame

I guess in your holiness
these undesirables cannot be known.

Is that why you were silent?

## AND FROM WHOM NO SECRETS ARE HIDDEN

but there were secrets
and they were hidden
embedded inside of me
for years and never once
did I hear you say
you knew what was going on.

Do you know how scary it is
to feel more knowing than you?

## CLEANSE THE THOUGHTS OF OUR HEARTS
## BY THE INSPIRATION OF YOUR HOLY SPIRIT

I had to do it myself
I could not wait
for your love and goodness
and the thoughts of my heart
are never free from memory
they crowd out even your Spirit
it is too soon to risk openness
even with you.

## SO THAT WE MAY TRULY LOVE YOU

God, this time it has to be my way
I have to start at the beginning
I want to know what love is
and when I discover it
it will be me
I will give my true love to.

This time God, you have to go second.

## AND WORTHILY PRAISE YOUR HOLY NAME

The naming was the hardest part
the words hung in my throat
I could not name the shame
that I felt
nor how unworthy I felt

of even just being alive.

But I did name it
the hiddenness and hurt
to name the unholy
to speak what had been
unspeakable
it was then I caught
a glimpse
of the possibility
of being holy.

## THROUGH OUR SAVIOUR JESUS CHRIST

Who are you that you ask me to call you Saviour?
When I really needed saving
from the sins of a sexual abuser
when I was locked up in silence
when I was isolated and surrounded by confusion
where were you, Saviour of the world?

Every Sunday I was told
he seeks and saves every soul
but I got overlooked or missed
can you imagine how small
that made me feel
as if I wasn't there at all?

## AMEN

I shall never again say
yes or so be it
to anyone
not unless it is healthy
and good for me
unless I choose it.

Not amen,
but No!
Not amen
but the yes
of a free and whole person
who is me.

Erice Fairbrother

**137**   *Womenspace midwinter song 1990*

Sun at stand -still, Black the night, Deep - est dark - ness shel -ters

light.__ 1. North   is   dark  -  ness,  South   is   song,__ West   be -
._____ 2. Past   re - mem  -  ber,   Fu - ture   see,__  Now   re -

-hind__ us,   East__   is   strong_____   Sun   at
-ceive_ it,   Stand - ing   free_____   (twice after v.2)

Jennifer Wild

**138**   *Song of awakening*

*As one lights a candle*

Listen, all you seeds in the earth,
    buried in your dark earthen tombs.
As this flame of my spring candle
    penetrates the darkness,
    may your young tender stems pierce the earth
    to dance in wind and rain
    just as this flame, like a tiny sun,
    now dances before me.

Father of fire, Mother of mystery,
    teach me the lesson of spring
    as all creation comes alive –
    tree and bush, flower and plant –
    in the alleluia richness
    of the resurrection of creation.
Grant me the gift, O God,
    to do the same.

Teach me, O glorious Spring,
    the lesson that nothing dies completely.

At the death of my body help me to know
that I have not entered an endless winter,
but simply a stage in the unfolding mystery
whose name is Life.

On this feast of the spring equinox
may I taste with delight
the freshness and vitality of new birth
and come forth from the womb of winter
youthful with hope
and fully alive
in the presence of my God.

Amen.

Edward Hays

## 139   *Act of thanksgiving and remembrance*

Everyone has a name
given to him by his parents
**Everyone has a name**
given to her by her stature
and the way she smiles
and given to her by her clothing
**Everyone has a name**
given to him by the mountains
and given to him by his walls
**Everyone has a name**
given to her by the stars
and given to her by her neighbours
**Everyone has a name**
given to him by his sins
and given to him by his longing
**Everyone has a name**
given to her by her enemies
and given to her by her love
**Everyone has a name**
given to him by his holidays
and given to him by his work
**Everyone has a name**
given to her by the seasons
and given to her by her blindness

**Everyone has a name**
given to him by the sea
and given to him by his death
**Everyone has a name**

## 140   *We cannot measure how you heal*

---

We cannot measure how you heal
Or answer every sufferer's prayer,
Yet we believe your grace responds
Where faith and doubt unite to care.
Your hands, though bloodied on the cross,
Survive to hold and heal and warn,
To carry all through death to life
And cradle children yet unborn.

The pain that will not go away,
The guilt that clings from things long past,
The fear of what the future holds
Are present as if meant to last.
But present too is love which tends
The hurt we never hoped to find,
The private agonies inside,
The memories that haunt the mind.

So some have come who need your help
And some have come to make amends,
As hands which shaped and saved the world
Are present in the touch of friends.
Lord, let your Spirit meet us here
To mend the body, mind and soul,
To disentangle peace from pain
And make your broken people whole.

*Tune: Ye banks and braes (Scottish traditional)*

**John L. Bell and Graham Maule**

## 141    *We shall go out with hope of resurrection*

We shall go out with hope of resurrection,
We shall go out, from strength to strength go on,
We shall go out and tell our stories boldly,
Tales of a love that will not let us go.
We'll sing our songs of wrongs that can be righted,
We'll dream our dream of hurts that can be healed,
We'll weave a cloth of all the world united
Within the vision of a Christ who sets us free.

We'll give a voice to those who have not spoken,
We'll find the words for those whose lips are sealed,
We'll make the tunes for those who sing no longer,
Vibrating love alive in every heart.
We'll share our joy with those who are still weeping,
Chant hymns of strength for hearts that break in grief,
We'll leap and dance the resurrection story
Including all within the circles of our love.

*Tune: Londonderry Air*

Joyce Boyce-Tillman

## 142    *The anointing*

Give thou to me, O God,
The healing power of oil,
Give thou to me, O God,
A place beside the Healer of my soul.
Give thou to me, O God,
The health of joy and peace.

Give thou to me, O God,
To know the death of Christ,
Give thou to me, O God,
That I may contemplate Christ's agony;
Give thou to me, O God.
The warming love of Christ.

O thou great God of heaven,
Draw thou my soul to thee,

That I repent aright
With upright, strengthened, pure and straightened heart,
A broken heart, contrite
That shall not bend nor yield.

Of angels, thou art God.
Bring me to dwell in peace.
Of angels, thou art God.
Preserve me from evil magic charms.
Of angels, thou art God.
Please bathe me in their pool.

*Tune: Healing*

June Boyce-Tillman
(adapted from Celtic sources)

## 143    *'All shall be well, in love enclosed'*

'All shall be well, in love enclosed',
An anchoress says in her cell.
Her revelations clearly tell
Of love that lives in heav'n and hell.

All shall be well, in love enclosed.
A God of judgement stands condemned
By One who only love can send,
Whose breath can heal, whose touch can mend.

All shall be well, in love enclosed
By One who holds us in his palm,
Who made us, shields us with his arm,
Redeems us, keeps us from all harm.

All shall be well, in love enclosed.
The ring of fire will meet the rose
In One who all our suffering knows,
Sweet Mother Jesus, our repose.

*Tune: Breslau*

June Boyce-Tillman

**144**  *Beginnings and endings*

We bless ourselves with love. *(hands crossed in front)*
We bless one another with strength. *(joining hands)*
We bless our world with joy. *(hands raised in the air)*

Let us go forward on the journey
rejoicing in all that we have
and open in trust and faithfulness
to all that is to come.

**Jan Berry**

# 9

# Give me your hand . . .
## The Christian vision

Jesus' request to Thomas leads Thomas to faith through touching someone else's wounds. The liturgies and prayers in this chapter are all concerned with woundedness, whether the open bleeding wounds of war or the scars on a landscape made by pollution. But they are also marked by hope, whether they address social injustice or whether they seek to celebrate and proclaim God in creation. The material which relates to creation is refreshingly unsentimental; human failure to respect and see itself as a part of the created world is all too obvious. There is a justice for the environment as well as for human society, the awareness of which prevents us being soppy about 'nature'; at the same time there is a move away from the huge suspicion of the natural world sometimes found in Christianity.

Much of this section is about the Christian vision of a kingdom that is both here and to come, a commonwealth of justice, peace and freedom. Some very specific liturgies are included which are capable of wider application: the peace preachers' commissioning liturgy, for example, is included to illustrate the notion of people's being *commissioned* to work for the kingdom. Number 153, 'We are not alone', highlights the value of many of these liturgies in reminding us that we struggle and hope *together*. The visionary themes of this chapter have been banded together under the story of Thomas as a reminder that the resurrected body still carries the scars.

## 145 *Blessed be the New Year*
### *A ritual of hope*

### Preparation

*Pick your favorite candle and put it in a special place. Or gather many significant candles and arrange them to please yourself. Choose a quiet time of the day for your lighting. Your candle(s) joined with those of others around the world illuminate new hopes, dispel old fears.*

*Invite a friend or several to join you if you like. Put on music if you wish. Rest your body in a comfortable place and relax.*

## Centering

*(Light your candle(s).)*
This is the season of hope!
Let the Spirit of Hope surround you.
Let your spirit rise to bless this new year.

## Blessing

O Great Spirit of Hope, blessed be your holy seasons.
Blessed be this season when we move to a new year.
Blessed be this magical time for new beginnings and fond farewells.
Blessed be this 'crack between the worlds' that we encounter at the
    New Year.
Blessed be this threshold place of transition between inside and
    outside.
Blessed be this transformation when spirits of hope and change
    gather.
Blessed be this passage from past securities to uncharted uncertain-
    ties.
Blessed be this shifting of emotions.
Blessed be this letting go of old hurts and pains.
Blessed be this reliable balancing act of nature.
Blessed be this rededication of values and meaning in life.
Blessed be . . . *(add others)*
O Great Spirit of Hope, blessed be your holy seasons.

## Reflection

What are the transitions that I experience as a new season of a new year
dawns?

What new goals for health, social change and sharpening my focus do I set
for myself?

*(Pause to reflect, journal, converse, draw or dance as you wish.)*

## Closing

This is the season of hope!
Let the Spirit of Hope surround you.
Let your spirit rise to bless this new year.

*(Blow out the candle(s) knowing you can rekindle one or all at any time.
Happy New Year!)*

**Diann L. Neu**

## 146  *A ritual to invite light into areas of darkness*

This can be used in large or small acts of worship. I first used this with several friends as we invited people to name political and ecological concerns at the beginning of Advent. It can be used on any occasion when people sharing worship will feel helpless at the size of the issue, and have to wait speaking, acting only a little at a time.

> *A speaker raises consciousness on an issue.*
>
> *A representative of the worshippers comes forward, lights a candle, says:*

I light this candle as a sign of the Light of Christ that will be with us as we commit ourselves to hear, wait and in time act upon what we have heard.

> *This is repeated after each speaker.*

For example, issues we spoke about were:
   Poverty in the world, and world banking.
   Seduction to over-spend, by the media and materialism.
   Justice for women.
   Recession: who pays the price?

**Mary Robins**

## 147  *A Pentecost celebration*
*Norwich M.O.W. (Movement for the Ordination of Women), 1992*

*This service moves from meditative singing through penitence to prophecy and hope. We shall move about from one part of the church to another, symbolizing the journey we all make, and the different spiritual places in which we find ourselves.*

### Opening prayer

Loving God,
Open our hearts,
so that we may feel the breath and play of your Spirit.
Unclench our hands
so that we may reach out to one another, and be healed.
Open our lips
that we may drink in the delight and wonder of life.

Unclog our ears
to hear your agony in our inhumanity.
Open our eyes,
so that we may see Christ in friend and stranger.
Breathe your Spirit into us,
and touch our lives with the life of Christ, Amen.

## Welcome

LEADER The angel of the Lord appeared to Moses in the flame of a burning bush.

ALL     The place where we are standing is holy ground.

## Hymn *Praise to God, the world's Creator* (**22**)

*During the singing of the hymn the congregation is invited to move through to the sanctuary to stand or sit around the altar.*

LEADER Our God is like a refiner's fire.

ALL     We will be purified like gold and silver.

## Prayers of penitence (As in 'A Confession' (Jan Berry) in **156**)

LEADERS
        In your mercy and love

ALL     Forgive us, change and renew us.

## Hymn *She who would valiant be (adapted from John Bunyan)*

*During this hymn the congregation move back through the screen to stand facing it.*

LEADER She reaches forth her hand to the needy.

ALL     Her candle goes not out by night.

*The candles at the screen are lit.*

## Intercessions

LEADER 2
        You call us like Miriam, to dance for freedom;

ALL    We remember those whose freedom dance is costly and dangerous. Give us wisdom to use our freedom for your kingdom.

LEADER 2
You call us, like Deborah, to judge our world, to make decisions and offer counsel;
ALL    We remember law-makers, and law-breakers, those who work for peace, for a sane environment, and for fresh understandings of your healing love.

LEADER 2
You call us, like Naomi and Ruth, to love one another;
ALL    We remember families who have lost their ground of love, and children who have never known love. Give us a true love for you, for our neighbour, for ourselves.

LEADER 2
You call us, like Mary, to be faithful bearers of your word;
ALL    We remember all women called to serve you as priests, especially in England at this time of waiting. Make us, like Mary, trusting and strong.

LEADER 2
Let us now remember aloud or in our hearts, those who have guided, nurtured, or prophesied for us . . .

*When the naming is over, a short silence shall be kept.*

LEADER 2
For all the saints who went before us,
who have spoken to our hearts and touched us with your fire,
ALL    We praise you, O God.

LEADER For all the saints who live beside us,
whose weaknesses and strengths are woven with our own,
ALL    We praise you, O God.

LEADER For all the saints who live beyond us,
who challenge us to change the world with them,
ALL    We praise you, O God.

*Return to pews.*

## Reading *Acts 2.1–18*

*Reflection, led by two of those present.*

### Hymn *We sing a love that sets all people free* (166)

*During this hymn all leave the pews and move to the font. Rose petals and rosemary will be distributed.*

LEADER Let the wilderness and the thirsty land be glad;
ALL    Let the desert rejoice and blossom as the rose.

## Word of prophecy

## The dismissal

May the God who dances in creation,
who embraces us with human love,
who shakes our lives like thunder,
bless us and drive us out with power
to fill the world with her justice.

(Janet Morley)

*All raise their rose petals and rosemary, saying loud and clear:*

**We remember with honour!**

**We believe and hope!**

**We trust in God!   Amen!**

Norwich M.O.W.

## 148    *Communion service on the theme of justice, peace and the integrity of creation*

### Entry into worship

1ST VOICE

Praise God, who has set bounds to the universe,
and brought each one of us to birth,
who has been at work in our history
and in every living thing.

2ND VOICE

Praise God, whose will is justice and love,
who marks out no one for privilege
and whose favours cannot be bought.

3RD VOICE

Praise God, who redresses the balance
in favour of the defenceless and the poor,
and calls on us to do the same.

4TH VOICE

> Praise God, who loves the foreigner
> and finds a home for the stranger
> and reminds us that we have been outsiders.

5TH VOICE

> Praise God, who has brought us happiness
> and looks only for humility in return,
> for wondering minds and thankful hearts.

ALL We stand in awe of you, our God;
your thoughts are beyond our understanding
and your love puts us to shame.

ALL We hear your commandments, our God,
and ask your forgiveness
because we have fallen so far short
of the love for you and the generosity
which you ask us to show to others.

ALL We offer ourselves in your service, our God,
whole-heartedly and without condition.
Whatever merit we have comes from you,
all that is worthwhile bears your stamp.
For you are our praise, our voice, our being.

(Stephen Orchard)

## Hymn *Creator of the earth and skies*

## Prayer and responses

6TH VOICE

> O God, the source of our being,
> and the goal of all our longing,

ALL **we believe and trust in you.**
The whole earth is alive with your glory,
and all that has life is sustained by you.

ALL **We commit ourselves to cherish your world,
and to seek your face.**

7TH VOICE

> O God, embodied in a human life,

ALL **we believe and trust in you.**
Jesus our brother, born of the woman Mary,
you confronted the proud and the powerful,
and welcomed as your friends those of no account.

Holy Wisdom of God, firstborn of creation,
you emptied yourself of power,
and became foolishness for our sake.
You laboured with us upon the cross,
and have brought us forth to the hope of resurrection.

ALL    **We commit ourselves to struggle against evil
and to choose life.**

8TH VOICE

O God, life-giving Spirit,
Spirit of healing and comfort, of integrity and truth,

ALL    **we believe and trust in you.**
Warm-winged Spirit, brooding over creation,
rushing wind and Pentecostal fire,

ALL    **we commit ourselves to work with you
and renew our world.**

(Janet Morley)

## Litany of Holy Wisdom and reflection on justice (J), peace (P) and the integrity of creation (C)

J    Let us praise God, Spirit of Holy Wisdom.

ALL    Let us praise God, for she is Justice.

J    She is like a mother who makes no favourites among her children.

Let us give thanks that, as Jesus observed, rain falls on the deserving and the undeserving; that earth's resources are meant for all.

P    Let us praise God, Spirit of Holy Wisdom.

ALL    Let us praise God, for she is Peace.

P    She is the Go-Between God, the reconciler.

Let us give thanks that the Prince of Peace rode a symbolic donkey; that he taught the offered cheek and the extra mile; that in our own time the Spirit of Peace moves and is acknowledged, not least through the initiatives of women.

C    Let us praise God, Spirit of Holy Wisdom.

ALL    Let us praise God, for she is the Integrator of Creation.

C    She is the source and sum of life.

As the Colossians and Ephesians heard, in union with Christ all things have their proper place: Christ completes things everywhere. Let us give thanks for new global visions of our time, for a world awakening to its need for health and wholeness.

J       I speak for Justice.

I was a nameless concubine from Bethlehem.

I was expendable, because justice was not extended to women.

1ST BIBLE READER   *Judges 19.20–8 (a modern translation)*

P       I speak for Peace.

I was Jephthah's daughter.

I too was expendable, because war takes no account of women.

2ND BIBLE READER   *Judges 11.30–9 (a modern translation)*

C       I speak for the Integrity of Creation.

I was Ruth. I was more fortunate.

A foreigner and a woman unprotected, I found myself accepted, loved, integrated into a community. Corn and water were freely shared with me. It was as though the earth and its conflicts were already harmonized.

3RD BIBLE READER   *Ruth 2.1–12 (a modern translation)*

J       I speak for Justice and for Christ.

I was Josephine Butler, wife of a cathedral canon in the nineteenth century. I fought against Acts of Parliament which 'as far as women are concerned remove every guarantee of personal security which the law has established and held sacred . . . because it is unjust to punish the sex who are victims of a vice, and leave unpunished the sex who are the main cause of it.'

P       I speak for Peace and for Christ.

I was Gladys Aylward, a missionary in China. Because of the atrocities of war, I was forced to flee with almost a hundred children. We travelled for a month, nearly 500 miles as the crow flies – and we were no crows. Twelve days of it was hard walking over mountains, with almost no food. Must women and children suffer so from the wars men make?

C       I speak for the Integrity of Creation and for Christ.

I was Julian, an anchoress of the fourteenth century. In my visions God showed me 'a little thing, the size of a hazelnut, on the palm of my hand, round like a ball. I looked at it thoughtfully and wondered, What is this? And the answer came, It is all that is made. I marvelled that it continued to exist and did not suddenly disintegrate, it was so small. And again my mind supplied the answer: It exists, both now and for ever, because God loves it.'

J  Let us pray to God, Spirit of Holy Wisdom, for Justice.
With loving concern we intercede for those suffering injustice
  – because they are women or children
  – because they are black
  – because of their political opinions
  – because they are poor, unemployed or of little account.

ALL May love redeem them.

P  Let us pray to God, Spirit of Holy Wisdom, for Peace.
With loving concern we intercede for those suffering from violence
  – for victims of war and prolonged unrest
  – for victims of hooliganism and mob riot
  – for victims of rape and abuse and battering
  – and also for the brutalized perpetrators of violence.

ALL May love redeem them.

C  Let us pray to God, Spirit of Holy Wisdom, for the Integrity of
Creation.
Let us pray for those who widen our vision
  – for ecologists, and scientists of all disciplines
  – for prophets and spiritual leaders of all faiths
  – for educationists, writers and broadcasters
  – for leaders of governments and industry ...

ALL ... that this groaning creation may not disintegrate but reach its
fulfilment in unity, redeemed by love.

## Hymn *Pour down thy Spirit from above*

## The Offering

1ST CELEBRANT

  This bread we offer:
    made out of rain and soil and green plant;
    brought by the work of women and men;
    staple of health, symbol of matter.
  This is for us the Body of Christ: the integrity of creation.

1ST VERSE SPEAKER

    Take, eat this body life, this bread,
    The daily unremarkable. Here feel
  With teeth and fingers stubborn matter's form,
    Texture of timber, plastic, linen, steel,
      The concrete poetry
      Of earth's variety.
  Eat this for Martha. Martha must be fed.

Lord of the bread, who art
The wheat germ in the heart,
Let Martha's days
Be praise:
Give us our daily breath.

2ND CELEBRANT

This wine we offer:
made out of rain and soil and green plant;
brought by the work of women and men;
signal of celebration, cup of sorrow.
This is for us the suffering and glory of Christ.

2ND VERSE SPEAKER

Drink of this cup. Take willing part
In this Gethsemane. Accept
Love's heartburst. Strain imagination dry.
The vinegar and hyssop sponge reject.
Hope. Wonder. Dare
The groaning prayer.
Drink this for Mary. Mary needs her hurt.
Lord of the wine, the love
In which we breathe and move,
Let Mary's pain
Remain:
Give us our daily breath.

**The Communion** *(Words and actions according to the preferences of the two celebrants.)*

FIRST CELEBRANT

In the body broken and the blood poured out,
we restore to memory and hope
the broken and unremembered victims
of tyranny and sin;
and we long for the bread of tomorrow
and the wine of the age to come.

SECOND CELEBRANT

Come then, life-giving spirit of our God,
brood over these bodily things,
and make us one body with Christ;
that we may labour with creation
to be delivered from its bondage to decay

into the glorious liberty
of all the children of God.

(Janet Morley)

## The Covenant

ALL *(holding hands)*

As we hold each other's hands; so we hold one another with strength. We remember where we have been, and are strengthened for the journey ahead. As we affirm our past; so we will affirm and shape our present and our future.

And so we go forth to continue our journeys.
In our separateness, we remain together,
and in our togetherness, we find strength.

(Lesley Hitchens)

## The Blessing

FIRST CELEBRANT

May the God who dances in creation,
who embraces us with human love,
who shakes our lives like thunder,
bless us and drive us out with power
to fill the world with her justice,
Amen.

(Janet Morley)<br>**Anne Ashworth**

## 149 *Mother earth, fruit of God's womb*
*St Hilda Community gathering, October 1993*

---

### Introduction and reflection on the theme

*Shared reflection from the group follows.*

### Petitions of prayer for those to be remembered

### Sharing of thanksgiving and sacrament

All life is your own,
All fruits of the earth
are fruits of your womb,
Your union, your dance.
Lady and Lord.
We thank you for blessings and abundance.
Join with us, Feast with us, Enjoy with us!
Blessed be.                                              (Starhawk)

    My friends, let us give thanks for Wonder.
    Let us give thanks for the Wonder of Life
    that infuses all things now and for ever.

Blessed is the Source of Life, the Fountain of Being
the wellspring of goodness, compassion and kindness
from which we draw to make for justice and peace.
From the creative power of Life we derive food and harvest,
from the bounty of the earth and the yields of the heavens
we are sustained and are able to sustain others.

    All life is holy, sacred,
    worthy of respect and dignity.
    Let us give thanks for the power of heart
    to sense the holy in the midst of the simple.

                                (Rami Shapiro)

Blessed are you, strong and faithful God.
All your works, the height and the depth,
echo the silent music of your praise.

In the beginning your Word summoned light:
night withdrew, and creation dawned.
As ages passed unseen,
waters gathered on the face of the earth
and life appeared.

When the times at last had ripened
and the earth grown full in abundance,
you created in your image man and woman,
the crown of all creation.

You gave us breath and speech,
that all the living
might find a voice to sing your praise.
So now, with all the powers of heaven and earth,
we chant the ageless hymn of your glory:

Holy, holy, holy Lord, God of power and might,
heaven and earth are full of your glory.
    Hosanna in the highest.
Blessed is he who comes in the name of the Lord.
    Hosanna in the highest.

All holy God,
how wonderful the work of your hands!
You restored the beauty of your image
when sin had scarred the world.

As a mother tenderly gathers her children,
you embraced a people as your own
and filled them with longing
for a peace that would last
and for a justice that would never fail.

Through countless generations
your people hungered for the bread of freedom.
From them you raised up Jesus, the living bread,
in whom ancient hungers were satisfied.
He healed the sick,
though he himself would suffer;
he offered life to sinners,
though death would hunt him down.
But with a love stronger than death,
he opened wide his arms
and surrendered his spirit.

(ICEL)

So we who live by his spirit
are bound to each other and to all people,
and in this to Jesus himself;
who in the night that he was handed over
took bread and gave you thanks.
He broke it and gave it to his friends, saying:
Take, eat, this is my body, my very self, given for you;
do this to remember me.
In the same way he took the cup of wine,
gave you thanks and gave it to them saying:
Drink this all of you; this is my blood, my very life.

This is the food we eat together,
this is the wine that brings us alive in the world.

And so we are bound to all people of faith,
those who share our love of Jesus,
and those who seek justice, truth and liberty in different ways.
We offer our thanks and praise
for all who work to enliven this world.

God of the living and the dead,
bring to the never-fading light of your peace
those who have died in faith,
especially the unloved and unmourned.
Gather us into one communion with our forebears
with all who have walked this earth before us,
so that at last all creation may be whole.
As we eat this bread and drink this wine,
enrich our lives to make your kingdom, here and now, a reality.

ALL AMEN!

We break this bread recalling the body of Christ broken for us.
Help us to accept the cost of discipleship and to take the risk of
faith.

*The bread and wine are shared with one another.*

The body of Christ, broken for you.
The blood of Christ, shed for you.

## Prayer

We eat not simply to satisfy our own appetites,
we eat to sustain ourselves in the task we have been given.
Each of us is unique, coming into the world
with a gift no other can offer – ourselves.
We eat to nourish the vehicle of giving; we eat to sustain
our task of earth repair, our quest for harmony, peace and justice.
We give thanks to the Power that makes for Meeting,
for our table has been a place of dialogue and friendship.
We give thanks to Life, to this earth, our Mother,
for continual Rebirth and Renewal. (Rami Shapiro)
And as the earth is generous to us,
let us embody our gratitude in a firm resolve to change the world:
that those who are hungry may be satisfied with food
and those without hope find courage. Amen. Amen!

**Jane Pitz**

## 150    *A winter solstice observance*
### *Northern hemisphere*

### A ritual of the winter solstice fire

LEADER Let us take into our hands a solstice candle.

*or*

Let us light the sacred solstice fire.

We pray on this night of ancient fear,
    when those who have gone before us were fearful
    of what lurked outside the ring of fire of light and warmth.
They feared all that prowled in the darkness:
    evil, disease, death, beasts that might destroy them
    and the hidden dangers of winter.

*Fire is lighted.*

As we light this fire,
    we ask that God who is the fullness of light
    would protect each of us on this night
    from what we fear most.

*A silent pause for reflection, then the leader walks around the dining room
table with a lighted candle, saying:*

May we all be encircled by the magic of fire,
    by the warmth of the light and love of God
    and the flame of our friendship with one another.
May we who sit at this table be protected
    from all harm and disease, all evil and wickedness.

On this holy night that welcomes the season of winter,
    it was the ancient custom to exchange gifts of light,
    symbolic of the gift of the new light of the sun.

*Candles are exchanged and perhaps the greeting, 'Light be with you'; then
all are seated at the festive table.*

### A blessing of the solstice feast

As our great star, the sun,
    graciously shares light, warmth and energy with us,
    may we, as children of the earth and the sun,
    share with one another the life and joy of this meal.
We acknowledge that the food and drink before us
    is sun-soaked and filled with star energy.

In this food and drink is the taste of the heavens;
    may we partake of it in peace
    with each other and with all the earth.
A winter solstice toast to the sun
    and to the joys of this winter season.

*Food and drink are now shared in an evening of friendship, entertainment and enjoyment*

## Concluding prayer after the solstice feast

Tonight we stand at the threshold of the feast of Christmas,
    the birth of the Son of God.

May tonight's celebration be in harmony
    with that most holy day of our tradition.
May it help us to truly rejoice
    in the birth of the Light of the World.

May this our winter solstice celebration
    bring us into communion
    with all those who prepare to celebrate
    the feast of the Nativity of Jesus Christ.
May we also be in communion
    with our Jewish brothers and sisters
    who in this time of darkness
    celebrate their holy feast of light, Hanukkah.

ALL RESPOND   Amen *or* Amen, let there be light!

*Lighted candles in the windows of various rooms of your home can add a great deal to the mood of this celebration. Guests may take home the candles used in the celebration. Even flashlights may be used as gifts and ritual objects of this feast.*

**Edward Hays**

---

**151**   *Ash Wednesday Service* 1991
*Bristol Churches Coalition of Justice and Peace Groups*

---

LEADER May the grace and peace of God our Father and the Lord Jesus
    Christ be with you all.
ALL    And also with you.

LEADER Lord God, whose judgement is shown in the disasters which we
    bring upon ourselves, show us your mercy now: put a stop to war,

save the lives of the innocent, teach us better ways to live with one another, through Christ our Lord.

ALL    Amen.

## Song *When you walk through the waters I'll be with you*

## Reading *Hosea 6.1–6: I want mercy, not sacrifice, knowledge of God, not holocausts.*

## Penitential litany

LEADER    Let us ask God to forgive us our personal sins and the shared sins of our nation which have led us to the judgement of this war.

– the *indifference* to the plight of the poor which has allowed us to spend so much on armaments and so little on welfare and jobs:

ALL    **Forgive us Lord.**

– The *greed* for cheap energy and food, which has made us wreck the economies and lives of other peoples:

ALL    **Forgive us Lord.**

– The *pride* which has allowed us to assume superiority over other races and right of intervention in their affairs:

ALL    **Forgive us Lord.**

– The *laziness* which tells us that the destruction of the environment is none of our business:

ALL    **Forgive us Lord.**

– All our sins, even those hidden from ourselves, which for the sake of a peaceful life we dare not renounce:

ALL    **Forgive us Lord.**

LEADER    Lord, listen to the prayers of those who call on you to forgive their sins and omissions. Give us the intelligence and the heart to make the changes which are needed for true repentance. Through Christ our Lord.

## Our Father . . .

## Hymn *Lord Jesus think on me*

## Blessing the ashes

LEADER    Sisters and brothers, let us pray to God to bless us with abundant grace as we take these ashes on our heads as a sign of repentance.

God of mercy, who do not desire the death of sinners and hate nothing you have made, blot out the sins of those who repent and raise up those who are bowed down with grief. Turn the hearts of men and women back to you and bring peace to the war-torn world. Through the observance of this penitential season of Lent, make us ready to celebrate with pure hearts the resurrection of our Lord Jesus Christ.

ALL    Amen.

## Imposition of the ashes

*With the sign of the cross on the forehead, we mark each other with the ashes, using the following words:*

Remember you are dust and to dust you will return.
Repent and believe the gospel.

## Homily

**Hymn** *Dear Lord and Father of mankind*

**Roger Ruston**

## 152 *Peace preachers' commissioning liturgy* as used in the Peace Preachers' Course

### Introduction

Although we use some symbolic gestures and words in this brief ceremony, we want you to remember that it is not a sacrament, but only something we have devised. It is an act of prayer. Also, we have no power to send you out as preachers. Only God can do that, perhaps through the agency of your churches. By your baptism you are already commissioned to represent Christ to the world and it is already your duty to speak for him. Being a trained preacher of the Word is something we can help you to prepare for. We like to think we have made you ready to be sent if and when the call comes to preach.

### Act of repentance

We all belong to a world which has, in various ways, caused the violent deaths of many millions of innocent people in the past fifty years. None of us can escape the material benefits of belonging to a rich part of that world which protects its riches by threats to annihilate others.

Let us ask God to forgive us for failing to raise our voices against
– the idolatry of war
– the massacres of the innocent
– the idolatry of money
– the wilful creation of poverty and hunger.

Let us do again what we did in our baptismal promises and reject Satan and all his empty promises.

ALL    Lord have mercy,
        Christ have mercy,
        Lord have mercy.

May almighty God have mercy on us, forgive us all our sins, save and strengthen us in every good work and lead us to everlasting life. Amen.

## Readings

OT *reading: Isaiah 52.7–10*
Ps *129: with the refrain,*

Awake, O sleeper, arise from the dead, and Christ shall give you light.

*Gospel reading: Mark 4.26–9*

## Prayer

*The peace preachers kneel.*

God our Father, you have made yourself known to us as the one who desires mercy, not sacrifice: neither the sacrifice of the child Isaac nor the slaughter of the Holy Innocents, nor any of the holocausts caused by the idolatry of this world. And as you yourself became a child for us, a Lamb of God for our redemption, making peace by the blood of your cross, so make us servants of your gospel so that we do not turn aside while the innocent are killed.

We remember the victims and martyrs of all ages and all who have paid for the truth and justice with their lives:

*Affirmation (all say)*
    The torturer shall not triumph over his victim.

The executioner shall not have the last word,
For the Word of the Lord gives life
And raises the victim from the dead.

*The peace preachers are touched on the shoulder, with the words:*

Arise and have no fear.

*The peace preachers receive lighted candles, with the words:*

In your baptism you received the light of Christ. So let your light shine before men and women that they may see your good works and give glory to God.

*Prayer:* Christ our only true light
The light of revelation to the Gentiles,
The morning star which heralds the dawn of the resurrection,
Banish the darkness of sin and error from our hearts
So that we are able to speak the truth that has been given to us in your name.

ALL Amen.

Let us pray with the holy women and men of the Old and New Testaments: With Abel, the first of the innocent slain, our mothers in faith Sarah, Rebecca, Rachel and Leah, our fathers Abraham, Isaac, Jacob, the prophets Moses, Miriam, Deborah, Samuel, David, Elijah, Isaiah, Jeremiah, John the Baptist, Mary the mother of Jesus, Mary Magdalene the first preacher of the Resurrection, Peter and the apostles, Paul the preacher to the nations.

## Profession

As Mary Magdalene received the good news from the risen Christ, and became the apostle to the apostles; as these first teachers of our faith preached the good news to the ends of the earth; as the evangelists, like the prophets of old, wrote it down for our instruction; so may we also receive the Word of the Lord and become preachers of the gospel of peace.

EACH PEACE PREACHER PROFESSES

May I, N, receive the Good News of God for our salvation, and through the Wisdom and mercy of God, together with the martyrs and ministers of the Gospel of all the ages, may I become a witness of the Gospel to the people of this age.

SPONSORS

May N receive your Spirit, and become a truly wise preacher of the gospel. May *she/he* go forth and preach the gospel of peace to all people.

ALL Amen.

**Hymn** *Come down O Love divine* (**168**)

**Final prayer**

God in whose judgement is mercy,
Prepare us for the Last Day,
When your justice is revealed to all nations,
Anoint us with the power of the Spirit,
That in our preaching
We may also prepare the world
To receive you at your Second Coming

Come, Lord Jesus, come.
ALL     Amen.

**Blessing**

May the blessing of the most holy one come upon you,
May the love of the Redeemer shine through all your works.
May the Comforter embrace and send you forth in the paths of
peace.
ALL     Amen.

**Hymn** *The people who stumbled in darkness* (**165**)

Angela West and Roger Ruston

## 153 *We are not alone*

### Introduction

*This service is prepared to encourage people who are involved in the
struggle for justice, peace and truth.*

### Opening sentences

Let us remember who we are:
LEADER We are the people of dignity.
Down the ages we have been the people of God,
the people who know themselves to be called
to freedom, courage and truth.
PEOPLE We light a white candle for that dignity
and the power of God in us.

LEADER We are the people who weep
for the suffering of the world.
We are the people who walk with the Christ
towards all who grieve,
who are oppressed and exploited.

PEOPLE We light a purple candle
for those who suffer with the people
and the power of Christ is in us.

LEADER We are the people of hope and faith.
In the Spirit we celebrate our energy
and strength, our power to heal
and our calling to work with God
in the recreating of the world.

PEOPLE We light a green candle
for our hope in the Spirit.
We are not alone.

## Naming our weeping

LEADER Where is the pain in our lives?
*The people name their fears, angers, areas of pain.*

LEADER You are not alone.

PEOPLE Your tears are our tears.

## Affirming our hope

LEADER Who are the people who have given us strength
and courage, who have created models for us?
*The people name the people.*

LEADER These people walk with us.

PEOPLE We have company on the journey.

## The Word *Reading from the Bible*

## Affirmation of faith

LEADER Let us afirm our faith in God:

ALL We believe in God
who created and is creating the earth,
who so loved the world that Christ was sent
to live life with us
and the Spirit to be our strength.

God has favoured us and appointed us
to be a light to the peoples
and a beacon for the nations;
to open eyes that are blind,
and release captives from the prisons,
out of the dungeons where they live in darkness.
In solidarity with the people of God
    around the world,
and in company with the other churches
    in this city,
we name ourselves as those who, in Jesus Christ,
are enough to do the task
in this time and this place.
We have heard the call of Christ
to follow in the way of the cross.
In faith we lay down our fear,
our weakness and our lack of worth
and announce again
with those who have gone before us that,
'Where the Spirit of the Lord is, there is liberty'.

## Intercession

LEADER Let us ask God for help along the way;
RESPONSE
    'Jesus, remember us' *(Taizé – sung)*

## The commitment to each other

*A symbol of common humanness is shared.*

LEADER In the face of all our realities:
ALL     We are the people who heal each other,
        who grow strong together,
        who name the truth,
        who know what it means
        to live in community,
        moving towards a common dream
        for a new heaven and a new earth
        in the power of the love of God,
        the company of Jesus Christ
        and the leading of the Holy Spirit.

## Blessing *(sung)*

**Dorothy McRae-McMahon**

**154**   *Litany for creation in travail*

---

The sufferings of this present time are not worth comparing with the glory that is to be revealed.
**I saw a new heaven and a new earth, for the former things had passed away.**

The creation waits with eager longing for the revealing of the children of God.
**I saw a new heaven and a new earth, for the former things had passed away.**

The creation was subjected to futility, not of its own will but by the will of him who subjected it in hope.
**I saw a new heaven and a new earth, for the former things had passed away.**

The creation itself will be set free from its bondage to decay and obtain the glorious liberty of the children of God.
**I saw a new heaven and a new earth, for the former things had passed away.**

The whole creation has been groaning in travail together until now; and not only the creation, but we ourselves, who have the first fruit of the Spirit, groan inwardly as we wait for adoption as sons and daughters, the redemption of our bodies.
**I saw a new heaven and a new earth, for the former things had passed away.**

> Lord,
> God of justice and peace
> who stands with those who are poor,
> who asks us to be the voice of the voiceless,
> we call upon you
> for those who have suffered the injustices of war and greed.

From the depths of our being we cry to you, Lord.
**Hear our cry, and listen to our prayers.**

> For those of Hiroshima and Nagasaki,
>     Bikini and Eniwetok,
>     Kwajalein and Mururoa,
>     Fangataufa and Christmas Island,
>     Johnston Island and Monte Bello,
>     Emu and Maralinga:

Those Pacific people whose precious land and sea have been ravaged by nuclear explosions.

From the depths of our being we cry to you, Lord.
**Hear our cry, and listen to our prayers.**

For those who are suffering this day from disease, genetic malformation and the loss of those they love, as a result of nuclear radiation.
May their spirits not be broken by their bodies' pain.

From the depths of our being we cry to you, Lord.
**Hear our cry, and listen to our prayers.**

For those whose land and sea are today being put at risk through radio-active pollution, from the dumping of nuclear wastes, and the passage of nuclear ships.
May their livelihood and health be preserved and may they live in peace and hope.

From the depths of our being we cry to you, Lord.
**Hear our cry, and listen to our prayers.**

We pray that your promise of justice may become real to those for whom we pray.
May they be released to live in freedom and love.

From the depths of our being we cry to you, Lord.
>    **Hear our cry and listen to our prayers,**
>    **for you are gracious, and there is in you**
>    **that which is to be feared, that which forgives,**
>    **that which strengthens, and that which comforts. Amen.**

>    (Pacific Conference of Churches)
>    from *Jesus Christ, the Life of the World*

## 155    *Litany of the four elements*

LEADER Earth, air, fire and water are traditionally symbols of life. Our 'slavery to sin' has meant that these elements may equally contain and carry death.

LIFE    I am life. I offer earth to share between the daughters and sons of God – soil for bearing plants to sustain the planet's life and yield bread for all people.

*A bowl of earth may be presented.*

DEATH   I am death. I take earth away from the many and give it to the few. I exploit and over-use it. I waste its bread while many starve.

LEADER O God, who wore our clay in Christ,
we confess we have not shared the land;

we have broken our bond with the earth and one another.

ALL **Forgive us: we have chosen death.**
**We long for healing: we choose your life.**

*(Pause)*

LIFE I offer air to breathe:
for the endless energy of the wind,
for birds to fly and seeds to blow.
Air has no frontiers; we share the breath of life.

*A fan may be used to create currents of air.*

DEATH I fill the air with poisonous fumes which all must breathe, and which claw away the threads of the universe.

LEADER O God, who breathed life into the world,
we confess we have polluted the air;
we cannot sense the harmony of your creation.

ALL **Forgive us: we have chosen death.**
**We long for healing: we choose your life.**

*(Pause)*

LIFE I offer fire for light and warmth, for purification and power. Fire draws us together in fellowship, around a meal cooked and shared.

*A candle may be lit.*

DEATH I use fire for my own violent ends.
I burn the forests and choke the air.
I give the rich the earth's energy to waste:
I deny the poor their fuel to cook with.

LEADER O God, pillar of fire and pentecostal flame,
we confess our lack of inner fire
for your justice to be done,
your peace shared on earth.

ALL **Forgive us: we have chosen death.**
**We long for healing: we choose your life.**

*(Pause)*

LIFE I offer water to drink and cleanse;
to be the veins and arteries of the land;
I offer strong waves for energy
and still lakes for calm of spirit.

*A bowl of water may be presented.*

DEATH   I pollute water with the waste from mines and factories, that it may
          kill the fish, be bitter to drink, and carry disease.
        I withdraw water from the land and make a desert;
        I extend the waters of the sea and drown cities.

LEADER  O God, fountain of living waters,
        we confess that we are cracked cisterns,
        lacking stillness to listen to your word,
        and energy to act on it.
ALL     **Forgive us: we have chosen death.**
        **We long for healing: we choose your life.**

        *(Pause)*

LEADER  God of earth, air, fire and water,
        we surrender to you our old humanity:
ALL     **Christ, we would rise with you:**
        **we would be born anew.**

LEADER  Christ has died: Christ is risen.
        We are forgiven: we too may leave the grave.

                                                      Kate Compston

## 156   *A liturgy for women and men*

### Introduction

### A confession

MEN     We acknowledge that we have taken our power for granted as if
        our strength and privilege were the experience of all.
        We ask for forgiveness.
ALL     **We shall grow together**
        **as we share our struggles and our hope.**

WOMEN   We acknowledge that we have colluded with male power and
        privilege,
        accepting it without question or manipulating it without open
        challenge.
        We ask for forgiveness.
ALL     **We shall grow together**
        **as we share our struggles and our hope.**

MEN     We acknowledge that we have denied our vulnerability, or looked
        to women to restore to us our buried feelings.

We ask for forgiveness.

ALL   **We shall grow together**
**as we share our struggles and our hope.**

WOMEN We acknowledge that we have denied our strength, hiding it from
ourselves and fearing the cost of change.
We ask for forgiveness.

ALL   **We shall grow together**
**as we share our struggles and our hope.**

ALL   We acknowledge that we have too easily accepted established
patterns,
and evaded our own responsibility for change.
God, forgive us.
Help us to grow together
as we share our struggles and our hope.

## Readings

## Prayers of intercession

## Act of affirmation and commitment

Sister God, you have given women strength,
    to make and sustain the beauty of creation
    to claim the wholeness of your image
    to live and grow in freedom and courage.
**Sister God, we thank you for your gifts.**

Brother God, you have given men strength
    to make and sustain the beauty of creation
    to claim the wholeness of your image
    to live and grow in freedom and courage.
**Brother God, we thank you for your gifts.**

Brother God, you have given men vulnerability
    to admit pain and weariness
    to know the frustration of helplessness
    to weep and touch with tenderness.
**Brother God, we thank you for your gifts.**

Sister God, you have given women vulnerability
    to rage with the pain of injustice
    to know anger and a desire for change
    to suffer and labour with you for the freedom of the world.
**Sister God, we thank you for your gifts.**

### Anointing and affirmation

### Close

May the God in whose image we are made,
strengthen us in our struggle,
embrace us in our weakness,
and inspire us with hope for a different future:
as we work, separately and together,
for the freedom of the whole creation. Amen.

**Jan Berry**

## 157   *A litany*

In the Samba Schools of Carnival, the Brazilians sing and dance of the hardships they live.

LEADER We must let our heart, soul and mind sing and dance a little, not to rid us of our problems and suffering, but to remember and live our faith in balance.

PEOPLE Join us in the celebration, O God.
Free us to the singing and the dancing.

LEADER Perhaps the harder we work, the more joy we will experience in our celebrations.

PEOPLE You work with us in all the creation.
Release us to your joy, O God.

LEADER But we can only truly celebrate at the party of all parties, when all have bread, freedom and opportunity – when all live abundantly and fully.

PEOPLE But, even now,
we celebrate the life in our midst.

LEADER We see women who sort through rubbish for a living, and jump for joy at the discovery of a new pair of shoes . . . at the birth of a new life in a poor community . . . in a shanty town of Rio.

PEOPLE May we share in their joy.

LEADER Along our journeys, we celebrate as we go, marking special occasions, victories, and celebrating along with others.

*The people light small candles and name the points of their hope and celebration.*

LEADER Join us in the celebration, O God.
PEOPLE Free us to the singing and the dancing
as we name every small sign of your reign.

**Group 3 Youth Interns in Mission, Uniting Church in Australia**

## 158 *Prayer rosary*

Hiroshima,
Bosnia,
Belfast,
the names slip through our fingers,
like blood-stained beads.

As we tell the story,
tell us,
tell us,
tell us,
the way
to peace.

Beirut,
Nagasaki,
Nurenberg,
still they come,
countless numbers:
people hounded,
refugees tramping the road
out of hell, into hell.

Where will it stop?
Show us,
show us,
show us,
the way to peace.

Five for sorrow,
ten for joy,
may what has been sown in pain
be reaped in hope.

Kate McIlhagga

## 159    *A prayer for all creative people*

Divine Artist of the universe,

Too often vapid cynicism and unfair criticism
crush the creative spirit.
Therefore, fill us with the passion to make,
and make again, where such unmaking reigns.
Give us the courage to go on
> painting
>> writing
>>> sculpting
>>>> composing
>>>>> singing
>>>>>> acting
>>>>>>> gardening
>>>>>>>> and dancing

that we may help to build a rainbow bridge of hope to span the gulf
between the peoples of your world;

And may your peace, your justice and your joy cover the earth from
pole to pole.

Jean Gaskin

## 160    *God in the struggle*

Living God,
When we find ourselves struggling,
in fear or pain or worry,
help us to feel you close by,
sharing our warm and fragile flesh.
And when we see *you* striving on the cross,
help us to join with you,
to take the pain,
to cry for justice,
to work for peace,
and share your victory of love.

Bob Warwicker

**161**    *Prayer of approach*

---

Loving God,
out of our homelessness,
we turn to you;
out of our helplessness
we come to you;
out of our hunger
out of our pain,
we return to you.

In love
deep love
we come.
Stand beside us,
comfort our helplessness,
feed our hunger,
tend our pain,
hear our cry
and welcome us home.
                    Amen.

                                        **Kate McIlhagga**

**162**    *God of light and warmth*

---

O God, star kindler
kindle a flame of love within me
to light my path in days of darkness.

O God, sun warmer
warm me with your love
to melt the frozen hand of guilt.

O God, moon burnisher,
burnish my shield of faith,
that I may seek justice
and follow the ways of peace.

                                        **Kate McIlhagga**

## 163   *Blessing of the Stew Pot*

Blessed be the Creator
and all creative hands
which plant and harvest,
pack and haul and hand
over sustenance –
Blessed be carrot and cow,
potato and mushroom,
tomato and bean,
parsley and peas,
onion and thyme,
garlic and bay leaf,
pepper and water,
marjoram and oil,
and blessed be fire –
and blessed be the enjoyment
of nose and eye,
and blessed be colour –
and blessed be the Creator
for the miracle of red potato,
for the miracle of green bean,
for the miracle of fawn mushrooms,
and blessed be God
for the miracle of earth:
ancestors, grass, bird,
deer and all gone
wild creatures
whose bodies become
carrots, peas, and wild
flowers, who
give sustenance
to human hands, whose
agile dance of music
nourishes the ear
and soul of the dog
resting under the stove
and the woman working over
the stove and the geese
out the open window
strolling in the backyard.

And blessed be God
for all, all, all.

Alla Renée Bozarth

## 164 *Thomas*

Put your hand,
Thomas,
on the crawling head,
of a child,
imprisoned,
in a cot,
in Romania.
Place your finger,
Thomas,
on the list of those,
who have disappeared
in Chile.
Stroke the cheek,
Thomas,
of the little girl,
sold into prostitution,
in Thailand.
Touch, Thomas,
the gaping wounds
of my world.
Feel, Thomas,
the primal wound,
of my people.
Reach out your hands,
Thomas,
and place them at the side of the poor.
Grasp my hands, Thomas,
and believe,
when you feel me
in the world's pain,
and in the world's glory.

Kate McIlhagga

**165**   *The Prince of Peace*

---

The people who stumbled in darkness –
Their eyes have seen the light.
And those who sit in the deepest pit,
On them has the day shone bright.
Like those who bring in the harvest,
They will laugh and they will cheer.
You have broken the guns of the violent ones
Who kept the earth in fear.

For every plane and every bomb
And every boot and gun,
And every blood-stained battle-dress
Will be burned in the fire to come.
A child is born who will put an end
To the killing and the grief.
The Holy One has given a son,
Our brother, our Prince of Peace.

His justice and care will be everywhere
And all terror and lies will cease.
The poor and the lame will praise his name
In truthfulness and peace.
And the nations will rise and learn to prize
The laws that he will teach.
And the world will rejoice when they hear his voice
And the gospel that we preach.

*Tune: Traditional Irish*

**Roger Ruston** (based on Isaiah 9.2–7)

**166**

---

We sing a love that sets all people free,
That blows like wind, that burns like scorching flame,
Enfolds like earth, springs up like water clear.
Come, living love, live in our hearts today.

We sing a love that seeks another's good,
That longs to serve and not to count the cost,
A love that, yielding, finds itself made new.
Come, caring love, live in our hearts today.

We sing a love, unflinching, unafraid
To be itself, despite another's wrath,
A love that stands alone and undismayed.
Come, strength'ning love, live in our hearts today.

We sing a love that, wand'ring, will not rest
Until it finds its way, its home, its source,
Through joy and sadness pressing on refreshed.
Come, pilgrim love, live in our hearts today.

We sing a burning, fiery, Holy Ghost
That seeks out shades of ancient bitterness,
Transfig'ring these, as Christ in ev'ry heart.
Come, joyful love, live in our hearts today.

*Tune: Woodlands*

**June Boyce-Tillman**

## 167

Make us true servants to all those in need,
Filled with compassion in thought, word and deed;
Loving our neighbour, whatever the cost,
Feeding the hungry and finding the lost.

Lord, make us prophets to cry out the way,
Telling the nations of mercy's new day.
Let us break barriers of hatred and scorn,
Speaking of hope to all people forlorn.

Lord, make us healers of body and mind;
Give us your power to bring sight to the blind;
Love to the loveless and gladness for pain,
Filling all hearts with the joy of your name.

from *One worship*

**168**

Come down, O love divine,
Fulfil the promised time
When we on earth shall see that Second Coming.
O Comforter, draw near,
Within our world appear,
For all creation waits with eager longing.

Alas the hour is late –
The world awaits her fate
As life to dust and ashes we are turning.
Now nature's pattern breaks,
And poison fills her lakes,
The forests of the future we are burning.

Earth groans amid her chains,
Consumed by famine's pains,
The Beast defiles the face of God's creation.
Behold the horsemen four
Ride to the final war.
Now breaks the seal upon God's revelation.

Come, Holy Wisdom, down,
See now her twelve-starred crown –
Here is redeemed God's lovely spoiled creation.
O holy city, come!
Peace rules Jerusalem,
And all God's creatures share in Christ's salvation.
*Tune: Down Ampney*

Angela West

**169**   *Hymn for Peace Pentecost*

Come, Holy Spirit, in this hour,
With peace your gift our souls empower;
May this our act of worship be
Witness against a blasphemy.

Give us the grace your truth to see
In nations' power futility.

Shall we a million deaths intend
And claim that we Christ's truth defend?

For this our sin the Lord once died,
Man's trust in power God crucified.
Shall we bring twice to Calvary
This Lord of our humanity?

O Spirit, may this sin be healed,
In weakness is your power revealed;
No power have we ourselves alone,
Yet in Christ's body we are strong.

Love's spirit our security,
Our freedom is God's charity
Now may we stand where Christ has stood
And trust alone in his dear blood.

Through you God's promise we shall know,
When in Christ's power of peace we go;
Though our resistance seem to fail,
These gates of hell shall not prevail.

Angela West

## 170 *Worker God*

Written for Unemployment Sunday 1992, and used for 1992 and 1993.

Worker God, who planned creation –
complex splendour held in one;
spoke out threads of light and matter,
weaving what your word had spun,
then, with proper satisfaction,
rested when the work was done.

Who are we to spoil the pattern,
make redundant hands and mind;
tarnish pleasure in achievement
which your pleasure undersigned,
crushing lives, and wasting talent,
uncreating humankind?

Many see the sudden ending
of their deeply cherished plans
through the failure of a system
which no longer meets demands,
and the fruit from years of effort
slips away from helpless hands.

Helplessness fuels bitter anger –
home and loved ones bear the cost.
Voices raised create a Babel,
countermanding Pentecost;
and by this disintegration,
whole communities are lost.

Worker God within creation,
weaving what our hands have spun,
give to us consistent strength
to speak your word and see it done.
So through humble human triumphs
may your victory be won.

*Tune, Rhuddlan, or Rhuddlan for the first and last verse and Oriel
(transposed to G) for the middle three verses.*

**Janet H. Wootton**

## 171    *Cleansing the Temple*

Is this the gentle Jesus
Whose healing touch is balm,
Consoler of the broken
And messenger of calm?
Is this the friend of children
At whom the tempests cease,
Are these his hands of blessing,
Is this his voice of peace?

His eye is bright with anger,
His workman's arm strikes clear;
The traders cringe and scatter,
Torn by unholy fear;
The mighty temple totters
For all its golden wealth:

The Spirit blows a tempest
Of cleansing, a new health.

This is the day he promised
Of good news to the poor –
Cast out the old corruption
That blocks the temple door!
Throw wide the gate of freedom,
Let all God's children come!
Through Jesus' broken body
God's people shall come home.

*Tune: Aurelia or Ewing*

**Mary Ann Ebert**

## 172 *God the strengthener*
*[written for the first eucharists of two women ordained to the Anglican priesthood)*

Praise to you, our great Creator,
You rejoice when we are strong;
Fill our hearts with loving power;
Bring us Wisdom with your song.
Alleluia, Alleluia,
It's to you that we belong.

Praise to you, the Christ, Transformer,
You have shared our wilderness;
Lead us to the streams of mercy,
Purify our bitterness.
Alleluia, alleluia,
Human God of gentleness.

Praise to you, the Holy Spirit,
You can scorch us with your flame;
Forge our love within your furnace,
Burning guilt, destroying shame.
Alleluia, alleluia,
Dancing fire we cannot tame.

*Tune: Praise my soul*

**June Boyce-Tillman**

# 10

# Go into all the world . . .
## Good news to all humanity

The Ascension is where we all begin, or a signal to return to the starting-point of this collection, the bearing of good news to all the world, so that the love of Jesus may be made present and efficacious in word and action in human lives. A people on the move seek signposts, in worship as in the affairs of everyday life. Discerning needs in oneself and others brings into action gifts of the Spirit that can only serve to build up the household of God.

## 173 *Lost in wonder, love and praise!*
### *Eucharist for Ascension Day*

> *The people come in and sit down.*
> *Silence.*

v   We have a great high priest who has passed through the heavens, Jesus the Son of God.

R   Alleluia! Christ is gone up on high and is with us to the end of time. Alleluia!

### Collect for Ascension Day

O God,
you withdraw from our sight
that you may be known by our love;
help us to enter the cloud
where you are hidden,
and to surrender all our certainty
to the darkness of faith
in Jesus Christ, Amen.

(Janet Morley)

**Hymn** *Hail the day that sees him rise*

**Prayer of praise and adoration:** *a setting of Psalm 8*

A    O Sovereign, our God,
       how majestic is your name in all the earth!

B    You whose glory above the heavens is chanted
       by the mouths of babes and infants,
       you have founded a bulwark because of your foes,
       to still the enemy and the avenger.

A    When I look at your heavens, the work of your fingers,
       the moon and the stars which you have established;

B    What are human beings that you are mindful of them,
       and mortals that you care for them?

A    Yet you have made them little less than God,
       and crowned them with glory and honour.

B    You have given them dominion over the works of your hands;
       you have put all things under their feet;

A    All sheep and oxen,
       and also the beasts of the field,

B    The birds of the air, and the fish of the sea,
       whatever passes along the paths of the sea.

A&B    O Sovereign, our God,
       How majestic is your name in all the earth!

**Prayer of confession**

V    Lord, our God, in baptism you have given us a part in the life, death, resurrection and ascension of Jesus Christ.
    We confess before you that we have not fully lived according to the true image of the new humanity.
    Therefore we cry to you:

R    **Kyrie eleison** *(sung to Russian Orthodox melody reprinted in* With All God's People).

V    Lord, our God, in baptism you have called us to drown day by day our old Adam, that we may rise as new men and women in righteousness, justice and holiness.
    We confess before you that we are too lax in striving to realize your will in all realms of life.

Therefore we cry to you:

R   **Kyrie eleison**

V   Lord, our God, in baptism you have incorporated us into the worldwide body of Christ, so that we may witness before the whole world to your healing and reconciling love.

We confess before you that we are too lazy in overcoming the division between the churches and in making visible our God-given unity within the body of Christ.

Therefore we cry to you:

R   **Kyrie eleison**

V   May almighty God have mercy upon us,
forgive us our sins for the sake of Jesus Christ,
and lead us to renewed and everlasting life
in the power of the Holy Spirit, Amen.

## First Reading *Daniel 7.13–24*

## Epistle *Acts 1.1–11*

## Acclamation of the Gospel *Holy God, holy and strong, holy and immortal* (sung to Russian Orthodox melody reprinted in With All God's People)

## The Gospel *Matthew 28.16–20*

## Homily

*Silence*

## The Offertory

*during which we sing 'Lo, I am with you to the end of the world'.
We stand as the gifts are brought forward.*

## The Peace

V   The risen Christ came and stood among his disciples and said,
Peace be with you!
They were glad when they saw the Lord.
Alleluia! The peace of the risen Christ be always with you.

R   And also with you. Alleluia!

V   Let us offer one another a sign of peace.

## The Thanksgiving

## The Prayer of Jesus

Beloved, our Father and Mother, in whom is heaven,
Hallowed be your name,
followed be your royal way,
done be your will and rule,
throughout the whole creation.
With the bread we need for today, feed us.
In the hurts we absorb from one another, forgive us.
In times of temptation and test, strengthen us.
From trials too great to endure, spare us.
From the grip of all that is evil, free us.
For you reign in the glory
of the power that is love,
now and for ever, Amen.

(Jim Cotter)

## The Breaking of Bread

## The Sharing of bread and wine *during which are sung*

*'Jesus is with God'* and *'Alleluia! sing to Jesus'*

*When all have received we stand.*

## The Dismissal

v The Lord be with you.
R And also with you.

v Christ our lover,
to whom we try to cling:
as you have reached into our depths
and drawn us to love you,
so make us open, freely to let you go;
that you may return in unexpected power
to change the world through us,
in your name.
R Amen.

(Janet Morley)

v And now go away from this place, to love and serve the Risen and
Ascended Christ through all the world. In the name of the most
holy, glorious and blessed Trinity, Creator, Redeemer and Sustainer, Father, Son and Holy Spirit, Mother, Friend and Lover; who

was and is, and is to come, for all time and for ever.

R    Amen.

Alec Balfe-Mitchell

## 174    *A Eucharist for people on the move, seeking signposts, living with change*

### Opening

V    Eternal Spirit, flow through our being and open our lips that our mouths may proclaim your praise.

R    Let us worship the God of Love.

*From Psalm 119:*

V    Blessed are those who are honest in their ways,

R    who walk in the paths of God's Law.

V    Those who do no evil deeds

R    are those who tread the way of justice.

V    May my ways be kept steadfast

R    on the narrow road of your Love.

V    With my whole heart I have looked for you:

R    let me not wander from your Commandment.

V    I am a traveller upon earth:

R    hide not your Guideposts from me.

V    I have chosen the way of faithfulness,

R    and your Justice is before my eyes.

V    Take from me the way of lying,

R    and graciously teach me your Truth.

V    I shall run the way of your Commandment

R    when you have set my heart at liberty.

(Jim Cotter)

### Prayers of intercession

For people forced to travel – refugees, homeless, wayfarers:
that they will know you with them on the road
**Lord, go with them.**

For people beset by danger – living in war zones, victims of crime, working on the front line:
that you will bring them safe through all the troubles
**Lord, go with them.**

For people lacking direction – the confused, the listless, the despairing:
that they will find their way with you
**Lord, go with them.**

For people whose way is barred – the hungry, prisoners, the unemployed:
that you will set them free and set their feet on the road
**Lord, go with them.**

For people who want to turn back – the persecuted, the failed, the
  discouraged:
that they will gain comfort and strength from you
**Lord, go with them.**

For people who refuse to move – the smug, the contented, the satisfied:
that you will give them hunger for righteousness and longing for change
**Lord, go with them.**

For people who wander in darkness – the depressed, the bereaved, the
  dying:
that they will see light in you
**Lord, go with them.**

For people who walk alone – the isolated, the housebound, the
  handicapped:
that you will be their companion on the way
**Lord, go with them.**

For all your people as we journey – ourselves, our friends, and all your
  church:
that we may move ever closer to you.
**Lord, go with us.**

## Prayer of thanksgiving

v   The Lord is here.
R   God's Spirit is with us.
v   Let us lift up our hearts.
R   We lift them to the Lord.
v   Let us give thanks to the Lord our God.
R   It is right to offer thanks and praise.

We give you thanks and praise, O Lord, for all that you have made,
for all the signs of your love seen in your creation,
for your provision for us, pointing us to you.

**We give you thanks and praise.**

**We give you thanks and praise.**

We give you thanks and praise, O Lord,
that you have always shown us the way to go.
Through law and custom you have shown us how to live together.
Through prophets and people of prayer you have made yourself known.
**We give you thanks and praise.**

Above all, we give you thanks and praise for coming to live among us,
as one of us, in Jesus: his life, a sign of faithful service;
his death, a sign of selfless love;
his rising, a sign of everlasting hope.
**We give you thanks and praise.**

We praise you for all that you have done.
We give you thanks for all that you do now,
your Spirit at work in the world.
We glory in the hope of what you will do,
more than words can express, more than we can dream.
We join with all your people –
past and present, here and everywhere –
and with all your creation as we sing:

**Holy, holy, holy is the Lord. Holy is the Lord God Almighty!**
**Holy, holy, holy is the Lord. Holy is the Lord God Almighty!**
**Who was and is and is to come. Holy, holy, holy is the Lord!**

We thank you for the sign that Jesus gave us, the sign of our unity with him,
the sign of our community with each other.
On the night before he died, he shared bread and wine with his friends and
said: This is my body. This is my blood. They are given for you. Eat and
drink together in remembrance of me.

**Jesus, Jesus, Jesus is the Lord. Jesus is the Lord God Almighty!**
**Jesus, Jesus, Jesus is the Lord. Jesus is the Lord God Almighty!**
**Who loved and died and rose again. Jesus, Jesus, Jesus is the Lord!**

As we remember Christ's death, let us live by his presence.
As we recall Christ's life, let God's Spirit help us to live as he did.
As we share Christ's gifts, let us give ourselves to him and to each other.
As we receive Christ's body and blood, let God's Spirit make us one body in
  him.
As we celebrate Christ's feast, let us look forward to the great celebration,
  prepared for all people, when God's rule is established in glory.

Glory, glory, glory to the Lord. Glory to the Lord God Almighty!
Glory, glory, glory to the Lord. Glory to the Lord God Almighty!
Who gives us life and lives in us. Glory, glory, glory to the Lord!

V The gifts of God for the people of God.
R Though we are many, we are one body,
  for we share together this bread and wine.

## Communion

### Prayers of departure

We are wayfarers, following roads
to the ends of the earth, pilgrims on our way to the end of the age.
'Behold, I am with you
to the end of the age.'

We are travellers on the road to freedom,
a community of grace
with good news for all we meet.
'Behold, I am with you
to the end of the age.'

We'll travel lightly, travel together,
learn as we go; we are disciples,
our mission is love,
the journey is long.
'Behold, I am with you
to the end of the age.'

We travel with authority
fearful of none;
we are sent, opponents of evil,
heralds of hope.
'Behold, I am with you
to the end of the age.'

We'll travel with humility,
no task is too small;
we are servants, the cross is our compass,
love is our sign.
'Behold, I am with you
to the end of the age.'

When the way is uncertain,
shadows are sinister,
and dangers threaten,
we'll not be afraid, but take heart.
**'Behold, I am with you
to the end of the age.'**

> (from *Peace, Justice and Integrity of Creation*, Advent '86 Campaign Kit
> (Centre for Mindanao Studies, Philippines))

May the road rise to meet you.
May the wind be always at your back.
May the sun shine warm upon your face.
May the rain refresh you on your way.
May you go with God for all your journey,
now and for ever. Amen.

**Anonymous**

## 175    *Litany: Go into the world*

LEADER Go into the world:
　　　　Dance, laugh, sing and create
PEOPLE **We go with your encouragement, O God.**

LEADER Go into the world:
　　　　Risk, explore, discover and love
PEOPLE **We go with your encouragement, O God.**

LEADER Go into the world:
　　　　Believe, hope, struggle and remember
PEOPLE **We go with the assurance of your love, O God.
Thanks be to God!**

**Group 3 Interns in Mission, Uniting Church in Australia**

## 176    *Prayer*

Go-between God:
inweave the fabric of our common life,
that the many-coloured beauty of your love
may find expression in all our exchanges.

**Jennifer Wild**

# Acknowledgements

We wish to thank all those who have contributed to this anthology and given permission for their writing to be used. In particular, although nothing appears here over his name, Fr Bill Kirkpatrick most generously allowed us to look through his vast collection of material, and to use several pieces from it.

We have made every effort to trace and identify pieces and parts of liturgies correctly, and to secure the necessary permission for printing. If we have made any errors in text or in acknowledgement, we apologize sincerely. Copyright for the most part remains in the hands of the authors named. Please address the author, c/o Mowbray, Cassell Plc, Wellington House, 125 Strand, London WC2R 0BB for permission to reproduce, marking the envelope clearly: PERMISSIONS: HUMAN RITES. For items marked with an asterisk, permission should be sought from the publisher specified. Publishers' current addresses are given in the first instance only. (It should be noted that, even if it were desirable to copy whole liturgies, in most cases more than one copyright source is involved, and our aim has been to offer inspiration rather than blueprints.)

Material in this collection first appeared as follows:

*'Christ Crucified and risen', copyright 1987 Kate Compston, in *Encounters*, the Prayer Handbook 1988, published by the United Reformed Church in the United Kingdom, 86 Tavistock Place, London WC1H 9RT.

'A celebration of faith development', copyright Nicola Slee, in *All the Year Round 1992: Resource material for public worship*, published by The Standing Conference on Unity in Prayer of the CCBI.

*'There's a season for everything', by Miriam Therese Winter, in *WomanPrayer, WomanSong*, copyright 1987 by Medical Mission Sisters, Philadelphia PA 19111, reprinted by permission of HarperCollins Publishers, 22–24 Joseph St, North Blackburn, Victoria 3130, Australia.

*'Light of God to give us light', copyright 1994 David Adam, in *The Open Gate: Celtic prayers for growing spiritually*, reprinted by permission of Triangle/SPCK, Holy Trinity Church, Marylebone Road, London NW1 4DU.

*'God of tender compassion and mercy' in *The Promise of his Glory*, copyright 1991 The Central Board of Finance of the Church of England, Church House, Great Smith Street, London SW1P 3NZ; reprinted by permission.

*'God our deliverer', 'God our mother', 'God of intimacy', 'Eucharistic Prayer for ordinary use', 'And you held me', 'In the body broken' (part of the 'Eucharistic prayer for Good Friday'), 'May the God who dances in creation', 'O God who brought us to birth', 'Christ our lover', 'O God, you withdraw from our sight',

reprinted by permission.

'A Celtic baptism' in the Association for Inclusive Language *Bulletin* 1/94. Reprinted by permission of the author.

'The blessing of the most Holy Trinity', adapted from 'The Women's Agape' devised from the early Christian *Didache* by Liz Campbell in *Greenham Vigil Office*, copyright Greenham Peace Vigil 1986.

'A retirement service', 'A service for a family who are emigrating' and 'A service signifying the end of a close relationship', copyright Roger Grainger 1987, in *Staging Posts: Rites of Passage for Contemporary Christians* (Merlin Books Ltd); reprinted by permission of the author. ('A retirement service' was also published in *Change to Life: The Pastoral Care of the Newly Retired*, Darton, Longman and Todd 1993.)

*'A children's ritual', 'Becoming a new family', 'Parents' remarriage', 'A liturgy for the blessing of a couple', 'The celebration and blessing of a Jewish–Christian wedding', 'Liturgy at the time of choosing whether or not to have an abortion', 'Rituals for abortion', 'Litany for AIDS Sunday', 'Liturgy for divorce', 'At the time of divorce: a children's liturgy', 'Preparing for death', 'At the time of death' and 'Remembering the dead', copyright 1991 Vienna Cobb Anderson in *Prayers of our Hearts in Word and Action* (Crossroad Publishing Company); reprinted by permission.

*'Come, cradle all', copyright Brian Wren in *Faith Looking Forward* (Oxford University Press 1983 and 1993); reprinted by permission of Stainer and Bell Ltd.

*'God be with us', copyright 1985 David Adam in *The Edge of Glory* (Triangle/ SPCK); reprinted by permission.

*'Come host of heaven's high dwelling place', 'A touching place' and 'We cannot measure how you heal', by John L. Bell and Graham Maule in *Love From Below* (Wild Goose Publications 1989), copyright 1989 WGRG, Iona Community, Glasgow G51 3UU; reprinted by permission.

*'Unless the Lord builds the house' and 'May God give blessing' altered and abridged from *The Iona Community Worship Book*, 1988 edition (Wild Goose Publications), copyright 1988 WGRG, Iona Community; 'Come, Lord Jesus, be our Guest', abridged from *A Wee Worship Book* (Wild Goose Worship Group), copyright 1989 WGRG, Iona Community; used by permission.

*'Be present, Spirit of God', 'We grieve and confess', 'God be in my head', 'The prayer of Jesus' (adapted), copyright Jim Cotter, in *Prayer at Night* (Cairns Publications); reprinted by permission.

'House blessing' and 'Partnership declarations', copyright Hazel Barkham, and *'Partnership promises', adapted from Jim Cotter, *Exploring Lifestyles: An Introduction to the Service of Blessing for Gay Couples* (Gay Christian Movement 1980) in Elizabeth Stuart, *Daring to Speak Love's Name: A Gay and Lesbian Prayer Book* (Hamish Hamilton).

'Celebrating the new family' and The Family Medallion are copyright Roger Coleman. Further information from Clergy Services, Inc., 706 West 42nd Street, Kansas City, Missouri 64111, USA.

*'You may give them your love', from Kahlil Gibran, *The Prophet*.

*'A rite of blessing at adoption' and 'Service of healing after a miscarriage' (114 and 115) in *Our Baby Has Died*, copyright The Board of Christian Education, Diocese of Auckland, Chandler Avenue, Royal Oak, Auckland 3, New Zealand; reprinted by permission.

*‘A litany of sorrow’ (words: Christopher Armstrong and Martin Dales; music: Martin Dales) in *Three Canticles*, copyright 1994 M.D. Music Co., Priory Cottage, Old Malton, North Yorkshire, YO17 0HB [USA/Canada distribution Boosey and Hawkes Inc., New York].

*‘Praying our farewells’, copyright 1992 The European Province of the Society of St Francis, in *Celebrating Common Prayer: The Daily Office SSF* (Mowbray); used by permission.

*‘Loving God’, ‘We need your healing’, ‘God forgives you’, ‘God of the dark night’, ‘God be your comfort’ (adapted), ‘God of all consolation’ (adapted), ‘Gracious God’ (adapted) and ‘Creator of all’ (adapted), in *A New Zealand Prayer Book: He Karakia Mihinare o Aotearoa* (1989); reprinted by permission.

‘A liturgy for release from marriage vows’, copyright the Right Reverend Roger Herft, Diocese of Newcastle, NSW, Australia.

*‘The unfinished symphony’, copyright Marjorie Gray in *Code Care: Prayer Poems of a Nurse* (Ave Maria Press, Notre Dame, Indiana 46556).

*‘Blessing for a deceased baby’, copyright Ingrid Kohn and Perry-Lynn Moffitt, *Pregnancy Loss: A Silent Sorrow* (Headway, Hodder and Stoughton Educational, 338 Euston Road, London NW1 3BH).

‘Death is nothing at all’ by Henry Scott Holland, in ‘The King of Terrors’, sermon preached on Whitsunday 1910, in *Facts of the Faith* (1919).

*‘Prayer following pregnancy loss’, copyright Diane Cohen in *Pregnancy Loss: A Silent Sorrow* (see earlier entry).

*‘A psalm for the dying’, ‘Song of awakening’ and ‘A winter solstice observance’ are reprinted with permission from *Prayers of a Planetary Pilgrim* by Edward Hays, copyright Forest of Peace Publishing, Inc.

*‘How shall I sing to God’, copyright Brian Wren, in *Praising a Mystery* (Hope Publishing Company); reprinted by permission of Stainer and Bell Ltd.

*‘All Souls: An evening of remembrance and thanksgiving’ in *Sharing Faith in the Countryside: A Resource Handbook*, copyright Council for Mission and Unity, Diocese of Chelmsford, 53 New Street, Chelmsford, CM1 1NG; reprinted by permission.

*‘By his wounds you have been healed’, in *No Longer Strangers, A Resource for Women and Worship*, WCC Publications, 150 Route de Ferney (PO Box 2100) 1211 Geneva 2, Switzerland; reprinted by permission.

‘Give thou to me’, copyright 1992 June Boyce-Tillman, in *In Praise of All-Encircling Love* (Hildegard Press and the Association for Inclusive Language), reprinted by permission.

*‘We shall go out’, ‘All shall be well’ and ‘We sing a love’, by June Boyce-Tillman, in *Reflecting Praise*, copyright 1993 Stainer and Bell Ltd and Women in Theology; reprinted by permission.

*‘Blessed be the New Year: a ritual of hope’, copyright 1992 Diann L. Neu (WATER, 8035 13th Street, Silver Spring, Maryland 20910).

*‘Praise God, who has set bounds to the universe’, copyright 1988 Stephen Orchard, in *All the Glorious Names*, the Prayer Handbook 1989 (URC).

‘Litany of Holy Wisdom’, copyright Anne Ashworth, in the Words for Worship series (Women in Theology).

‘O God, the source of our being’, copyright Janet Morley, and ‘As we hold each other’s hands’ and ‘And so we go forth’, copyright Lesley Hitchens, in *Who Are You Looking For?* (Women in Theology).

# Authors and compilers

(It should be noted that the name that appears at the foot of each liturgical piece is that of the compiler, who may also have written a greater part of the liturgy in question. Work by other writers within a liturgy is clearly marked as such, as far as we have been able to ascertain authorship.)